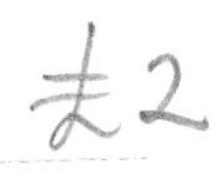

CASTLES OF WALES

For My Family,
With whom I've visited many castles in Wales.

CASTLES OF WALES

JOHN PAUL DAVIS

First published in Great Britain in 2022 by
PEN AND SWORD HISTORY
An imprint of
Pen & Sword Books Ltd
Yorkshire – Philadelphia

ISBN 978 1 39901 887 6

A CIP catalogue record for this book is available from the British Library.

Typeset in Times New Roman 11.5/14 by
SJmagic DESIGN SERVICES, India.
Printed and bound in the UK by CPI Group (UK) Ltd.

Pen & Sword Books Limited incorporates the imprints of Atlas, Archaeology, Aviation, Discovery, Family History, Fiction, History, Maritime, Military, Military Classics, Politics, Select, Transport, True Crime, Air World, Frontline Publishing, Leo Cooper, Remember When, Seaforth Publishing, The Praetorian Press, Wharncliffe Local History, Wharncliffe Transport, Wharncliffe True Crime and White Owl.

For a complete list of Pen & Sword titles please contact
PEN & SWORD BOOKS LIMITED
47 Church Street, Barnsley, South Yorkshire, S70 2AS, England
E-mail: enquiries@pen-and-sword.co.uk
Website: www.pen-and-sword.co.uk

Or
PEN AND SWORD BOOKS
1950 Lawrence Rd, Havertown, PA 19083, USA
E-mail: Uspen-and-sword@casematepublishers.com
Website: www.penandswordbooks.com

Contents

Introduction

When I was five years old, my parents took my brother and me on a caravan holiday to Pembrokeshire. The year was 1990: the earliest of my life that I can remember in any great detail. Thirty years later, it's impossible to look back on that period without a sense of nostalgia. The weather was perfect. The sandy beaches endless. The world was still a decade from reliance on the Internet and mobile phones. As a child growing up in a low- to middle-income household, it was a time when imagination was a child's best friend, and even when it rained, the two-week seaside holiday was the indisputable highlight of the year.

As I briefly recalled in the introduction to my previous book, *Castles of England*, that trip proved an important one for me. Such was the lack of educational progress shown by my brother and I – he a future Oxford grad preparing for secondary school, and me still getting to grips with writing my own name – my parents wisely decided to expose us to the sights of the great outdoors. An investment was also made in a Cadw pass, allowing us free access to many of Wales's incredible ruins. I remain convinced that I learned more during this two-week stay than I did that entire first year of school. I've often wondered whether the same was true of sixteen years of schooling.

While my early struggles can undoubtedly be put down to my poor attitude and a lack of interest as much as my early teachers' limited talents, things worked out to my advantage. As I look back, few memories compare with the joy I felt exploring those beautiful castles. From the moss-covered walls of Carew to the amusingly named Kidwelly, there was no shortage of mighty medieval bastions on which I could feast my imagination. Whether it was a game of darts or pool inside the damp walls of the eighteenth-century castellated mansion of Amroth Castle, where our caravan park was sited, a glance at the untidy desk of Dylan Thomas's writing shed in the shadow of the boathouse and castle at Laugharne, or a walk through the flower-covered gardens of

Manorbier, my enthusiasm never wavered. Even now, there are few things I remember more fondly than the unique sensation of eating a bowl of chips in the great hall of Caerphilly, on whose walls the arms of many great families hung proudly. My, I felt a proper little knight.

On my return from that two-week paradise, my reception teacher invited me to present on my visit. On our final night, my father and brother had helped me put together a scrapbook of our time away, the content of which formed the heart of my 'show and tell'. With the possible exception of hiding my teacher's favourite whistle and cutting another boy's hair to the point of near baldness, that talk was the highlight of infant school.

Little did I know, it would be the only public talk I ever gave in primary school.

More than thirty years later, I still have the scrapbook close at hand. Even as I write, I struggle to turn the pages without a genuine sense of awe and wonder. The tattered cover may have given way to a newer one, but the pictures have survived, as have the memories. Seated at my computer, I can't help but smile to think that the motley collection of pages would form the basis of a published book.

Ever since that trip to Amroth Castle, from which I began a lifelong acquaintance with the castles of Great Britain, Wales has held a special place in my heart. Growing up in England, yet never more than a stone's throw from the border, trips were regular back then and remain so to this day. As someone who regards himself as much a Brit as an Englishman, the subject of patriotism and national identity is of great interest to me. When driving from England, only the signposts offer any persuasive evidence that one has passed into a different country. However, such things become increasingly obvious the farther one travels. A visit to one of the historic towns or villages is often enough to realise that Wales is a nation where the past forms a treasured part of the modern identity. From the historic pub to the wattle and daub cottage, reminders of centuries past can be found in every nook and cranny of the local architecture. Be it the walls of the local church, pub, library, village hall or town square, all contribute in their own way to preserving a culture that shows little sign of diminishing.

Even at the time of writing, parts of Wales remain little changed since the days of St David. The more I see of Britain, the more I come to learn how rare this is. The Welsh language is one of the oldest in Europe and is still widely in use. The country is also blessed with a treasure trove of early medieval literature. According to legend, Merlin was born in Wales. Except perhaps for Glastonbury and Cornwall, nowhere in Britain is more deeply intertwined with the tales of King Arthur. Many a song has been written of the verdant Welsh valleys; no less true is this of the misty mountains and soaring headlands. While the modern-day tourist must accept regular rain as the necessary cost for the natural vibrancy of the vegetation, water was sacred to the ancient dwellers of this land of deep rivers, rugged coastlines and beautiful lakes. Nearly every water source has a story dating back to mythology. It has also been told that the breaking of a wave represents a tormented cry of one of the thousands of Welshmen to have become victim to the sea. In the 'Dark Ages', tales were told of terrifying dragons lurking at the bottom of deep lakes, guarding a pot of gold and bewitching passing travellers to their deaths. Throughout its history, the dragon has held a central place in Welsh culture. Since the Middle Ages, the emblem of Wales has been *Y Ddraig Goch*, The Red Dragon. As long as there has been civilisation, fact and folklore have co-existed. Even now, Wales is a land where the present meets the past. The home of a unique people with a proud and passionate spirit. A land of mountains, mist, and rugby.

As an Englishman by birth, I realise some will be sceptical of an 'outsider' commenting on their heritage. I believe that's precisely the way it should be. With this in mind, may I set out my intentions for this book clearly from the start? This is not a book about Wales alone. It is a book about Wales and her neighbours. More than ten years of concentrated research on the thirteenth and fourteenth centuries have thoroughly convinced me that the evolution of Wales, as an independent nation, a collection of minor kingdoms and one annexed by England, is one of the Middle Ages' essential composites. It is baffling to me that this is so frequently overlooked, or at least downplayed in the context of England's relations with her neighbours to the north or across the Channel. As next-door neighbours, it is impossible to understand the history of one without the other – especially as skirmishes between the two, if not invasions of one by the other, were relatively common.

Concerning the great Welsh castles, stories of English dominance over Wales tend to be relatively well known in England. Yet examples of the opposite are also easily found. For some, the national rivalry never ended, albeit it is now channelled on the football and rugby pitches instead of bloody siege. From a personal perspective, let me be equally clear: I haven't written this book to curry favour or for purposes of political correctness. Nor have I done so to ruffle feathers. A lifetime of visiting Wales has instilled in me a genuine love for the country. More importantly, it has whetted a genuine interest and passion for understanding its history. I've climbed Snowdon, Cadair Idris and Pen y Fan on multiple occasions, yet never without being humbled along the way. I've enjoyed the hospitality of many establishments between Warwickshire and Anglesey; not once have I personally received any form of anti-English sentiment. The opposite is true of amusing banter, again usually sports-related. As a frequent holidayer and lover of Welsh heritage, I hope that my best attempts at constructive objectivity will be rewarded with the typical sense of hospitality. The Welsh, in general, are rightly famed for it.

Further to its abundant natural beauty, no country on Earth has a higher concentration of churches and castles than Wales. The most famous date from the late 1200s and are rightly associated with one man above others. On defeating Llywelyn ap Gruffudd in 1282, Edward I of England commissioned the construction of what is now often known as the 'Iron Ring' to act as a sign of dominance over the kingdom of Gwynedd. Assisting Edward was his master mason, James of St George, whose expertise benefitted many of these castles. Of James's background, little is known. Judging by the appearance of much of the Iron Ring, a Savoyard or crusader pedigree seems highly probable. The castles' appearance may indicate that he often spent time in the Holy Land and may have been a contemporary of the crusader king there. Coupled with the castles that have survived from the eleventh century or later eras, Wales boasts some of Europe's genuinely great fortresses. While some of the less sophisticated structures pay testament to the brave resistance of the native rulers against English usurpers, the 'Iron Ring' has come to emblemise the expansion of England's second great empire. Though most now lie in ruin, few have lost their sense of majesty. Rare indeed is it for any tourist site to compare with the appeal of the magnificent shells such as Caernarfon and Harlech.

As I set out on my journey back in time – both my own and that of Wales itself – I am faced with many conundrums. Few would dispute that the castles of Wales have become a priceless part of Welsh culture. Yet, it is a bizarre irony that an Englishman put down many to augment

English dominance over the native. More ironic still, Henry V, the man immortalised by Shakespeare as the hero of Agincourt and perfect English military ruler, was himself Welsh-born. The fact that the royal Tudor line began with a Welshman, Henry Tudor – later Henry VII – also seems even more bizarre considering that, in recent centuries, the Prince of Wales, heir to the throne of England, is invariably an Englishman.

One of the earliest challenges one must deal with when writing about castles is the definition of the castle itself. As I set out in the introduction to *Castles of England*, I find myself much in agreement with that offered by R. Allen Brown in his *English Castles*. In short, a castle is a 'residential fortress' and 'a fortified residence'. That this definition should be considered correct for every country is perhaps worthy of debate. In France, for example, *chateau* has become an umbrella term for everything and anything from a castle or castellated mansion to a grand home. Does it, therefore, apply that the definition of a castle can vary with variations of style, culture, architecture, construction materials and history?

While I believe this to be worthy of extended investigation, I am satisfied that Allen's description remains the most appropriate in the case of this book. A prime reason for this is that many castles of Wales were built by the Norman and Plantagenet rulers of England. They were also the product of similar building patterns and purposes. True it is that other fortresses were erected throughout Wales before Edward I's subjugation, many on the orders of the princes of Gwynedd in a bid to augment their rule over their ancestral heartlands or launch a counteroffensive against the English invaders, not least the earls of Pembroke, they were often vastly more primitive. Nevertheless, most, if not all, fit the definition of a residential fortress and fortified residence.

It was mainly due to the early exploits of the Norman and Plantagenet rulers that war between England and Wales was a recurring theme throughout the Middle Ages. The areas immediately on either side of the border, often known today as the Welsh Marches, were particularly volatile. The March was a unique region in England. Defined by the *Welsh Academy Encyclopaedia of Wales* as a 'frontier region', it was technically independent of the Crown and immune to the threat of royal writs. The precise boundaries are difficult to establish, not least as its position varied throughout the centuries. For simplicity's sake, concerning castles not located in modern Wales, I have decided to extend the definition to the neighbouring English counties, namely Herefordshire, Gloucestershire and Shropshire, which at one time all formed part of the Welsh Marches. Due to their existence being inexorably linked with border security issues, the area gave rise to many important castles. As well as residential fortresses and fortified residences, they were the seats of local government: the domains of kings within kingdoms. Such was their importance to the history of Wales, I have decided to include these castles in this book instead of *Castles of England.*

There is little doubt that the English castles of the Welsh Marches share much in common with their Welsh counterparts – often far more than their English siblings. At times, they were subject to invasion and conquest by the Welsh. Such patterns were a regular occurrence until the reign of Edward I and even after. Not until the Marcher lordships fell into the Crown's hands, notably following the accession of Henry IV, himself lord of Brecon, Monmouth, Kidwelly and the three castles of Gwent, did this change. Not until the Act of Union in 1536 was the jurisdiction of the Marcher lords officially abolished.

By including the English castles of the Welsh Marches in this book, I hope that several additional facets of the story of the castles of Wales will become apparent. As is always true of war, there are at least two sides to every story. Depending on the reasons for the conflict and the period in which it took place, gaining a clear insight is often a significant challenge. It has often been said that history is written by the victors. If this is true, this may well be a prime reason why the significance of the wars with Wales often tends to be overlooked or its importance understated. True, these events were often concurrent with war with Scotland, France or the Crusades, yet this alone should not account for it being maligned.

Another significant challenge is separating fact from fiction, or in many cases: folklore. Perhaps unsurprisingly, considering Wales's unique collection of myths and legends, combined with such a colourful history, this ancient land remains rich in mystery. Few places have such a reputation for being haunted. Passionate and expressive in life, it is also perhaps no surprise that many of the country's former residents reputedly continue to be so in the afterlife. Equally unsurprising, with more castles per square mile than anywhere else in the UK, it is within their ruined walls that their spirits are said to linger.

Like *Castles of England*, an attempt to gain a firm grip on these stories is a subject I feel especially worthy of investigation. True it may be that no one book can ever solve every mystery nor prove – or disprove – the existence of the paranormal, it is in such tales the mighty bastions of Wales often find great allure. The border wars between the English and Welsh were among the bloodiest in recorded history. No less gruesome is the history of many other Welsh castles. Reading this book, many of you will notice that, in some cases, the stories are more concerned with past sieges and rebellion, and in others, the unsolved legends. There is a simple explanation for this. The history of these castles is what it is, and like all writers, I get my motivation from what interests me. Be it the scars of war, the forgotten stories of former inhabitants or treasures that remain undiscovered, I hope it interests you too. By delving deep into their history and throwing light on their tales, we allow ourselves the opportunity to enter that lost world. A world that, though long gone, remains an inescapable part of our past, present and future.

Preface

The Castle in Wales

Wales is a land littered with historic fortifications. In common with its old enemy to the east, no matter where one ventures, there is rarely any shortage of Iron Age hill forts, Roman ruins, or pre-Norman settlements around which the history enthusiast can enjoy a leisurely ramble. This is equally true of the post-Norman: no fewer than 600 castle sites have been recorded in Wales and the Welsh Marches.

As I recalled in *Castles of England*, the castle's story in Britain is a complicated one. While military fortresses can be traced back to the Bronze Age, the castle's birth can confidently be dated to an obscure citing by a monk at Canterbury in 1051. Writing in the *Anglo-Saxon Chronicle*, the cleric noted a structure put down in Herefordshire by French members of the king's party. Separate from a Saxon *burh*, but with apparent similarities, the word he used was *castellum*. As time would tell, the chronicler had recorded not only the happenings of the year but also a glimpse of the future.

Within four years of the Norman invasion, dozens of these so-called 'castles' had sprouted up all over England. From William the Conqueror's initial trio at Hastings, Pevensey and Dover – in addition to the now lost structure in Herefordshire – further motte and baileys shot up as far apart as Exeter and York. In 1068, William subjugated England's west. Two years later, the same was true of the north. By 1070, it seemed nowhere in Britain would escape the Conqueror's fiery march. As the predominantly Viking population of the north experienced themselves, the Norman onslaught was quite literally 'harrowing'. To augment his dominance, William built more than forty castles. By the time the *Domesday Book* was compiled, a year before the king's death in 1087, the castle had already changed England for good.

In Wales, the pattern was similar but not identical. Even before the Norman invasion, the natives of this mountainous land were no stranger to the threat of the would-be usurper. Writing of the year 61AD, the ancient historian Tacitus referred to the marauding natives of Anglesey instilling the fear of God into the Romans' hearts with their terrifying curses and smearing of altars in blood. A combination of limited source material and modern archaeology suggests that the Romans crossing the River Severn around 47AD had been the first step of many in dominating the entire country. A further thirty years would separate them from total victory.

The Welsh had been a hard nut to crack, but broken they were. So difficult had the Romans found this maverick bunch that a force of some 30,000 soldiers was required to bring them to order. Once they did, however, there was no going back. From 79AD onwards, Roman roads, villas, forts and amphitheatres accounted for just a portion of the construction all over the country. Many of these can still be visited. The amphitheatre at Caerleon, whose nearby baths and accompanying structures still survive in some detail, was one of the largest to be built outside Rome. It has even been suggested as a possible inspiration for King Arthur's roundtable.

For the next three centuries, the Roman colonisation of Wales was ongoing. However, this would change in the mid-fourth century with the empire's declining fortunes. Exactly what state Wales was in when Magnus Maximus led his retreat in 383AD is impossible to determine. Unanswered questions also concern the exact date of Christianity's arrival. Regardless of the precise origins, over the coming two centuries, the period often known as the 'age of saints' would dramatically influence Welsh culture. In some instances, evidence for the juxtaposition of the old and the new is also present. Indeed, modern archaeology has confirmed Roman villas in Wales a century after the Romans' departure.

As is sadly typical in early medieval Britain, reliable sources concerning what came next are scarce. More comfortable to establish are some of the more general trends. Just like in England, the creation of forts often meant churches, if not abbeys. St Deiniol's monastery, a precursor of Bangor Cathedral, can be dated as early as 525AD and has been dubbed the oldest in Wales. Later that century, David founded a *clas* – cloister – in his native Pembrokeshire. Aided by the Irish missionaries, the fledgeling nation became a centre of Celtic Christianity.

The following century would prove particularly significant in the context of Wales's development. While the English were doomed to suffer ongoing carnage at the hands of Angle, Saxon, Jute and Viking, the Welsh enjoyed a period of relative security in their mountainous terrain. Unlike their Roman counterparts, the Germanic tribes that had enjoyed eventual success in England were less skilled in navigating the tricky landscape. What Wales gained in withstanding an invasion, however, was not followed by a blitz of construction. In the absence of building activity, which the Romans had excelled at, Wales's advancement as a centre of architecture followed a different direction. Any fortifications that were built have not survived. In the absence of historical certainties, the 'Dark Ages' brought an era of myth and legend. It was a time when the writings of chroniclers such as Gildas and Nennius were guided as much by hearsay as reality. It was also a time of legendary kings. The time of King Arthur.

Not until the eighth century can any degree of clarity be gained from the myriad of sources. The great Mercian King Offa's legacy lies mainly in the magnificent 150-mile dyke that once denoted the border with England. By the mid-800s, Rhodri ap Merfyn (often known as Rhodri Mawr), King of Gwynedd, had conquered much of modern Wales, not least courtesy of his annexation of Powys and Seisyllwg. Following in his footsteps, his grandson, Hywel Dda, governed Gwynedd, Powys and the newly formed Deheubarth through a combination of inheritance, war and marriage. Peace was also constructively formulated with the English earls. Among Hywel's crowning achievements was an elegant legal code that was among the most liberal in Europe. A rarity for the time, it was also sensitive to the rights of women.

A century later, Welsh unity reached something of a zenith. During the reign of Gruffudd ap Llywelyn, King of Gwynedd, Welsh rule extended across Hywel's kingdom to Morgannwg in the south. Hywel's great-grandson, Gruffudd, was both opportunistic and ruthless. The writers of the *Welsh Academy Encyclopaedia of Wales* believed that this era marked the first occasion when one man officially ruled a united Wales. Yet, such progress ended abruptly in 1063 when Gruffudd was murdered, most likely by one of his rivals, after a dispute with the Saxon Harold Godwinson. Exactly who performed the deed was never discovered. Also unrecorded is the look on Harold's face when the dead man's head was placed before him. For Godwinson, of course, recent successes would prove limited. When the victorious William the Conqueror marched across England, Wales was presented with a new problem. A nation already blighted by internal uncertainty was now the target of an external attack.

As the Norman invaders would learn to their great cost, subjugation of Wales would not be achieved quickly. Indeed, as the Romans had already discovered, the Welsh would prove a typically formidable opponent, even as a divided country. In 1070, around the time of the 'Harrowing of the North', the Conqueror completed his first step by establishing what the *Domesday Book* would later describe as the March of Wales. With this, the battle lines – albeit murky ones – for the next two centuries were drawn.

Such developments, notwithstanding the uncertainty surrounding the sovereignty of Wales, would be far from insignificant concerning the destiny of the castle. Had the Welsh surrendered meekly to their new overlords, the history of Wales and the development of the fortified residences and residential fortresses would almost certainly have been very different. In contrast to his mandate for the conquest of England, William sought peace with Wales. As a sign of his benevolent intentions, he undertook a pilgrimage to St David's in 1081 and enjoyed warm relations with the king of Deheubarth, Rhys ap Tewdwr. However, during his son's reign, whatever peace had previously been achieved gave way to wanton vandalism and pillage. Worse still, Tewdwr's death in 1093 had a demoralising effect on his people. The latest enemy was the new breed of 'Marcher lords', whose role in the ongoing feuds would be of both great benefit and frustration to the monarch. As William (Rufus) II's successors would realise to their great peril, not only did the dream of complete control of Wales leave little choice but to embark on expensive military campaigns, but due to the unique power of the Marcher lords, control of their borders would require great diplomacy.

A better legacy of the Marcher raids was the erection of the first Norman castles. Within a year of the Battle of Hastings, the Normans made their first march into the heart of Wales under the leadership of William's trusted ally, William FitzOsbern, 1st Earl of Hereford. Chepstow was one of several castles built on his watch. A rarity in British history, it appears to have been of stone foundation. By the start of Rufus's reign, no fewer than eighty motte and baileys had been erected across the south of Wales. Alongside about seventy of these, the Normans also established a series of 'fortified colonies', usually of rectangular Romano-French design. It was here, from around 1108, that immigrants from Flanders were granted special mercantile privileges in exchange for their help defending the castles.

While control of the south of Wales – the easiest route for crossing to Ireland – was of immense value to the English monarchs, effective military raids, coupled with a series of unstable alliances with local Welsh lords, provided profitable returns for the Marcher lords. Key to the associations were marriages between Norman lords and Welsh royalty. The most famous was Henry I's mistress, Princess Nest ferch Rhys – daughter of Rhys ap Tewdwr – who was granted to Gerald de Windsor, the first castellan of Pembroke Castle.

English luck would change for the worse under Henry's nephew and successor, Stephen of Blois. As England struggled throughout nineteen years of 'Anarchy', the Welsh took control of many early Norman fortresses. A notable exception was Pembrokeshire, which Richard I granted in earldom to William Marshal, later Henry III's regent. The mighty bastions of Pembroke and Cardiff owe some form of origin to the late eleventh century, albeit as timber motte and baileys. Both were also the subject of comprehensive reconstruction in the following centuries, notably Pembroke's rise under Marshal's guardianship.

As the influence of the Marcher lord broadened, the title became more financially valuable. Gaining the lordships proved particularly lucrative for many powerful Anglo-Norman families looking to cut new paths on leaving the ancestral motherland. Despite the clear gains at the nobility level, relations between the English Crown and Welsh rulers were rarely straightforward. During the reigns of Henry II and the marauding Rhys ap Gruffudd – a grandson of Rhys ap Tewdwr and *de jure* Prince of Deheubarth – peace was often on a knife-edge, not least as Rhys drove out most of the English from the south of Wales. Military conflict was also at the mercy of the weather. On Henry's death, Lord Rhys's relationship with the Crown broke down beyond repair.

While the perpetual threat of violence strengthened the Marcher lords, their rising power was often to the king's peril. Llywelyn ap Iorwerth's earlier decision to marry off his daughters to Marcher lords confirms his acknowledgement of their importance. Similarly, John's granting of his illegitimate daughter, Joan of Wales, to Llywelyn clearly illustrates his recognition of Wales's importance. This view was shared by the rebel barons, who demanded in the strongest terms that 'the law of the march' be made distinct from that of England at Runnymede in 1215. Though John famously showed no intention of abiding by the first charter, at the time of his death a year later, support for his nine-year-old son, crowned Henry III, among the Marcher lords was more or less unanimous.

By the beginning of the young Henry III's reign, only the mountainous region of Gwynedd in the north had survived the Norman onslaught. Famed by future historians as the most militant area of Welsh identity in the Middle Ages, Gwynedd remained '*Pura Walia*' well into the 1200s. Under the leadership of their charismatic princes, North Wales enjoyed its own period of castle building. Fortresses such as Criccieth and Dolwyddelan proved useful in defending the coast and the Snowdonia pass. At times, the two Llywelyns – Llywelyn ap Iorwerth 'the Great' and Llywelyn ap Gruffudd 'the Last' – were also successful in uniting their country against the English. Helped by the pressures placed on Henry III by his own subjects during the Second Barons' War, the Treaty of Montgomery in 1267 affirmed Llywelyn ap Gruffudd as Prince of Wales.

Sadly for the prince, his efforts proved in vain. Arguably the most remarkable feat of constructional engineering in Henry III's reign – with the possible exception of Westminster Abbey – commenced in 1268 with the building of the mighty Caerphilly. Inspired by parts of Kenilworth, it was the first castle of concentric design; even including Kenilworth, it was the first to have been designed that way from the start. Fourteen years on from the commencing of work on Gilbert de Clare's masterpiece, Edward I's initial plan to reclaim the lost lands of the south ended with the conquering of Gwynedd. Throughout the period 1283–95, Caerphilly's younger siblings sprouted up rapidly. While Llywelyn ap Gruffudd's palace perished, giants such as Conwy, Caernarfon, Harlech and Beaumaris rose on its foundations. In 1284, Edward penned the Statute of Rhuddlan in which 'Divine Providence' transferred to the English monarch 'the land of Wales with its inhabitants'. With this, the era of the princes of Gwynedd gave way to the English princes of Wales.

The land now adoringly known as the 'Land of Castles' was officially born.

Chapter 1

Denbighshire and Flintshire

Bodelwyddan

Famed as one of the most haunted buildings in Wales, Bodelwyddan Castle is the classic site of many purposes. A recuperation hospital in the First World War, in recent times, it has served as an all-girls school, museum and visitor attraction.

As of 2021, the castle is sadly one of many plagued by financial complications. Since Lowther College closed in the 1980s, the Bodelwyddan Castle Trust has looked after the castle. In partnership with the National Portrait Gallery and Royal Academy of Arts, its rooms displayed many fine pieces of their collections. During that time, the interior was impressively refurbished in the style of the Victorian era. Sadly, in 2017 the partnership ended with the deeply disappointing decision of Denbighshire County Council to cut funding. As of 2019, the museum and gardens have been closed to the public. A sad set of circumstances for a beautiful building nominated 'Museum of the Year' as recently as 1989. One can only hope that the right buyer will come.

Located near the village of the same name, a stone's throw from the seaside town of Rhyl, Bodelwyddan Castle was founded around 1460. Its first owners were the Humphreys family, who hailed from Anglesey. What started life as a humble manor house has been improved and upgraded many times. In 1690 the Humphreys sold the castle to Sir William Williams, 1st Baronet, who briefly served as Speaker of the House of Commons in 1681. In later years the family merged with the Wynns (see Gwydir Castle).

It was under Williams's descendants that the present castle was born. Around 1830 a period of remodelling took approximately two years under the ownership of Sir John Hay Williams. Intent on creating a masterpiece in the Greek Revival style, Williams enlisted famed architects Edward Welch and Joseph Hansom (the man behind the Hansom Cab). Their combined ambition was somewhat unprecedented. As such, the site has been labelled 'wildly dramatic' and 'owing nothing to its predecessors'. Further to the grand redesigns and addition of an estate wall, Sir John Hay's passion for horticulture saw the creation of formal gardens.

Sadly for the estate, a deterioration in the family's lead mining prospects saw it fall on hard times. Consequently, Sir John's relative, Sir Herbert, 7th Baronet, inherited the castle on his cousin's death and took on the refurbishments. Thomas Hayton Mawson undertook the last great work done on the gardens in 1910. His creations complemented the earlier addition of many exotic plants from Sir John's time.

By the early twentieth century, the castle's time as a family home was nearing an end. Following the assassination of Archduke Ferdinand, the house was redeployed as part of the war effort. As well as tending to the wounded, the grounds were used for training troops in trench warfare, physical evidence of which can still be found. By 1920 further financial pressures saw the Williams-Wynns lease the property to Lowther College, followed by a sale five years later. Prior to the college's closure in 1982 (another to be cursed by financial mishaps) the school had established a reputation for talented musicians. It was also unique for being one of the first all-girls schools to own a swimming pool and private golf course. Concurrent to the museum and gardens, the owners leased a large part of the site to create a luxury hotel independent of the museum and grounds.

A fact common for sites of regular reconstruction, Bodelwyddan has established a reputation for being haunted. In recent years, the castle has become of particular interest to advocates of 'stone tape theory': the notion that the surroundings can record past happenings. Indeed, it is said that the hammering and hubbub of comings and goings were not the only occurrences during the Victorian era. Inspired by the wave of spiritualist mediums in Britain, the castle played host to many séances. Ghostly children have been heard playing, and there have been many reports of clothes and hair being pulled in the Toy Room. Chief among the alleged sightings are two Victorian girls, usually peering out into the courtyard.

A particularly famous sighting at Bodelwyddan is the 'blue lady'. Sporting a flowing dark blue dress, she wanders what was previously the Sculpture Gallery. She has also reputedly been seen to pass through a wall where a doorway once was. Whether the blue lady is the same spirit as that described as a two-dimensional, reddish-brown, or sepia tone is unclear. Both have been said to sport a long dress, seemingly of the same period.

The ghost of a soldier in World War One uniform has been witnessed strolling one of the galleries. Despite fitting the broader profile of a former inhabitant, his identity remains unknown. Perhaps he was brought to the castle to undergo treatment and rehabilitation. A far darker spirit is said to dwell in the cellar and has been described as unfriendly to women.

By far, the strangest haunting is that of disembodied legs. Seen by a security guard as he opened a door that led from the entrance hall to Watts Hall, the sight of black shoes with gold buckles below white stockings was clear enough to report. What had become of the spirit's torso remains one of the castle's more colourful mysteries.

Chirk

On first viewing, the modern façade of Chirk Castle has more in common with a stately home than one of Edward I's great citadels. Indeed, should a visitor arrive at the small town of the same name in the hope of finding a majestic Harlech-style ruin, the last thing they may expect is a well-rounded establishment with manicured gardens in the care of the National Trust. The reason for the discrepancy, of course, can be summed up in one word – Cromwell. While his name is often regarded as a swear word among castle lovers, on closer inspection, one will find Chirk a castle of reinvention and survival.

As indicated by its age, the original castle was another vital link in Edward I's strategy to cement his conquest of the north. On this occasion, the builder was Edward's loyal ally Roger Mortimer de Chirk, uncle and near-namesake of the famous 'greatest traitor', Roger Mortimer, 1st Earl of March. Mortimer erected the fortress around 1295 to guard the Ceiriog Valley. Being located within 200m of Offa's Dyke, which denoted the ancient Welsh border, and between the cold waters of the rivers Dee and Ceiriog, the castle became the administrative centre of the local Marcher Lordship of Chirkland. As the Marcher lordships declined following Henry IV's accession, Chirk's status wavered with it. In 1593 the castle was sold.

In addition to the Mortimers, two families are commonly associated with the castle: the Trevors and the Myddeltons. One could also add the Hugheses of Gwerclas to this list: an ancient Welsh family descended from the kings of Powys Fadog. Information about precisely what transpired during the period 1295-1593 is frustratingly sparse. In 1593, the Trevors sold the property for the hefty sum of £5,000 to Sir Thomas Myddelton, a merchant adventurer and future Lord Mayor of London. During his son and namesake's tenure, an initial allegiance to Cromwell spared the castle of Roundhead-related trouble. However, this changed when Myddelton defected during the Cheshire Rising of 1659 under George Booth, 1st Baron Delamer.

Exactly when Chirk was partially demolished is unclear. The third Sir Thomas Myddelton, styled 1st Baronet of Chirke, inherited the castle after Charles II's accession. The chain continued until the male line died out in 1796. The final Myddelton to inherit the castle was Charlotte, later Mrs Robert Biddulph, who joined their respective surnames. Their son and successor was Robert Myddelton Biddulph, whose descendants inherited it. Except for the first half of the twentieth century, when the castle was leased to Baron Howard de Walden, Chirk remained a Myddelton property until 2004. With this, an arrangement with the National Trust that began in 1981 became obsolete.

There is little doubt that the castle's present appearance offers a greater connection to more recent times than medieval conquest. Before serving as a refuge for evacuees in the Second World War, the country house-style façade made it the perfect setting for the film *Victory and Peace* in 1918. Today, under National Trust ownership, the estate is popular among visitors for its clipped yew hedges, attractive terraces, rich collection of art, carpets and tapestries, and Georgian parkland.

Yet should one dig a little deeper, surprises await. Approximately 300m from the castle, the remains of an ancient tree can be found close to the earthworks of Offa's Dyke. According to legend, the tree dates from the reign of the ninth-century Saxon king Egbert of Wessex. In the twelfth century, it is believed to have been used as a grave marker for victims of the Battle of Crogen, fought between Henry II and Owain Gwynedd. It has been described as the 'only living witness of the battle' and earned the nickname 'Oak at the Gate of the Dead'.

Joining the veteran tree, many other reminders have survived of the castle's dark past. The original dungeon and tower remain from the medieval period. Records from 1422 tell of the transfer of 15 French prisoners there from the Tower. That they are among the castle's ghosts is a tantalising thought. The apparition of a lady in a black Victorian costume has been seen on the grand staircase. Footsteps have been heard in the Long Gallery, while others have complained of being touched by unseen hands. Similar tales concern the sounds of children running along corridors. In the king's bedroom, a woman's shouting has been heard by multiple people. Noises and peculiar smells are also reported there.

Stories of paranormal activity are said to plague other parts of the castle. A happy man in a brown outfit has been seen on many occasions. A lady in an oversized dress, and another in green pyjamas, have also been reported. Even more bizarre was the moving of furniture and a conversation between two invisible forces. Among the most incredible sightings were two soldiers in First World War uniforms carrying a third on a stretcher.

A strange epilogue to Chirk Castle's catalogue of mysteries concerns the origin of the Myddelton family coat of arms. Local legend tells that a dispute occurred at some point in the castle's past when the elderly owner had to decide how to split his fortune between his twin boys. The pair agreed to partake in a race between the castle gates and the lake. As the more popular of the brothers closed in on victory, he was cut down by a supporter of his opponent, culminating in the origin of the 'bloody hand'. Various other editions of the story have also been passed down, including that they swam across the lake, at which point the first hand to touch the far shore was cut off. A more bizarre version tells that the less popular brother, trailing by a few metres, chopped off his own hand and tossed it across the line to win the race. A different story tells that a curse was placed on the family and would only be removed if a prisoner could survive ten years in the castle dungeons. The legend goes on to explain the likelihood that no prisoner ever could. Perhaps the strangest potential origin story still conjectured that he would inherit the castle if one could stay alive for twelve years without cutting his fingernails.

Perhaps the most likely point of origin is that a battle during the family's formative years led to the injury of an early Myddelton dressed in a white tunic. On touching the tunic with his bloodied hand, the heraldic symbol was born. The rest, as they say, is history.

Denbigh

Seated on a steep slope that towers above the county town of Denbighshire, Denbigh Castle was in every way a defensive masterpiece. Begun in 1282 by Henry de Lacy, Earl of Lincoln, to form part of Edward I's

Iron Ring, this imposing fortress occupies an almost perfect military position. Few castles enjoyed such excellent views of the surrounding area. Nor were many so challenging to besiege.

Like much of the Iron Ring, modern-day Denbigh is a castle of contrasts. Though Parliamentarian siege and father time has brought parts to the point of dilapidation, reminders of Denbigh's former grandeur are also clear to see. The great medieval gatehouse that famously stood guard against would-be invaders remains the initial greeting for any modern visitor. Similar is true of some of the surrounding towers. A combination of centuries of weathering and the colour of the local Gwespyr stonework has left the walls a slimy green, creating the strange impression that a great snakeskin has been shed. Carved into the stonework of these 'Green Chambers', a series of Gothic corbels achieve the chilling illusion that ancient eyes watch on. In the town itself, the remains of the old walls merge seamlessly with the modern: so much so, it isn't easy to see where the old ends and the present begins. The Burgess Gate that offered entry to the old town remains a jewel in the North Wales crown. Reminiscent of nearby Conwy and Caernarfon, the construction of Denbigh Castle and its town walls were a complementary project.

Situated within the ancient Welsh patrimony of Perfeddwlad, which controlled the Denbigh Moors' farmlands and led to the creation of Gwynedd's royal palace, Denbigh was always destined to become an important location in the context of local government. When Edward I toasted early success in the region in 1277, the king granted Perfeddwlad to the Welsh prince Dafydd ap Gruffudd, brother of Llywelyn ap Gruffudd, but not always the prince's ally. Dafydd clearly rated the site, as he adopted the improved castle and settlement of Dinbych – an abbreviation of Dinas Fechan, which translates as 'little fortress' – as his chief residence.

Many legends surround the area's earliest times. Ancient folklore records that a fire-breathing dragon once terrorised the area until one Sion y Bodiau defeated it. A giant of a man, Bodiau was reputedly possessed of two thumbs and eight fingers on each hand, earning him the English nickname, Sir John of the Thumbs. On killing the dragon, he repeatedly cried '*Dim bych*', meaning 'no dragon'. From this, Denbigh was born.

On firmer historical ground is what followed Dafydd's construction. By 1282 the feuding brothers had resolved their differences and entered an alliance. Concerned by Dafydd's perceived treachery, Edward marched on North Wales with a large force and took the castle in October. Edward later created a new Marcher lordship there and granted the renamed Denbigh to Henry de Lacy.

Consistent with the building of the other great citadels of Edward's 'Iron Ring', the influence of the king's master mason, James of St George, proved of intrinsic importance. As with nearby Conwy, great emphasis was placed on defence and surveillance: a feat achievable due to the castle's lofty location. Complementary to both factors, Edward's decision to rebuild atop a former Welsh stronghold was symbolically of great importance and proved detrimental to the Welsh morale.

As the king probed ever deeper into the Snowdonia wilderness, de Lacy worked hard on his new fortress. By 1285, the castle and town were already prospering. The town walls followed the castle's southern and western sides, around which time Henry granted the town its first charter. A census from no later than 1286 reveals that the 9.5-acre town held sixty-three burgesses, mostly of English birth. Work on the remaining defences and nearby buildings continued throughout the next decade. Despite possessing many fine features, the castle remained incomplete when Madog ap Llywelyn laid waste to the area in September 1294. Though the rebellion saw the castle change hands, it was swiftly recovered before the end of the year, thanks chiefly to de Lacy's relief force. Once back in control, the earl subsequently improved the defences.

On de Lacy's death in 1311, and with his son having predeceased him, the castle passed to his daughter, Alice. Wife of Thomas, Earl of Lancaster – grandson of Henry III by Edward I's younger brother, Edmund – Alice's situation became complicated by her husband's execution for treason against Edward's son and heir, Edward II, in 1322. Further to Lancaster's deprival of estates, a stunning insight into the instability of the time can be found in the knowledge that Denbigh's owners in Edward II's reign included royalists Hugh le Despenser the Younger and William Montagu, as well as the king's usurper, Roger Mortimer.

Despite the toing and froing of fortunes, work on the castle and town walls progressed well. In 1355 Mortimer's descendants regained the lordship, after which Denbigh's prospects soared. So impressive had the joint castle and town defences become, rebellion by Owain Glyndŵr achieved little beyond raids of the town. Due to the young age of Edmund Mortimer, 5th Earl of March – he was only seven years old on the death of his father, Roger, the fourth earl, in 1398 – Henry IV subsequently bestowed Denbigh's command to Sir Henry 'Hotspur' Percy. Under Hotspur's guidance, Denbigh stood firm, and Edmund held the castle until dying childless in 1425. For the first time in almost a century, Denbigh left Mortimer hands and became the property, through marriage, of Richard, 3rd Duke of York.

Under York, Denbigh's role in the Wars of the Roses was more or less assured. In 1457 Henry VI placed the castle under the constabulary of Jasper Tudor, Earl of Pembroke, albeit still technically in York's possession. When the Lancastrians achieved victory at Ludford Bridge in 1459, Jasper finally forced the garrison to surrender. As the war ebbed and flowed, Yorkist control resumed in 1461 under Sir Richard Herbert. In 1467 William Herbert was appointed constable and steward a year before Jasper's return saw the town razed. Somewhat predictably, this resulted in a widespread exodus, which eventually led to new suburbs. Writing in 1586, the antiquarian William Camden recorded that the 'old town is now deserted'.

Though the castle became a centre of county administration, its condition improved little. The gatehouse and accompanying towers were used primarily as a courthouse and prison. In 1563 Elizabeth I leased the castle to Robert Dudley, who built a church in the town, yet little changes were made to the castle beyond minor repairs. Dudley died in 1588, the year of the Spanish Armada.

Denbigh's final date with destiny would occur the following century. Like most castles, when the English Civil War encroached into Wales, the castle's garrison was stoutly Royalist. Charles I was even recorded as having sought refuge at Denbigh for three days in September 1645 following the Battle of Rowton Heath. In October, a force led by Sir William Vaughan was attacked at Denbigh Green, a stone's throw from the old friary, as they sought to relieve the royal troops at Chester. As the Roundhead body led by Sir Thomas Mytton approached the castle, they also took parts of the suburbs. After failing to infiltrate the main town, Mytton returned with reinforcements the following year. A siege that began in April 1646 battered the east side with heavy artillery. Only on hearing word of the king's willingness to concede did the valiant Royalist Colonel William Salesbury finally enter negotiations to surrender. When terms were agreed, Parliament installed a small garrison under Colonel George Twistleton, who used it chiefly to incarcerate political prisoners. A Royalist gaol break in 1648 came to nothing.

Unlike many castles of Royalist persuasion, Denbigh initially avoided destruction or slighting. This changed in 1659 when Sir George Booth targeted the castle and town as part of a rebellion against Cromwell's commonwealth. In August, they successfully seized the castle and imprisoned the Roundhead garrison. Unfortunately for Booth, defeat at Winnington Bridge a few weeks later put paid to any chance of further success. No sooner was the castle back under Ironside's control than General Monck ordered its slighting. Over the coming six weeks, at least two towers and parts of the curtain walls were flattened by gunpowder. As was the custom, part of the stonework was used to build new houses.

With this, Denbigh's period of prominence came to something of an end. In 1696 it was returned to the Crown after a brief period under the Earl of Portland, yet little effort was made to ensure its future. A further 150 years of neglect saw this once magnificent fortress slowly crumble. In the Victorian era, a castle committee was created to look after the ruins, and repairs gradually took place. Some of the more contemporary buildings were destroyed to allow room for new research. Care, like most, now lies with Cadw.

Though the castle has been uninhabited for many years, local legend tells that the ghosts of its past remain. In contrast to the destroyed areas, the strangely named 'Goblin Tower' remains mostly unchanged from the castle's heyday. Surrounded by woodland, a natural spring flourished here. It was to protect this vital water source Henry de Lacy built the tower.

Sadly for the earl, the tower was also the site of a dreadful tragedy. During his tenure, de Lacy was left heartbroken after his son slipped from the scaffolding to his death. Of the exact circumstances, conjecture has been rife. It remains unclear whether the young lad hit his head or drowned. More than six centuries have passed, yet many locals still view the tower with trepidation. The petrified face of a pale boy has been reported looking through a void where a window once existed.

The imposing shell is also said to be haunted by the spirit of a lady. Over the years, the 'lady in white' has been reported floating around the Goblin Tower. In 1999 three local youths were reported to have spotted her, standing at the foot of one of the medieval towers. The figure reportedly stood silently before gliding slowly towards them. Local lore also tells that a child was dropped down the well, though this may be a corruption of the young de Lacy's story. Who the woman was and the possible identity of a second child remains unclear. With so many spirits of its eventful past reputed to interact with the living, it is no surprise that the castle is often avoided at night.

Dinas Brân

Perched on a hilltop above the Denbighshire town of Llangollen, the ruined Castell Dinas Brân is one of the great enigmas of Welsh history.

Unlike many of the nation's great citadels, the site's story begins long before the Norman Conquest of Britain. Indeed, its origins may date from around the sacking of Jerusalem by Nebuchadnezzar in 586BC. While chaos reigned over the Biblical city, in the north of Wales, the erection of a humble earthen rampart, probably surrounded by a deep ditch, wooden palisade and several roundhouses, was one of the significant constructions of the Welsh Iron Age. Sadly, little record has survived of its creators or its history during the Roman era. The best evidence suggests it was created by the Ordovices: a Celtic tribe that dominated the area prior to the Roman invasion. The first structure to succeed the primitive hillfort may have been the preserve of Elisedd ap Gwylog, a prominent Romano-British ruler of the eighth century. Similarly little is known of Elisedd except for a general acceptance that his inclusion on the Pillar of Eliseg near Valle Crucis Abbey illustrates his importance.

Although Elisedd was revered in ancient literature as a founder of the Kingdom of Powys, no evidence of any form of Saxon structure has been found. That this should be regarded as surprising is debatable. In general, the period between the departure of the Romans and the coming of the Normans has revealed little evidence of stone construction in Britain. Local evidence also indicates that some form of fortress was destroyed by fire. If a timber structure had been present, it would most likely have been commanded by the local Welsh prince, Madog ap Gruffydd Maelor, a lord of Powys Fadog. It was Madog who founded the magnificent abbey at Valle Crucis in 1201.

While the emergence of stone castles in the north of Wales mainly occurred under Edward I, Dinas Brân was one of many constructed by the Welsh after the 1267 Treaty of Montgomery between Henry III and Llywelyn ap Gruffudd. At the time, the Lord of Dinas Brân was Madog's son, Gruffydd II ap Madog – an ally of Llywelyn. Despite Henry III's agreement to recognise Llywelyn as Prince of Wales, the Welshman was only too aware that the last protection between England and Gwynedd would be lost if Powys fell. On Gruffydd II ap Madog's death, no later than 1270, his four sons shared inheritance, with the eldest, Madog II, taking control of the fortress.

As the early years of Edward I's reign demonstrated, Longshanks had far less interest in keeping the peace than his father. In 1277 Edward commenced his grand march from Chester, leading to peace negotiations with two of Gruffydd's sons, Madog and Llywelyn. The surrender documents, however, are strange. Among the terms cited was a specific mention of the need to recapture the fortress. A short time later, a counter attempt was led by the Earl of Lincoln, Henry de Lacy: the same man later entrusted with the command of Denbigh. However, on arriving, he learned that it had already been abandoned and torched due to Madog and Llywelyn's younger brothers – Owain and Gruffydd Fychan I – continued alliance with Llywelyn.

For the English, news that the castle had been deserted must have been a significant confidence boost, not least as its razing implied that the brothers had little faith in their ability to withstand any form of intense siege. Even better news for Edward was that de Lacy found the slightly charred castle in generally good condition. Some form of English presence was established and remained in place until Edward and Llywelyn made terms at the Treaty of Aberconwy in November.

What state the castle was in when war resumed in 1282 is not recorded. On Madog's death in 1277, his three younger brothers all carried their swords for the Prince of Gwynedd. When Edward granted custody of the castle to John de Warenne, Earl of Surrey, the earl chose to start work on nearby Holt Castle and leave Dinas Brân to the elements. Never again would it be inhabited by either English or Welsh. By the seventeenth century, the same was true of Holt.

An imposing ruin seated proudly on a lush hillock, its rugged walls frequently an extension of the gloom on a grey day, there is little doubt Dinas Brân is the ideal setting for a literary tale. In the absence of historical records, there are many legends associated with the site. The name itself is also something of a mystery. The word 'dinas' can mean both city and defended enclosure – the latter's origins are firmly established in Middle Welsh, and the former in modern. Brân, on the other hand, has been the subject of much discussion. The literal translation is crow, which may suggest it was the fortress of the crow. Another possibility is that the word was an epithet used to denote a ruler dubbed 'The Crow'.

Such a theory was posited by both the Tudor antiquarian William Camden and his contemporary, Welsh cartographer Humphrey Llwyd. Their candidate was the Gaulish chieftain 'Brennus'. An early legend linked closely with Arthurian lore is that Brân was the Duke of Cornwall's son. Other theories concern Brân the Blessed – Brân Fendigaid – an ancient Celtic king of Welsh and Irish mythology. An ancient myth tells that Brân's head was buried beneath the site on which the Tower of London was erected. From here, one can find a plausible origin for the legend of the Tower's ravens.

Many theories have been put forward over the years, including that the word derives from a hill or mountain stream – specifically a brook near Llangollen renowned for the blackness of the water. This wealth of suggestions aside, the evidence suggests that the contemporary English were convinced that the fortress was that of the 'Crow'. In Richard Gough's update of William Camden's *Britannia* in 1789, the name appears taken for granted. Within a century, an inn in Llangollen had the same name. In the Victorian era, the historian Walter Hawken Tregellas recorded that nearby Tower Farm once consisted of an outwork of the ancient defences.

Over the centuries, the site has also become deeply intertwined with Welsh literature. The famous Welsh song *Myfanwy* by Joseph Parry in 1875 is believed to have been inspired by a fourteenth-century love story of Myfanwy Fychan of the castle and the poet Hywel ab Einion. The subject was also behind the 1858 poem *Myfanwy Fychan* by John Ceiriog Hughes and *Howel's Song* by John Parry in 1822.

Of even greater intrigue is the castle's inclusion in the twelfth-century manuscript *Fouke le Fitz Waryn* or *The Romance of Fulk Fitzwarine*. Named in the literature as Chastiel Bran, the fortress is described as a ruin during the early years of William the Conqueror. Central to the tale is a bullish knight named Payn Peverel. Also mentioned in Arthurian lore, Payn takes a keen interest in the ruins on learning that the castle was abandoned due to its reputation for being haunted by evil spirits. Intent on putting his manhood to the test, Payn and fifteen 'knightly followers' took on the challenge. That night, a storm preceded the appearance of Gogmagog, a giant equipped with a mace. Payn not only protects his men but slays the giant by hitting him with his shield and cross before a fatal stabbing of the sword. With his dying breaths, the giant tells of the bravery of his great foe King Brân, who had built the castle to defend against him. According to the giant, the king proved no match for him and was later forced to flee the castle. With his dying breaths, the giant also told of a treasury of idols, including swans, peacocks, horses and a golden ox buried somewhere nearby. The location, alas, he took to the grave.

Ewloe

An air of mystery hangs over the ruins of Ewloe Castle. Situated on a rocky knoll set among dense woodland that grows close to the village of the same name in the heart of Flintshire, Ewloe is another rare breed of castle whose existence belongs to Llywelyn ap Gruffudd. Indeed, one could easily argue the walls represent the prince's last hurrah.

Like many of his grandfather's – Llywelyn ap Iorwerth – fortresses, Ewloe's exact origins are unknown. Begun, most likely, as a Norman manor house, records confirm a property on the site from shortly after Owain Gwynedd's victory at the Battle of Ewloe in July 1157. The Welsh triumph was a disaster for the English. Despite leading a considerable force, Henry II appears to have been caught off guard by a Welsh ambush as he focused on his march towards Rhuddlan. It was only thanks to Roger de Clare, Earl of Hertford's quick thinking that the king escaped with his life.

Whatever the original fortress's state for the next century, Llywelyn ap Gruffudd commissioned work to convert it into a castle almost immediately on his arrival in 1257. Due to the lack of records, the site's exact purpose remains uncertain. Contrasting theories exist on whether it was constructed as a defensive fortress or predominantly as a hunting lodge. The new castle was a rarity as it combined features from seemingly every phase of its past. Deep ditches cut into the rocks during the castle's time as a motte and bailey lie a short distance from the parapet-topped curtain wall that encloses two courtyards and an inner ward dominated by an 11-m high keep. The D-shaped design resembles Castell y Bere – constructed by Llywelyn ap Iorwerth in the 1220s – and differs considerably from the usual Norman or Plantagenet style. Two sections of the wall meet at a circular tower that combines to protect the lower outer wall. Due to the tower's layout, specifically, the gap between the curtain walls, the only way up to the parapets would have been using wooden ladders. There is also no clear evidence that the builders included gateways between the outer courtyard and inner ward. Therefore, access to the castle must have been by way of timber ramps. Though the move would have made infiltration difficult, it seems unlikely to have been popular among the garrison.

A site of ongoing skirmishes since the Norman invasion, Llywelyn's conversion of Ewloe was undoubtedly intended to build on his early successes in the north of Wales since inheriting the princedom. Progress was reversed, however, when Edward I's forces rendezvoused at Chester in July 1277. Following the establishment of a base at Flint, which led to the construction of Flint Castle, Ewloe's existence became somewhat redundant. A lack of mention in the chronicles has convinced some historians that Llywelyn had abandoned the area. Ewloe's lack of a seaport may have convinced Edward to concentrate on the new castles at Flint and Rhuddlan.

Following Edward's conquest, the only reference to the castle occurs in the Chester *Plea Rolls* of 1311 concerning the manor. Further to recalling that Llywelyn gained Ewloe in 1257 and built a castle in the woodland, the rolls state that much was still standing. By the Tudor period, however, much had changed. As was often the case, the need for building materials saw its walls ransacked. Today, the castle forms part of Wepre Country Park. Though it's now owned by a farmer, the ruins are under the ongoing care of Cadw.

To the delight of many modern visitors, the ruins very much deliver the aura of a fortress trapped both physically and in time. Amidst the dense vegetation, a deep melancholy pervades, as though the dilapidated walls themselves weep from years of neglect. Due to its location, parking on the main road's layby precedes a quarter-mile walk into the forestry. On occasions when one goes alone, the sound of flowing water dominates, attributable to the joining of two streams. A steep climb is the undoubted highlight of a perusal of the depleted sandstone walls. Disappointingly, the views fail to pass the treetops.

That the castle is altogether uninhabited is itself a matter of debate. Ghostly lights have been reported to glow above the ruins at night. From deep in the woodland, the sounds of soldiers talking, marching and the echo of iron on iron have also been heard. Local lore connects the soldiers to the battle of 1157 that took place close by. The shapes of soldiers have also been witnessed, most notably one of a headless horseman. A similar mystery surrounds the haunting tones from an unseen singer from the vicinity of the high tower.

None of the abnormal activity reported at Ewloe is surely more frightening than the strange presence believed to haunt the ramparts. This 'glowing wraith' in white is regarded as particularly unpleasant. On one sad occasion, a poor dog is believed to have been so frightened that it died of shock a few days later. Stranger still, the area is reputedly the haunt of ghostly dogs, many of whom were buried in the local pet cemetery.

Completing Ewloe's compilation of woeful tales is the local legend of Nora. A grey, nun-like figure has been reported either hovering close to a nearby stream or around a small pond. Despite her local renown, doubts about her identity remain. A common story is that she drowned after giving birth out of wedlock. Other reports suggest that she murdered the child or was decapitated following an affair with a monk.

Undoubtedly the most intriguing of these legends is that the holy lady was the princess Gwenllian ferch Llywelyn, daughter of Llywelyn ap Gruffudd. Following her father's death, Edward I placed the infant child in a convent. As the last Prince of Gwynedd's only child, her survival was potentially of great importance to the chances of Welsh insurrection. For fifty-four years, she lived a quiet life, effectively imprisoned in the Lincolnshire priory of Sempringham. The monastery's chronicler recorded her death in June 1337, just before her fifty-fifth birthday. Having been separated from her father at just a few months, it is unlikely that she remembered him, nor ever learned to speak her mother tongue. History nevertheless rightly recognises her as the last native princess of Wales.

Flint

Should one be faced with the question, which was the first castle in Wales to be created from scratch by Edward I, it is unlikely that Flint will spring to mind. The reasons for Edward's decision were practical. The site was located only a day's march from Chester and accessible via the River Dee. Of equal advantage, a nearby ford allowed for crossing on foot. Edward rightly realised that Flint would prove an important strategic point to establish control over Wales's north-east.

Unlikely it may be that the castle would ever feature in the top five of the great fortresses of Wales, its ruined walls are not without charm. Nor should its influence on Welsh history be overlooked. On completing his conquest of historic Flintshire in 1277, Edward wasted little time in commencing building work. The rocky ground on the edge of the Dee's marshland proved ideal. The project was undertaken initially by the future Mayor of Chester, Richard L'Engenour, assisted by approximately 2,000 workmen. In April the following year, when the ashlar/sandstone combination was beginning to take shape, responsibility was transferred to the legendary mason, James of St George. By November 1280, James appears to have arrived in person, beginning seventeen months of consistent progress. When the master mason moved on to concentrate on proceedings at Rhuddlan, Flint's construction was well underway.

Although the product of the same genius behind the rest of Edward I's Iron Ring, Flint's design is without precedent in Britain. Its appearance had an undeniable Savoyard feel, as illustrated by its independent keep. The possibility of a Middle Eastern influence can also not be ruled out. Whether Edward personally influenced the design, perhaps inspired by his earlier travels, or James of St George was inspired by his homeland's grand chateaux is unclear. Within a year or so of its beginnings, an outer bailey surrounded an inner ward comprised of three high towers and its imposing keep. Additional protection was also offered by a complex system of a tidal moat, gatehouse and drawbridge. The keep, or donjon tower, was used as the constable's residence, who from 1284 onwards also served ex officio as the town's mayor. A timber gallery was added atop the keep for the visit of the Prince of Wales, the future Edward II, in 1301. Beyond the walls, the origins of a permanent settlement were also well underway. In contrast to the vast expenditure rolled out for Caernarfon and Conwy, the bill for Flint was only around £6,000 (£5-6 million today).

Flint faced its first significant test when rebellion stirred in 1282 under the banner of Llywelyn's brother, Dafydd. Twelve years after surviving this initial onslaught, Madog ap Llywelyn provided a sterner test. So concerned was Flint's constable by Madog's charges, he opted to torch the fortress to prevent its capture. When Edward quashed the rebellion, a combination of rebuilding work and the allocation of property titles to the locals saw the town flourish. A relatively quiet century also brought relative stability in the north. Flint's next significant mention was its residence for the soon-to-be-dethroned Richard II in August 1399 before returning to London. The scene was famously imagined by William Shakespeare in his play *Richard II*. Richard most likely spent his time in the keep before Henry Bolingbroke's forces brought him to London.

By the Tudor age, successful English subjugation of the north of Wales brought the usual redundancy of purpose. A bystander in Owain Glyndŵr's rebellion in the early 1400s and the Wars of the Roses, Flint's final hurrah came during the civil war. After serving effectively as a Royalist fortress throughout its history, a three-month siege in 1647 culminated in a surrender. For the second time in its history, a garrison's reluctance to allow it to fall into enemy hands led to its slighting. By the early 1650s, the once-mighty citadel was already described as 'buried in its own ruins'.

Despite this, parts of the castle remained useable. Throughout the 1800s, the outer bailey served as the county gaol. In 1838 the ruins piqued the interests of romantic artists such as J.M.W. Turner, leading to its immortalisation in watercolour. Around this time, the town became the refuge of those afflicted by the Irish potato famine, leading to its being dubbed 'Little Ireland'. Sadly, a combination of a nearby lead works and a chemical factory, poor water and pollution severely impaired the quality of life. The castle became the property of the state around 1930.

A site that has seen the good, the bad and the ugly of Welsh history, and upon which the first link in Edward's 'Iron Ring' was founded, Flint's legacy in the conquest of Wales is evident. Regardless of whether any ghosts still appear in visitation, one thing for sure is that, in Flint, the community is blessed with a site of genuine importance. Its days of withstanding siege may be over, but thanks to the antisocial behaviour of a few locals, it has faced several unnecessary battles. Sadly, in life, especially in heritage matters, ignorance often serves as the greatest threat. One can only hope that in time more locals recognise the castle for the genuine treasure that it is!

Gwrych

Surrounded by a wooded hillside overlooking the north coast in the Vale of Conwy, the ruins of Gwrych Castle are a sad relic of a lavish dream blighted by continuous misfortune. Ravaged and weathered since its desertion, this once elegant home is now little more than a derelict shell possessed of collapsed floors and fire-damaged rooms.

The first stone castle on the site appears to date shortly after a timber fortress was seized in around 1170 by the fiery Rhys ap Gruffudd, Prince of Deheubarth. Gwrych itself means 'Hedged Castle', which probably indicates its origins lie in the valley's natural lushness. The remains of two Iron Age hill forts can still be found within the 250-acre estate, as well as a Roman shrine and mines that contain lead and silver.

The ancestral owners were the Llwyds of *Plas yn y Gwrych*, who were part of the royal house of Marchudd ap Cynan. Unsurprisingly, given the region's history, the estate has seen many battles, some of which were catalogued on stone tablets near the main entrance. After standing proudly above the rugged landscape for five centuries, the castle was gutted by Roundhead fire during the English Civil War. Rebuilt between 1812 and 1825, it then served as the home of the wealthy industrialist Lloyd Hesketh Bamford-Hesketh, grandfather of Winifred Cochrane, Countess of Dundonald. On his marriage to Lady Emily Esther Ann Lygon in 1825, the 4,000-acre estate contained 128 rooms and nineteen ruined towers. It was this site that Queen Victoria visited in 1832. On the death of the countess in 1924, George V declined an offer of ownership, and it passed to the venerable Order of St John. Four years later, the 12th Earl of Dundonald, Douglas Cochrane, bought the castle and used it to provide shelter in the Second World War for some 200 Jewish refugees. To meet the cost, Dundonald was forced to part with the contents.

As time went by, failure to provide for the castle's upkeep saw its condition deteriorate, and in 1985 it was shut up and fell into disrepair. An American millionaire's vision of turning the once-grand home into a hotel failed to live up to expectations. Within ten years of buying the castle in 1989 for £750,000, he had already sold up. In recent times the creation of a preservation trust and use for film and television, including the 1997 film *Prince Valiant* and the TV *series I'm a Celebrity Get Me Out of Here!,* has helped it turn a corner. Ravaged by fire, dilapidated from years of neglect, and plagued by looting, the halls of Gwrych have long been derelict. Yet, one must applaud the efforts of those who have taken on the mantle.

From the outside, the ruins are a chilling sight. A site of regular warfare and, more recently, countless false dawns, many familiar with the area's history are not surprised to discover that the empty shell is considered one of the most haunted castles in Wales. For many years, ghost hunters, new age travellers and alleged psychics have descended on Gwrych, a handful of whom have dared spend time alone within its walls. Throughout the ruins, an unearthly silence echoes like a forest devoid of life. The temperature has also been known to drop and rise inexplicably, as though a strange wind passed through.

A sombre thought pervades when contemplating the contrasting sights witnessed by the modern visitor compared to that of the Iron Queen two centuries ago. The entrance hall would have been the first part of the castle Queen Victoria saw. The windows, once lined with stained glass, have since become vacant, leaving its once splendid rooms largely unguarded against the forces of nature. Ominous gusts regularly enter through the ruined fireplaces, the frames of which have become dishevelled. Despite recent improvements, a nauseating stench of rot and decay plagues the walkways and floors. The plastered ceilings have long since crumbled, while the once celebrated wood panelling has been destroyed by fire. Light is largely prohibited from penetrating the ancient stone by breezeblock that shields uneven floors covered in dirt and broken glass even on the sunniest days. The banqueting hall, whose candelabras once illuminated walls lined with decorations that would have been the envy of many a noble home, now sits in darkness. According to local lore, the seven-foot oak door was ripped from its hinges by an unseen force.

Due to the lack of records connected with the castle, recounting specific individuals or happenings isn't easy. A lady in red has been seen in various parts. Another in a white dress has been spotted drifting throughout the long-abandoned halls. During the Second World War, a caretaker named Bill Price patrolled the corridors on the lookout for possible intruders. Possessed of a largely fearless deposition the caretaker may have been, a sense of unease always greeted him from the old library. After locking up for the night, he often returned to find objects moved and furniture rearranged, even though no sign of forced entry was found. A possible side note to the story is that the caretaker's relationship with the late countess was frosty.

One of the most fascinating hauntings at Gwrych concerns a butler who is believed to have died of a heart attack in 1915. The butler's tale went untold until a clairvoyant stayed at the castle for several weeks in the winter of 1970. She claimed to have successfully contacted many spirits, including the butler who lived in the servants' quarters. The butler allegedly told the medium of a secret passageway that led into the hillside. On reaching the staircase on her way to investigate, she felt a tightening sensation in her chest, as if she was repeatedly stabbed. The staircase is believed to be the exact spot where the butler suffered his fatal heart attack. The psychic never returned to the castle.

The 52-step Italian marble staircase is regarded by many as the jewel in Victorian Gwrych's crown. At the summit, a large window still provides outstanding views of the surrounding landscape. Near to the window, steps lead to what was once a chapel. Within it stands a door that is said to remain locked. It has never been known what lies behind it. Intriguingly, those who have entered are said to have met with a terrifying misfortune.

The tale of the secret passage is not without substance. Several miles of tunnels do indeed stretch deep into the hills and are known to end near the castle. Although the exact location has been lost, the castle's rebuilding during the Napoleonic Wars may indicate that they were put in as escape tunnels. The tunnels may also connect to a fascinating discovery made in the nineteenth century by a group of lead miners. Within the mountains, a series of Roman tunnels navigate deep into the earth. The mines, once quoted by the Romans as being 'the most perfect Roman mines in the whole of the kingdom', were found to house many interesting artefacts, including hammers, tools, and even the golden hilt of a great sword.

On the nearby mountain, Pen y Cefn, an empty cave was reportedly once the home of the Devil. The people of Llanddulas were ever wary of the Prince of Darkness, primarily because he had a peculiar habit of sneaking up on pregnant women. After his pranks became unbearable, it is said that the people visited the cave, and a priest performed the rite of exorcism. During the service, it is told that the Devil fell into a dark muddy pool after being cleansed by the Lord's Prayer.

In addition to the above, the area has many other strange tales. The western side of the Pen y Corddyn Mawr hillside has a steep cliff, which even the most experienced find challenging to climb. A large, isolated rock, known in Welsh as Craig Y Forwyn, lies on the ridge. Tradition states that any couple who successfully climb it will be married within twelve months.

A spring or lake in a nearby field is said to have once provided Gwrych with some of the purest water in the vicinity. According to legend, the beautiful lake is bottomless and once claimed the lives of several horsemen, whose souls remain forever trapped deep in the water. Similar to the lake story, a farmer in the Vale of Abergele became aggrieved when his beloved daughter fell ill. Tormented by her death, the grieving parent ventured to a holy well where he was said to have renounced his baptism vows by spitting out holy water. Sometime later, while ploughing one of his fields on a calm day, the sky darkened, the sky flashed with lightning, and the horses bolted. The steeds were later found near the holy well, but the farmer was never seen again.

Cefn Yr Ogof, the summit of the hill to the castle's west, is the setting of another great cave. Sometime in the distant past, the cave reputedly provided shelter for many British troops. A penniless squire later visited the area, fleeing Caernarvonshire to avoid his debtors. On his way, he passed a man in a sailor or soldier's uniform standing at the foot of the cave. The squire told him of his unfortunate situation, to which the stranger informed him of a bag of gold in the cave; however, under no circumstance must he touch the water. The poor squire was rewarded in his quest by finding the gold but slipped on his way out and put one leg in the water. The gold solved his debts, but his leg was forever blackened. Legend tells that one of the area's oldest families includes a black leg on its heraldic coat of arms as a reminder of their ancestor's fate. Local lore also connects the treasure with the Romans.

Perhaps the most bizarre of the claims surrounding the castle concerns a story from 1913. As was reported in several news articles, many travellers that took the nearby road leading to Colwyn Bay encountered sightings of a strange headless creature in a field beyond a hedge. Though the animal appears to have been a black and white sheep, whose head merely merged with the shadows, many avoided the road for a time. As is so often the case, the lesson is perhaps that the greatest fear is of the unknown.

Gwydir

One mile to the west of the medieval market town of Llanrwst and twelve miles south of the great castle town of Conwy, Gwydir Castle hosts many reminders of an intriguing past. Set in the Gwydir forest against the beautiful backdrop of the Snowdonia countryside, few would initially assume that the site was once the setting of many a bloody battle between post-Roman warlords. As early as 610AD, Llywarch Hen, a prince of the ancient kingdom of Rheged in northern England, fought a battle nearby. In 954, war was also waged between the realms of Gwynedd and Deheubarth.

The first building on the site originated around 1356, and many rightly regard it as one of the finest manor houses in Wales. The name is believed to derive from Gwy and Dir's combining, thus translating as 'water land'. The suggestion is plausible due to its lying on the edge of the River Conwy's floodplain. The first owner may have been Howell Coetmor, who commanded longbowmen under Edward, the Black Prince in the Hundred Years' War. His ownership of the original manor house coincides with his fighting at Poitiers on 19 September 1356 and may have been his reward. Half a century later, he reputedly supported Owain Glyndŵr's rising of the early 1400s. Assuming he had no son of the same name, this would have made him of old age. The original manor appears to have been destroyed during the Wars of the Roses.

In the 1500s, Gwydir became the seat of the Wynn family, around whom many of the castle's stories revolve. Alleged descendants of the princes of Gwynedd through Owain Gwynedd, the family enjoyed much prestige throughout the Tudor and Stuart periods. During the time of Maredudd ab Ifan ab Robert – the modern Wynn dynasty's recognised founder – Gwydir was purchased and rebuilt as a castle, albeit more reminiscent of a Tudor courtyard house. Following the Dissolution, Maredudd's son, Sir John 'Wynn' ap Maredudd, plundered the dissolved Maenan Abbey and reused some of the materials at Gwydir. Chief among the inclusions were the staircase in one of the square turrets and several beautifully carved stones.

Since Sir John's time, Gwydir has been the proud home of many. In the late 1500s, the castle was the residence of the Welsh noblewoman Katheryn of Berain. In Charles I's reign, it became the property of Sir Richard Wynn, 2nd Baronet, who served as Groom of the Royal Bedchamber and Treasurer to Queen Henrietta Maria. Charles himself is conjectured to have stayed at Gwydir in 1645. In 1899 George V and Queen Mary, while Duke and Duchess of York, also visited, by which time Lord Willoughby had overseen widescale demolition.

To visit the castle in the modern day, one cannot help raise an eyebrow in consideration of the castle's lost prestige. At its height, Gwydir was the centre of 36,000 acres of parkland, in which deer roamed freely.

The castle and estate became neglected when the Willoughbys took possession in 1678 following marriage to the Wynn heiress. Some thirty slate mines were developed within this mountainous region, most of which provided little more than roofing tiles. Such was the low quality and limited production that the estate struggled financially and was gradually sold off. When Charles Robert Wynn-Carrington, Earl Carrington, sold the castle in 1921, he broke a four-century chain of inheritance dating back to Maredudd. The panelled dining room, whose origins were traced to the 1640s, was stripped and bought at auction by William Randolph Hearst. At Hearst's bequest, the panels were later gifted to the New York Metropolitan Museum of Art, where they remained in storage for decades.

Ironically, the sale was somewhat welcome. The following year a fire gutted the Solar Tower, after which a further inferno in the West Wing rendered Gwydir derelict. In 1944 it was bought by a retired banker named Arthur Clegg, whose grand ambitions went unrealised. The modern renovations are a fine testament to the work of the present owners, Peter Welford and Judy Corbett, under who the carved and gilded dining room panelling has miraculously been restored to its rightful home.

Today, Gwydir is a castle of many curiosities. For the contemporary visitor, the Grade I-listed 10-acre gardens are likely to prove of similar intrigue to its revamped interior. A collection of ancient cedars includes one planted in 1625 to commemorate Charles I's wedding to Queen Henrietta Maria. Also worthy of mention are the 1590s Renaissance arch on the raised terrace, the ancient yew topiary, and the octagonal fountain in the Old Dutch Garden. Welsh oaks in the Royal and Stateman's gardens were planted to honour the royal visits of 1899 and 1911, while one yew tree, adoringly coined 'the Lovers Tree', is estimated to be around 1,000 years old. A chapel in the nearby woods dates to 1673 and stands as a family memorial founded by Sir Richard Wynn. Another chapel dates to an earlier Sir Richard Wynn about forty years previously. While the former is famous for its magnificent painted ceiling, the latter may owe its origins to Inigo Jones. Local legend tells that amongst the fine stone coffins is one containing the remains of Llywelyn ap Iorwerth, whose tomb was removed from Maenan Abbey during the Dissolution.

Without question, there is something undeniably special about Gwydir. It may lack the creature comforts or scars of battle associated with many Welsh castles, but it is not devoid of authenticity. The fact that the castle remains lived in, and something of a work in progress, only adds to its charm. No walk around the estate is complete without a chance encounter with one of Gwydir's muster (or ostentation) of peacocks. Indeed, some fifty peafowls still dwell there, all of which offers a tangible connection to the castle's past. According to legend, it isn't just the peacocks that provide such a connection. The ancient house is reputedly one of the most haunted homes in Wales.

In the castle's north wing, the walls that line the passageway that joins the hall of Meredith to the great chamber have been witnessed to bleed. In the nineteenth century, the room located behind the panelling – known as the 'ghost room' – was reputedly the setting of the strange process known as putrefaction – believed by some paranormal investigators to be the manifestation of a haunting. Visitors passing this area have reported a bizarre substance oozing from the panelling, accompanied by an overwhelming stench. Following the bubbling fluid's appearance, the apparition of a ghostly lady is reported to emanate. The phantom has been seen in both the corridor and the 'ghost room' wearing a long, grey dress. Accompanied by the same sickly smell, visitors walking the corridor have also reported being tapped on the shoulder by an unseen hand.

It is commonly believed that her story may relate to a tale from the 1600s and the 1st Baronet of Wynn, Sir John. A mighty man with a reputation as a scholar, an antiquary and Member of Parliament, Sir John was also somewhat loathed. Although married with several children, Wynn was said to have abused his power on at least one occasion by seducing a young maid. After the affair ended, Wynn reputedly killed her. Speculation has abounded that the servant was pregnant.

In the mid-1990s, when restoration work was being carried out, the present owners were shocked to discover the engraving of a heart and arrow accompanied by the letters JW and I in one of the chimneys. The initials are complemented by the number 1555, which indicates the inscription concerns the earlier Sir John, as opposed to the Jacobean baronet. Intriguingly, it was this chimney that harboured a void plagued by putrefaction. It is similarly something of a coincidence that the discovery backs onto the so-called 'ghost room'.

In keeping with question marks over the victim's background, the identity of the murderer has also been a cause for debate. The fifth and final baronet, also named Sir John, reputedly confessed on his deathbed in 1719 to murder at Gwydir in the mid-1600s. Due to no less than three Wynns sharing this name, it seems likely that elements of their stories have become merged if not made up altogether. Many locals believe the 1st baronet is the more likely murder candidate, primarily due to his loathsome reputation as a local tyrant. The ghost of at least one of these characters has also been seen haunting the spiral staircase that connects the Solar Hall to the great chamber.

Interestingly, it is not just inside the castle walls that the former despot has been seen. On visiting the area in the 1770s, the antiquary Thomas Pennant recounted an old tale that Sir John's spirit is trapped within a local waterfall known as the Swallow Falls, 'forever to be purged, purified and spat upon for the evil deeds committed by him in his days of nature.' For at least two centuries, his long-dead face has been reported in the falls.

Sir John and his alleged victim are not the only spirits said to haunt the castle. Another gentleman, dressed in an Edwardian suit, was often seen pacing across one of the rooms during the 1970s. A short lady sporting a yellow dress of the Elizabethan era has also been seen while crying children have been heard from the former nursery. Most fascinatingly, not just the spirits of humans have been witnessed within the ancient walls. A far friendlier ghost has also been reported: not a human, but a dog.

In her autobiographical account, *Castles in the Air*, co-owner Judy Corbett records the dog's appearance. Following a series of appearances by the loveable animal in 1995, her husband, Peter, made a surprising discovery while clearing floodwater from one of the cellars. Floating among the wreckage was a collection of small bones, nearly two hundred in total. The bones were later examined by the police and confirmed as belonging to an ancient hound. Sadly, the police later incinerated the bones, and the playful spirit has ceased to appear.

For the modern visitor, Gwydir is a pleasant sight in the day. But when night falls, the eerie formation of a phantom procession has been seen on the great terrace near Sir John's arch. Lit by torchlight, it moves silently, only to vanish without a trace. Such an event seems peculiarly in keeping with the magic of Gwydir. Like the castle itself, one is almost obliged to wonder whether such a thing could happen at all. Or whether such a magical place is itself not of this world but a castle in the air.

Rhuddlan

Beautiful Rhuddlan is undoubtedly one of Wales's most recognisable fortresses. Seated on a windy Denbighshire hilltop close to the small town of the same name, the castle famously formed part of Edward I's Iron Ring.

While post-fourteenth-century accounts of James of St George's masterpiece are well known, Rhuddlan's early history is steeped in mystery. Building on the natural defences and benefits of the River Clwyd, Edward the Elder established the town close to a Saxon burh. A nearby hill also served as the motte of an early Norman castle, *Twthill* in the local tongue. This castle may have been constructed atop Gruffudd ap Llywelyn's royal palace. The ruler of Gwynedd 1055-63, some historians regard Gruffudd as the only Welsh prince to rule over all present-day Wales. During Gruffudd's rule, Rhuddlan occupied the heart of the cantref of Rhos. From the royal palace, the lords of Rhuddlan administered the four local cantrefs that also included Rhufoniog, Dyffryn Clwyd and Tegeingl, which together formed Perfeddwlad.

Gruffudd's old palace overlooking the Clwyd was regarded as an important military site by the Normans. For this reason, the knocking down of the Welsh prince's stronghold was viewed with the inevitable symbolism. Though attempts by the earls of Chester failed to prevent Gruffudd's return from exile, which had begun when Harold Godwinson expelled him from the area, Gruffudd's retaking of the town was as good as it got. By the compiling of the *Domesday Book*, *Twthill* had been erected just to the south of the modern castle at the behest of William the Conqueror's key supporter, Robert of Rhuddlan.

No documents appear to have survived of the castle's appearance and later fate. Most likely the victim of an attack from the Welsh between 1086 and 1277, it is also possible that the English demolished it shortly after Edward I's accession. Financial records from Edward I's early reign confirm that a significant project was underway at Rhuddlan before the culmination of the war of 1277-82. Those records would seem to confirm that Rhuddlan was among the first castles Edward began constructing in the north of Wales. When the conflict started in 1277, Edward vacated his base at Chester in July and set about making a new one at Flint (see Flint Castle). By the end of the summer, and with work on Flint progressing well, he moved along the coast to Rhuddlan, at which point James of St George took over the mantle from the Gascon Master Bertram. On 9 November, a treaty was made at Aberconwy, after which the Welsh relinquished the town to Edward. A day later, the Treaty of Aberconwy was officially ratified.

Unsurprisingly, considering the influence of Bertram and James, the new fortress at Rhuddlan had much in common with the later members of the Iron Ring. No less than four stone types were used in the construction, the blending effect of which casts the castle's walls in an attractive purple-grey colour. Other oddities have also contributed to its distinct appearance. Though broadly concentric in design, placing the gatehouses at the joining of the walls of the square bailey achieved something of a diamond shape. Both gatehouses are double-towered and among the most recognisable in Wales. Complementary to both, a series of towers also mark the outer curtain wall. In the war with Llywelyn ap Gruffudd, earthen ramparts were also erected. At the castle's heart, a great hall sat adjacent to the kitchens, chapel and private apartments, parts of which no longer survive. The same is true of the granary, stables and a smithy in the outer bailey.

Being located just a few miles inland from the coast and connected by the River Clwyd, whose mouth merges with the Irish Sea to the north, Edward's builders chose to straighten its path. The chilly waters of the Clwyd joined up with a three-pronged moat to provide complete water protection of the outer curtain wall. Parts were also dredged to allow the castle to be reached by ship, which ensured supplies were always within easy reach. In 1282 its first test was passed when the walls withstood a minor rebellion. Building work stopped until a relief force led by Amadeus, later V Count of Savoy, ensured the castle's survival. A short time later, Edward authenticated a new borough to the north, from which the modern town grew.

When the rebellion was over and work was again underway, Edward sought to consolidate his early progress. Such was his faith in Rhuddlan's qualities that it was there his queen, Eleanor of Castile, gave birth to their daughter, Elizabeth. Whether or not the royal birth – 7 August 1282 – preceded the castle's completion is unclear. The completed castle was the setting of the Statute of Rhuddlan, from which the lands of the princes of Gwynedd officially passed to the Crown and English Common Law was introduced to Wales. Attempts by Madog ap Llywelyn to reverse the process a decade later failed. A year following Richard II's sojourn at Rhuddlan in 1399, on his road to Flint, Glyndŵr's forces laid siege to the castle, causing mayhem among the town but failing to pass its outer walls.

In keeping with most Welsh castles of English origin, Rhuddlan's purpose diminished during the Tudor age. This would continue until the English Civil War, when it accommodated a Royalist garrison. Throughout the first war, Rhuddlan held firm until the tide turned at the Battle of Naseby. Siege by Major-General Thomas Mytton in 1646 eventually forced its surrender. In 1648, what remained was slighted. The Welsh antiquarian Thomas Pennant remarked on passing the ruins in 1781 that one of the towers was named '*Twr-y-Silod*' – meaning Tower of Grain – and another '*Twr-y-Brenin*' – Tower of the King. It was likely within the latter that Edward I took up residence and Eleanor at Elizabeth's birth.

A famed fortress during the early days of English subjugation, a royal birthplace, and a key administration site, it is no surprise that Rhuddlan has amassed its fair share of stories. One of the castle's more colourful legends concerns Erilda, a daughter of a Welsh king, who was betrothed to Morvern. Though the father's identity is slightly unclear, Morvern's usual identification as the son of Bleddyn ap Cynfyn – Gruffudd ap Llywelyn's half-brother and successor – places him to the tenth century. After losing her way while out on a hunt, a handsome knight named Wertwrold rode out from the shadows and transported her back to Rhuddlan, her father's castle.

Only on her arrival did those present realise the black-clad knight whose helmet was capped with a red-plume feather was a demon. After convincing the knight to elope, the princess recoiled in horror when her captor revealed his true, slimy, grey form on reaching the river. The beast killed her with a stab of the tri-pronged spear at the peak of his helmet and flung her body into the Clwyd before disappearing beneath the surface. In one version of the tale, Erilda accidentally killed her father in the melee. In another, the demon entered the chapel just as vows were to be exchanged with Morvern. Initially delighted at her rescue, the maiden was never seen again. Over the centuries, Wertwrold's demonic laughter has reputedly been heard many times at Rhuddlan. Legend tells that his spirit is destined to chase the poor Erilda around the ramparts until hell freezes over.

Ruthin

Ruthin Castle now has little in common with the fortress of days past. For today's visitor, the mid-nineteenth century red sandstone hotel is a wonderful place to unwind from everyday stresses amidst the beautiful countryside of the Vale of Clwyd. Yet should one pay closer attention, beneath the surface glamour, the castle hides an underground labyrinth of dank, dark corridors and dungeons whose empty chambers are said to echo with the noise of past inhabitants.

A few rugged external walls are all that remains of Edward I's castle. When Edward took on his invasion of Gwynedd in 1277, the land was granted to Dafydd ap Gruffudd – Llywelyn's younger brother – as a token of the king's gratitude. There is some evidence that Edward's castle was situated on an Iron Age fort; however, it is unclear how much of the primitive structure existed when work began on Dafydd's new project. Like many castles of the time, the construction materials included multiple types of stone. The reddish hue evident among the grey was undoubtedly influential in the castle's original name, *Castell Coch yn yr Gwernfor*, which translates as 'the Red Castle amidst the Great Marsh'.

Five years after work commenced, the Red Castle was granted to the de Grey family, an influential clan of Anglo-Norman pedigree, who claimed descent from William Marshal, 1st Earl of Pembroke. Honoured by Edward II with the baronage Grey de Ruthin in 1324, Roger de Grey set up headquarters of his Marcher lordship of Dyffryn Clwyd (a cantref before 1282) within Ruthin's walls.

Two generations later, Roger's grandson, Reynold de Grey, 3rd Baron of Ruthin, took on the mantle. A favourite of Richard II and Henry IV, his influence in the Marcher lands has been claimed as the catalyst for Owain Glyndŵr's rebellion. Of particular importance was Reginald's issue – and enforcement – of royal grants in the Northern March. His problems with Owain also stemmed from his claim to some of Owain's property – a fact not helped by Henry IV's confiscation of the land after Richard II had favoured Owain's case. In 1410, after an ongoing legal dispute about the right to bear the arms of the Hastings family – from whom the de Greys were descended of the Marshal family – Reynold's success also entitled him to certain properties from the Earl of Pembroke's estate.

Consistent with most castles of north Wales, the quelling of Owain Glyndŵr's rebellion had a clear calming effect. After more than two centuries of little notable use – the imprisonment and torture of the Welsh poet, recusant and later saint Richard Gwyn being a notable exception – the creation of a Royalist garrison in the civil war found the fortress in disarray. After rapid repair work, it was able to withstand a Roundhead siege for eleven weeks. Only when the opposing force formed plans to lay mines beneath the walls did the garrison finally surrender. On Cromwell's orders, the remains were slighted.

For the next two centuries, what remained of Ruthin's walls entered the usual period of relative obscurity. In the early 1920s, a degree of refurbishment and rebuilding led to the castle becoming Britain's first private hospital for researching obscure diseases. Though it closed in the early 1950s, the building was updated again and reopened as a hotel. Its guests have included Prince Charles, who chose the hotel for his inauguration as Prince of Wales at Caernarfon (see Caernarfon Castle). At the time of writing, Ruthin continues to welcome both tourists and spa lovers, royal and non-royal alike.

A site that has endured such a varied history, it is perhaps unsurprising that the hotel is said to house a somewhat more permanent guest alongside its loveable peacocks. Dubbed 'the grey lady', the designation has more to do with her appearance than family. Ironically, the lady in question is believed to be the wife of either the first or third Baron Grey's deputy. Tradition tells that her husband had an affair with a local, after which the scorned wife axed the mistress to death. Found guilty of the murder, she was executed. As was customary at that time, she was buried outside the castle walls in unconsecrated ground. A pile of stones reputedly designates her grave. Her spirit is said to haunt the battlements and chapel.

Chapter 2

Anglesey, Caernarvonshire & Merionethshire

Beaumaris

Famed among castle lovers as Edward I's lost masterpiece, Beaumaris is a fascinating mixture of raw beauty and incompleteness.

To cement his hold on Gwynedd in 1282, Edward initially focused on securing the mainland, leading to the creation of the castles and town walls of Conwy, Caernarfon and Harlech. To augment his command of the north-east, the king also formulated plans to establish a castle near the village of Llanfaes on Anglesey, but this was delayed due to the spiralling costs. Like the rest of Wales, the isle was plagued by infighting. Even at the best of times, control by the princes of Gwynedd had been somewhat fragmented. Originally a Viking settlement named *Porth y Wygyr* – literally Port of the Vikings – the area became an important trading port with the Irish, which unsurprisingly piqued the interest of raiding pirates. By the time of Beaumaris's creation, Llanfaes was the wealthiest borough in the country and most heavily populated.

Construction was still to commence when Madog ap Llywelyn began his rebellion in 1294. The local sheriff, Roger de Pulesdon, was a notable loss who was killed by Madog's forces. On securing Anglesey in April 1295, Edward immediately prioritised the construction of a new fortress. The name 'Beaumaris' likely comes from the English 'fair marsh' and was located one mile from Llanfaes. As the native population were relocated, the creation of an English town followed. On the watch of the renowned James of St George, the castle was established in one corner of the new town, whose designs bore more than a passing resemblance to nearby Conwy, albeit without the town walls. Documents cite his title as '*magister operacionum de Bello Marisco*', which could translate as 'head of operations of the fair marsh'.

As with his other castles, St George appears to have kept a constant presence at Beaumaris. In keeping with the other castles of the Iron Ring, the scale was enormous. An estimated workforce of 2,000 of varying skills ensured progress was rapid. Records of the work have thankfully survived in a tremendous volume of pipe rolls. The following year, work began to ease off, which tallies with evidence that debt levels were rising. By 1300 the renewed war with Scotland proved a significant drain on the king's resources, bringing work on Beaumaris to a halt. Total costs neared £11,000, yet neither the inner walls nor towers had reached their projected heights. By Edward's death in 1307, the new castle had already become somewhat neglected, while work on the outer defences became an increasing concern. Such things continued under Nicolas de Derneford after James of St George's death in 1309. By the early years of Edward III, an outlay of £15,000 had still not seen the walls reach their intended heights. A royal survey taken in 1343 concluded that less than £700 could see the project completed; however, the money was never spent.

As the following years showed, Edward's decision was a poor one. A military genius and administrator of the highest order, his oversight was Owain Glyndŵr's gain. Beaumaris fell in 1403 and was held for two years. On its recapture, maintenance again proved inadequate. A report composed in 1534 during the constabulary of Roland de Velville reported most rooms were rain-soaked. Five years later, another account lamented a pitiful arsenal of fewer than ten guns and forty bows, an amount unlikely to withstand attack. A further report from 1609 decried the castle as 'utterlie decayed', which bode incredibly ill for the upcoming civil war.

Located on the sailing route to Ireland, Beaumaris was understandably considered of some importance during this period. Under the watchful eye of the Royalist Thomas Bulkeley, 1st Viscount Bulkeley, whose family had managed the site for some years, an estimated £3,000 was spent to reinforce it. How the improvements would have fared was never tested. As Roundhead dominance reached its zenith after Charles I's defeat at Naseby, Thomas's son, Colonel Richard Bulkeley, surrendered in June. A revolt on Anglesey in 1648 briefly saw Royalist resumption of control, yet this was also over by October.

By 1649 the slighting that afflicted so many royal fortresses in the post-civil war period had become a severe threat to the castle's future.

Fortunately for Beaumaris, following discussion in Parliament, the potential threat of invasion from the Royalists' Scottish allies ensured its refortification. On the restoration of the monarchy, the Bulkeleys were reinstated at the expense of Colonel John Jones. Lucky in the sense that the castle avoided slighting, the asset-stripping that cursed Conwy and Caernarfon followed. In 1807 a Bulkeley descendant, Lord Thomas Bulkeley, purchased the castle for £735 and incorporated it into the park that swallowed up his residence, Baron Hill.

As the ruins of Wales enjoyed the attention of famous artists, Beaumaris became the focus of Turner. Three years earlier, in 1832, the soon-to-be Queen Victoria also visited. While some of the stones may have been reused for the local gaol, renewed interest in the castle saw its restoration become a top priority. In 1925 custodian Richard Williams-Bulkeley handed the fortress to the Commissioners of Works. Classification of the castle in 1950 as 'one of the outstanding Edwardian medieval castles of Wales' seems self-evident. In 1986 UNESCO officially made it a world heritage site.

Plagued by crippling finances, neglect and civil unrest, the beautiful marsh would never live up to its true potential. Had that been reached, modern-day visitors may have been treated to a Harlech-style twin, if not a Caernarfon-like palace. Nevertheless, the Bodiam-esque shell that stands today, surrounded by an equally attractive moat, is no failure. The symmetrically arranged limestone and sandstone combination is a prime example of what some considered the ideal formula for a military fortification. Many who lament its incompleteness still consider the castle something of a work of art. Located on the coast with the main gate by the sea, the setting is indeed one of extreme beauty and functionality. Had the castle been completed and subsequently maintained, there is every reason to believe Beaumaris may well have been the finest of James of St George's works. Some would argue that it is anyway.

Be it a missed opportunity or a delightful accident, there is no doubt that Beaumaris's remains are a must-see for any castle hunter. By day the grassy courtyards and countless passages are a real treat that can genuinely bring out the best in one's imagination. At night, however, the feel is more oppressive. Ghostly sightings have plagued the castle throughout the centuries. The echo of religious chanting has been heard in the chapel and even recorded in some cases. Even the briefest moment inside is enough to establish the strength of the acoustics. Similar reports have concerned bizarre screams in other parts of the castle, a reminder, perhaps, of a forgotten tragedy, most likely during one of the sieges. Cold spots are said to occur at random. Like Carew in the south, the presence of bats in the dark corners can be a terrifying experience, especially if one should take a photograph with the flash on.

Though the castle's reputation for the paranormal is subdued compared to the nearby gaol, it is difficult to escape the feeling that one is walking in old footsteps, even on a quiet day. The feeling of being watched, the daunting noise of unseen footsteps and onsets of extreme loneliness are also common, especially in the inner courtyard. The occasional sighting of figures from a bygone time has also been witnessed. Who they were and why they remain tied to Beaumaris is another mystery unlikely to be solved. Like the castle itself, the tale of Beaumaris is one of extreme intrigue and beauty, but, ultimately, one never destined to be finished.

Caernarfon

Standing proudly on the Anglesey shoreline, nine miles south-west of the ancient city of Bangor, Caernarfon is architecturally one of Britain's finest castles.

Like many in Edward I's Iron Ring, the initial fortifications were Roman. A fort, *Segontium*, was constructed a short distance from the modern walls on the banks of the River Seiont. Early records dubbed the land *y gaer yn Arfon*, which means 'the stronghold in the land over against Môn' – Môn being the Welsh name of Anglesey. It was from this that the name Caernarfon originates.

Little documentation survives of *Segontium*. Most likely abandoned following the Romans' departure, the ruins were still visible when William the Conqueror made his first march into Wales. During the compilation of the *Domesday Book*, Norman command of North Wales was officially the preserve of Robert of Rhuddlan: the man behind the first castle at Rhuddlan. How much power this warlord wielded is a matter for speculation. At the time, most Norman power came from the Marcher lands to the south and border region. When the natives killed Rhuddlan in 1093, his cousin, Hugh d'Avranches, Earl of Chester, attempted to exert authority by establishing three castles, one of which was a typical motte and bailey on a peninsula flanked by the River Seiont and the Menai Strait. This timber motte and bailey fell in 1115 when the Welsh took Gwynedd. Contemporary evidence tells that both Llywelyn ap Iorwerth and Llywelyn ap Gruffudd made use of it.

Ongoing war with England, of course, ultimately culminated in total conquest. When a determined Edward led his charges into North Wales in 1282 the fall of the remaining castles under Welsh control preceded the building of new. Along with contemporaries Harlech and Conwy, no finer castle was constructed than the new fortress at Caernarfon. In place of the motte and bailey – the former of which was integrated into the new structure – the stone fortress marked a drastic transformation in the town's appearance. In addition to the new citadel, town walls and a new quay were added. The genius behind the progress was once again most likely James of St George. The castle's appearance again indicates that he often spent time in the Holy Land and may well have been a contemporary of the crusader king there.

Typical of the time, sources concerning the building work are something of a mixed bag. Work on the foundations and digging a ditch proved mammoth tasks, on which several hundred were involved. As the project became increasingly ambitious, rapid expansion required the mass clearing of local houses. Though the previous residences were cleared quickly, compensation for their owners was far from instant. Indeed, many had to wait three years before receiving their due. Edward also commissioned timber-framed apartments for himself and his queen, Eleanor of Castile. They are recorded as having stayed for more than a month after arriving no earlier than 11 July 1283.

Even in the castle's early days, legends were rife. One captivating story, recorded in the *Flores Historiarum*, states that the Roman emperor Magnus Maximus's remains were discovered during the construction work. He was buried in a local church on Edward's orders. Another intriguing tale concerns the castle's layout. Renowned for his fascination with the Arthurian romances, Edward took inspiration from the stories of Merlin. That he sought a palace worthy of remembrance in the company of the great kings, such as Arthur, is unsurprising. The castle also dates to a similar period to that of Winchester's great round table, which Edward most likely created for an Arthurian-themed tournament.

Edward's first son, later Edward II, was born on 25 April 1284 in one of the three small turrets of the Eagle Tower. When the king heard the good news, he knighted the messenger on the spot before hurrying to North Wales and summoning the chieftains to offer homage. A sixteenth-century legend cites that, on meeting with Edward, the recently conquered natives asked that the king appoint a prince who spoke neither English nor French. Better still, one of Welsh birth. To this, Edward presented his infant son. Whether the king had deliberately chosen that the young prince's delivery should occur in Wales or that this was a chance of fate is unclear. Regardless, in 1301 the teenage Edward of Caernarfon was invested Prince of Wales and obtained control of its incomes. Since that time the castle has been regarded as the palace of the new dynasty of princes. In 1911 Prince Edward, later to be crowned King Edward VIII, had his inauguration there. The same was true of Prince Charles in 1969.

Records suggest that the town walls were complete by 1285. Documents regarding the castle's building work also temporarily cease in 1292. Two years later, the Welsh rebel Madog ap Llywelyn targeted the castle with some success. On taking control of the ditch and temporary barricade, the latter was set alight, along with anything flammable. The inferno was of great consequence to the English. Further to losing the castle, significant damage was brought upon the town walls. Despite these high-profile mishaps, the English retook the castle no later than the summer of 1295 and began refortifying the town walls in November.

Work also recommenced on completing the fortress for the first time since 1292. As James of St George moved his attentions to Beaumaris, Walter of Hereford assumed the role of master mason. Walter departed in 1300, after which another lull in accounts suggests a labour hiatus until 1304. Whether this was directly related to Walter's absence, a shortage of funds or the complication of Edward's war with Scotland remains unclear. Work was continued after Walter's death in 1309 by his subordinate, Henry of Ellerton, and proceeded until 1330.

For all its magnificence, Caernarfon never fulfilled its potential. Even today, the interior remains littered with features intended for a sumptuous royal palace. Neither of the rears of the entrances at the King's Gate and the Queen's were completed. As was so often the case, overly ambitious plans and spiralling costs proved a wretched combination. Between 1277 and 1329 the total outlay on Edward's Welsh building projects stood at an estimated £95,000: approximately £58m in modern money. Of this, around £20,000-25,000 related to Caernarfon and the town walls. By contrast, work on Dover – often cited as the key to England – came in at well under £8,000.

By the mid-fourteenth century the castle was not so much a palace but an arms depot. Due to its importance as an administrative site, it was permanently garrisoned and became a frequent target of unrest. As the bulk of power remained with the English officials, the castle was forced to withstand countless Welsh sieges, including those of Owain Glyndŵr in 1401, 1403 and 1404. The Battle of Tuthill in November 1401 was fought nearby between the castle's defenders and besiegers.

With the coming of the Tudors, Caernarfon's need, like most of Wales's great castles, became less critical. Though the walls remained strong, the roofs were neglected; by 1620 only the Eagle Tower and King's Gate remained covered. The domiciles were emptied of their valuables, including raw materials such as glass and iron. Such deprivation did not, however, make the walls undefendable. When the civil war came to Anglesey, the Royalist garrison repelled two sieges before falling to a third in 1646. Orders that the castle and town walls be dismantled were fortunately never carried out.

Despite the reprieve, neglect remained ongoing until the 1870s. Thanks to the, at times misguided, work of the deputy-constable Llewellyn Turner, Caernarfon was both conserved and restored. Though it remains the property of the Crown, a combination of Cadw and the Welsh Government has ensured that the castle, now a UNESCO World Heritage Site along with the town walls, continues to be enjoyed by future generations.

A fine example of Plantagenet splendour, the area is also reputed to be plagued by dark tales from the past. Even before the Romans, stories of the ancient Druids, famous for their pagan rituals and bloody sacrifices, had been passed down. Since Edward I's time, the area's witnessing of hangings, murders, wars, and plagues has undoubtedly added to its gruesome reputation. Groaning and footsteps have been heard in the dead of night. Sightings of its former inhabitants have also been reported. One of the most seen apparitions is that of a woman, who appears a misty blue shape in the courtyard. Whether she is the same spirit that was once caught on camera outside the Eagle Tower is unclear. Ghostly soldiers have also been seen in various parts. Like the unknown lady, they have been seen marching the courtyard before vanishing without a trace.

Castell y Bere

Seated in the shadow of the mighty Cadair Idris on a rocky hillock that offers unrestricted views of the Dysynni Valley, the rugged ruins of Castell y Bere bear the scars of a castle plagued by war.

The castle's early days are somewhat unusual in Welsh history. Of native origin, the fortress was built due to a family dispute. Though the Welsh princes had erected many castles in the south, as a rule, they created austere palaces or courts instead of massive citadels. *llysoedd* in the native language.

By the 1220s, Llywelyn ap Iorwerth's dominance over the non-Norman parts of Wales was almost absolute. Indeed, large swathes of Norman land in the middle of Wales was in danger of falling for the first time since the days of William Rufus. Buoyed Llywelyn undoubtedly was by recent inroads against the English, whose situation had become increasingly complicated by the fallout surrounding Magna Carta – not least the surprise death of King John and the young Henry III's accession – the Prince of Gwynedd had become increasingly disappointed by his eldest son's performance in command of Meirionnydd. Shortly after imprisoning Gruffudd, with whom he fell out due to matters in Meirionnydd, Llywelyn swiftly started work building a castle to protect Gwynedd's south-west border, along with the mountain trade routes around Cadair Idris.

The result was impressive. In addition to establishing a degree of control over the roads that connected Gwynedd, Deheubarth, and Powys Wenwynwyn, Castell y Bere was the only native Welsh castle except for Criccieth that appears to have included decorative sculpture. The majority that have survived are either statues of soldiers or floor tiles. The castle proved the first in a spate of new fortresses Llywelyn ordered and consisted of several towers around a courtyard from which views continued as far as the eyes could see.

As the following years would show, Llywelyn's death would prove a significant turning point for both castle and kingdom. By 1240 a combination of Llywelyn's passing and Henry III's coming of age saw both a decline in Gwynedd's power and the loss of the eastern lands by 1247. In 1255, a power struggle between Llywelyn's grandsons, Llywelyn and Owain ap Gruffudd, saw the former imprison the latter. Among his many developments throughout Gwynedd, Llywelyn extended his grandfather's castle at Castell y Bere by adding the south tower.

His best efforts, alas, would prove in vain. As Edward I marched further inland, the castle fell to the English in April 1282 following a brief siege by Roger Lestrange and William de Valence, 1st Earl of Pembroke. That same year a violent skirmish resulted in Llywelyn's death near Builth. No sooner had the prince's little remaining power passed to Llywelyn's brother, Dafydd, than Edward's rampant march forced their retreat to Snowdonia. Deployment of 7,000 troops finally saw Dafydd's capture and execution in 1283. Though Llywelyn's epithet, 'the last', would ensure immortality, for Gwynedd and Wales, the cause was lost.

Back in mid-Wales, Edward I viewed Castell y Bere worthy of consideration. After visiting three times in 1284, he employed five masons and five carpenters to expand the castle and establish a small town. Among the improvements, £47 was spent on a luxury chamber, most likely for private accommodation. The other rooms relied on central hearths instead of fireplaces. Edward also spent an additional £262 to combat Rhys ap Maredudd's revolt by constructing a barbican, gate towers, and interlinking walls. With Walter of Huntercombe at the helm as constable, the castle also faced Madog ap Llywelyn's rebellion in 1294. Besides the king ordering Richard Fitzalan, Earl of Arundel, to help reinforce the defences, what happened next remains something of a mystery. The Welsh appear to have taken the castle around October and razed it; however, the circumstances are unclear. Edward never repaired it and left the fortress and town to crumble. A combination of the castle's isolated location and lack of access by water undoubtedly swayed Longshanks's decision.

In the 1500s, this native-Plantagenet hybrid was already in a state of decay. The contemporary poet Gruffydd Hiraethog noted what was once, 'a large strong building but which is now destroyed and cast to the ground.' In the 1850s, the undergrowth was finally cleared, after which archaeological investigations were carried out. In 1949 the final owner passed it over to the state. It is now in the care of Cadw.

Dominated by wild vegetation and seated against such an impressive background, Castell y Bere's ruins retain a splendid aura. A candidate for the most picturesque mountain in Wales, Cadair Idris itself is not without legends. Perhaps the finest is that the reward for a nightly camp is either poetic brilliance or insanity – something this author fears to test. Ghostly screams have been reported on the wind. The apparition of a soldier has also been noted, usually patrolling the ruins at sunset.

Close to the castle, the local thirteenth-century church is also a source of interest. A small window close to the vestry was known as the Leper Window and allowed inmates of a local leper colony to witness services. Another local, Mary Jones, was also renowned for her piety. Local lore tells that she once walked barefoot from Llanfihangel-y-Pennant to Bala, about 26 miles. The purpose of her hike was to purchase a Bible. She is famed in the locality as the inspiration for the British and Foreign Bible Society.

Conwy

It is Cadw's view that 'Conwy is by any standards one of the great fortresses of medieval Europe'. Few words do better justice to this incredible citadel. Designed by James of St George, that same enigmatic character credited with responsibility for much of Edward I's 'Iron Ring', the castle and surrounding town walls remain as instantly recognisable today as they were seven centuries ago. Few sites are more deserving of the label UNESCO World Heritage Site.

Even before the castle and town walls, Conwy was already a revered location in Welsh history. Before the coming of the English, the Cistercian abbey of Aberconwy had found considerable fame among the Welsh princes. It was here Llywelyn ap Iorwerth was laid to rest in 1240. The reason Llywelyn picked it undoubtedly concerns the location of the nearby palace or *Llys*, which was similarly enjoyed by ancient Welsh royalty. When the castle and the town walls were built in 1283-89, one wall and a tower of the old palace formed part of the new defences. Identifiable from four window openings, the features were contemporary to Llywelyn and date from no later than the early thirteenth century.

As history would show, the castle and surrounding walls would play an equally decisive role in Wales's destiny. Located on the north coast, close to the River Conwy, the fortress was ideal for keeping watch over an important strategic location. Before Conwy's construction, the ageing Deganwy had carried out the same purpose. The exact date of Deganwy's construction is unclear. Rebuilt in stone for Henry III in the 1220s, its origins may have been Roman. Aberconwy fell when Edward marched north with a large army in March 1283, after which plans to erect the new castle were put in place. With the mighty settlement established in place of the Cistercian monastery – whose monks were relocated to Maenan – and Deganwy rendered redundant, Edward had achieved a double thunderbolt. Not only had he created the ultimate physical defences, but crushed the symbols of the ancient dynasty. For Edward, the astronomical cost of £15,000 for the castle and walls was money well spent.

In 1294 the imposing walls faced their first test. As with nearby Caernarfon, Conwy was a chief target of the rebellious Madog ap Llywelyn. Madog was of a junior branch of the House of Aberffraw, whose line descended from the ninth-century Rhodri ap Merfyn 'the Great'. A distant relation of Llywelyn ap Gruffudd, he was recognised as Prince of Gwynedd, albeit not a direct heir. On commencing his siege in December, Edward struggled to repel his opponent until a large relief force arrived in February. The chronicler Walter of Guisborough speculated that due to the conditions, the king was extra generous with his private supply of wine and shared it among the garrison. Perhaps partly due to its location and the unfinished state of Caernarfon, Conwy became the main port of call for esteemed visitors. Among them was the future Edward II, then Prince of Wales, on receiving the homage of the native leaders in 1301. It was the view of Jeremy Ashbee, a former curator of the Tower of London, that the royal lodgings included the 'best preserved suite of medieval private royal chambers in England and Wales'.

As highly as Edward I viewed Conwy, his son did not maintain the same standards. A survey conducted in 1321 highlighted a lack of regular maintenance, with criticisms ranging from leaking roofs to a lack of provisions. This would continue until Edward III granted Conwy to his heir, Edward, the Black Prince, in 1343. Among the repairs were new support arches, notably those in the great hall. Sadly for Conwy, the Black Prince's death led to further failings. Later that century, Conwy provided a haven for Edward's son, now Richard II, as he attempted to flee Henry Bolingbroke. On 12 August 1399, Richard met his cousin's emissary, Henry Percy, 1st Earl of Northumberland, for peace negotiations. It was also within the chapel that Percy swore no harm would come to him. A week later, Richard surrendered at nearby Flint on the condition he would spare his life (see Flint Castle). As history, and Shakespeare, would relate, the promise was not kept.

Within a year of Bolingbroke taking the throne of England as Henry IV, rebellion broke out under the flag of Owain Glyndŵr. In March 1401, Conwy was subject to a surprise attack from Owain's cousins, Rhys and Gwilym ap Tudur. By posing as humble carpenters in town to carry out necessary repairs, they infiltrated the castle Trojan horse-style and killed the duty watchmen. No sooner had the castle fallen than the rebel attack commenced. A short time later, the town was also under Welsh control. For three long months, the dynamic brothers held the town and castle before eventually surrendering. To ensure lasting peace, Henry IV granted them royal pardons.

As the following years would show, Conwy's time in the limelight was already coming to an end. Although it was reinforced during the Wars of the Roses, the castle played no active role. Henry VIII carried out some work in the 1520s and 30s, but the castle's purposes evolved little beyond that of a prison, armoury, depot, or place for visitors. Such was its impoverished condition when Charles I sold it to Edward Conway in 1627 for a mere £100. Inherited by his son four years later, the castle was requisitioned by John Williams, Archbishop of York, for the English Civil War. After installing a garrison at his own expense, a dispute arose between the cleric and governor, Sir John Owen. Consequently, the archbishop defected to the Roundheads, and the town fell in August 1646 to Major-General Thomas Mytton. In November, the castle followed.

When the war was over, Colonel John Carter was appointed governor. On his watch, long-awaited repairs finally took place. In 1655 the Parliament-appointed Council of State ordered the castle's slighting. The destruction of the Bakehouse Tower probably occurred in the immediate aftermath. At the restoration of the monarchy, the fortress was returned to Edward Conway, Earl of Conway, who performed a ruthless asset stripping. This confirmed Conwy's slide into the realms of picturesque ruin. Excellent works by Turner and many others successfully immortalised the castle's beauty. As the communications links improved, visitor numbers increased. In 1865 the castle passed to the town's civic leadership, and the process of restoration began in earnest. Along with Edward I's other castles and town walls in Gwynedd, Conwy was officially declared a world heritage site and placed under the watchful eyes of Cadw.

Even as a ruin, there is something undeniably special about Conwy. Indeed, set against the stunning backdrop of the north coast, it is no surprise many of Welsh birth view the town as second only to St David's in its ability to connect the living and dead. Situated at the heart of the modern town and dominating the local landscape as it has for more than seven centuries, the rugged walls juxtaposed with the sights and happenings of the modern world convey the very essence of a fortress lost in time. It is perhaps no surprise when the great doors close and the tourists go home, numerous spirits are said to dwell within this great ruin.

Legend tells that the eight large towers on the castle's outer rim all have their resident ghosts. An intriguing insight into the superstitions of the time can be found in the story that when Edward I's workmen were building the castle, they were recommended never to leave their tools unguarded overnight. On the third night of construction a fire started mysteriously in the great hall. The workmen abandoned the castle to seek refuge from the blaze, leaving their tools within the burning walls. On returning, the builders were apparently hindered by unseen forces. Whether eight spirits of the eight towers really possessed the tools, one can only speculate. Unlike Caernarfon and Beaumaris, the castle was eventually completed.

Outside the castle, the town itself is rich in legend. One from the Middle Ages tells that local fishermen caught a mermaid while out in the estuary. Despite begging for release, she was paraded through the streets before the astounded crowds. Prior to her waterless death, the siren put a curse on the town. Her cackling laughter is believed to accompany local tragedy.

Of the town's many hauntings, few compare with the strange tale believed to have involved one of Robert Wynn's successors – or even Robert himself – at the nearby Elizabethan manor house Plas Mawr. When the new laird left his wife and child to fight overseas, the man's wife longed for his return and entered the habit of gazing out for any sign of him. After watching till after darkness one night, she sadly slipped on the stairs with her child in her hands and the pair fell to the bottom. It was not long before mother and child were found by the servants and taken to what was known as the lantern room. In urgent need of medical attention, a doctor named 'Dic' was called to attend. Despite doing all he could, his best efforts were in vain. Fearing his master's wrath on his return, the servant refused to allow the doctor to leave and locked him with the dead wife and child in the lantern room.

Only when the lord returned did the strange story reach a conclusion. Unlocking the door, he found his wife and child dead in the room, but, strangely, there was no sign of the doctor. Among the theories put forward is that the doctor escaped by one of the chimneys. Haunted by the loss of his beloved wife and child, the Wynn lord is said to return to the lantern room, searching for the elusive doctor.

Criccieth

Such is the multitude of great fortresses scattered throughout Gwynedd, it is easy to forget that wonderful Criccieth lies sandwiched among them. Due to its position on a rocky headland between two glorious sandy beaches, the thirteenth-century citadel offers excellent views over the town and across Tremadog Bay.

The present castle was not the first structure to be erected at Criccieth. Prior to the thirteenth century, a timber motte and bailey existed nearby, which was later destroyed and superseded by the new castle. Unlike the more famous neighbouring Edwardian fortresses overseen by James of St George, work on the inner ward at Criccieth began in the 1230s at the behest of Llywelyn ap Iorwerth. In contrast to most contemporary Welsh fortresses, Llywelyn went to great lengths to make Criccieth defensively capable. The D-shaped towered gatehouse and portcullis were both of the Norman style – a detachment from the usual poorly guarded palatial structures typical of the natives. Equally Norman were the murder holes and arrow slits. Indeed, so Norman is the design that it's difficult to miss the similarities with Hubert de Burgh's Montgomery, or Ranulf, Earl of Chester's Beeston in Cheshire.

Further work on the castle occurred during the reign of Llywelyn's grandson, Llywelyn ap Gruffudd. Throughout the late 1260s and 70s, Llywelyn improved the defences with a new gateway and outer ward. Though impressive, the prince's additions failed to withstand the might of Edward I. In 1283, Edward recognised Criccieth's potential and employed James of St George to strengthen it. Among the additions, a second double-storey rectangular tower, 'The Engine Tower', was added to complement Llywelyn's earlier work. Many have speculated that the structure might have originally formed part of a siege engine. After strengthening the walls, other additions included adding a further storey to the gatehouse and a barbican. Within the walls, several timber buildings included a great hall.

Eleven years after Edward conquered Gwynedd, the strengthened walls faced their first test. When Madog ap Llywelyn's forces arrived in the winter of 1294, a prolonged siege followed. Fortunately, unlike several English towns whose buildings were pillaged and set alight, the castle held till spring when supplies arrived.

The following century saw more comfortable relations for Criccieth and the broader settlement. As the Welsh threat subsided, the castle was used to hold local felons. Among its constables was the warrior Hywel ap Gruffydd, 'The Axe', who fought bravely at Poitiers in 1356. Criccieth's era of relative peace would end with Owain Glyndŵr's rebellion around 1404. In league with the French, Owain blocked the Irish Sea route for potential reinforcements, leaving the garrison little choice than surrender. Rather than use the castle as a base to conduct future rebellion, Owain had it razed, along with the town. Such was the ferocity of the flames, it permanently burned some parts red.

Criccieth's time in the spotlight appears to have ended with Owain's fiery rebellion. Though it may have been used as a residence following this, the English never repaired it. Due to its westerly location, it also avoided the Wars of the Roses and the English Civil War. As such, the fortress quietly slipped into ignominy.

Today, the castle is thankfully in good hands. Whether or not the ghosts of its past remain in residence, a visit to Criccieth is more than capable of stimulating the imagination. Not for the first time, Turner's masterpiece, displaying the rugged walls as the backdrop to his scene of shipwrecked mariners, is unlikely to be bettered. Legend has long spoken that every breaking wave represents the cry of a Welsh life lost at sea. Should one witness the scene personally, it is easy to see why Turner chose it. Nor is it difficult to wonder just how many brave souls plunged to the watery depths.

Dinas Emrys

Seated proudly on a high hillock, dense in woodland, and set against the spectacular backdrop of the clear waters of Llyn Dinas and the vast Snowdonia wilderness, Dinas Emrys is another of those magical fortresses that could have been plucked straight from the pages of a fairy tale.

For the modern visitor, a trip to Dinas Emrys may well come into the 'worth it for the scenery' category rather than for the stonework. Intended no doubt to keep watch over the Glaslyn River Valley, from where views continue seemingly into eternity, little remains of the structure. Indeed, should one not be aware of the area's history, the stone ramparts and ruined keep could easily be overlooked.

Precisely who oversaw the early work remains a mystery. Archaeological excavations at the site appear to confirm a medieval pedigree, yet records are sparse. Llywelyn ap Gruffudd may have built the castle to guard the Snowdon Mountain pass; however, this is speculation. Regardless of its point of origin, Edward I saw little reason to maintain it.

Archaeological excavations have confirmed that fort builders have been attracted to the area since the early second century. Proof of an artificial pool has also been found on the site. The pool is significant, not least as it appears to date from the same period. It is from the early medieval period that the castle has achieved lasting fame. No fewer than three early chroniclers recorded that it was at Dinas Emrys that the world was introduced to a young Merlin.

The tale is a famous one in Welsh mythology. As *Historia Regum Britanniae* recalls, on fleeing England to evade the Anglo-Saxons, the fifth-century warlord Vortigern was advised to construct a fortress on the summit. Though work began smoothly, every night after the builders left, their creations were reduced to rubble. Sensing evil, Vortigern was advised by his sorcerers to locate a young boy born not of a human father. Vortigern's magicians found such a boy, named Myrddin Emrys, or Merlin Ambrosius, on the streets of Carmarthen. Summoned before Vortigern, the boy's mother admitted she knew not how her child had come to be born. Local druids believed him to be the product of an incubus.

When Merlin asked why the king had him brought there, Vortigern told him of the predicament and showed him evidence of the fallen masonry. Merlin denounced the sorcerers' idiocy and informed Vortigern that a strange pool existed deep beneath the site, in which two dragons lived: one red, the other white. The red, so Merlin claimed, represented the Britons; the white, the Saxons. It was on account of their continuous fighting that the towers continued to collapse. The fight, he prophesied, would remain ongoing until the red dragon ultimately prevailed.

The masons dug deep into the hill and discovered the pool and within it the dragons. In a trance, Merlin revealed that the sons of King Constantine, who Vortigern had usurped, were preparing an attack. He also predicted that the elder brother, Aurelius Ambrosius – another possible origin for the historical Merlin – would be crowned king but ultimately succumb to poisoning and be succeeded by his younger brother, Uther. In time, Uther would also be dispatched by poison, and the crown fall to his eldest son, Arthur.

The story of the dragons has, of course, been the subject of much scorn and scepticism. Clearly symbolic, it also provides an origin for the adoption of the red dragon as the symbol of Wales. Regarding the dragon's original containment, legend has also been rife. The tale of *Lludd and Llefelys* as recorded in the *Mabinogion* – a collection of early Welsh prose – tells that Lludd ruled Britain in the first century BC. Once a year, on May Eve, a piercing scream, for which no source could be found, disturbed the people of the kingdom. On seeking out his brother Llefelys, Lludd learned that the noise was the cry of battling dragons. On his brother's advice, he captured both dragons in a cauldron of mead, then buried it at Dinas Emrys, where the fort and castle were later built.

The story of the dragons is not the only one synonymous with the site. Ancient legend also tells that Merlin once hid treasure in a local cave. The prophecy states that the lucky discoverer shall be golden-haired and blue-eyed. When that person is near, a bell will toll before the cave's opening at the touching of that person's foot. Local lore relates that once upon a summer's moon, a local from the village of Beddgelert climbed the hill with a pickaxe and sought to dig out the site around the tower. After a time, the ground began to shake, and the sky darkened. The man made a run for it as lightning flashed overhead. He never returned for his pickaxe.

Close by lies a field in a grove named Cell y Dewiniaid – the Grove of the Magicians. According to tradition, it was here that Vortigern's council once met and that their bodies lie in a nearby field. In days gone by, a stone marked their graves, and a white thorn tree blossomed over them.

The scant remains of the castle that still occupies the wooded hill may be a far cry from the stories of Arthurian romance, yet even now, there is something truly special about the area. There may be no dragons living beneath the pool's remains or hidden treasures nearby, but a trip to the summit is not totally devoid of magic. Amidst the stunning scenery, it is easy to let the mind wander. In so doing, we can at least appreciate the site on which many myths and legends were born.

Dolbadarn

Erected to guard the Llanberis Pass at the foot of the mighty Mount Snowdon, Dolbadarn Castle is another of Gwynedd's beautiful sites. A rarity among the fortresses of North Wales, the structure does not appear to owe its origins to either the primitive palatial style of the early princes or the imposing foreign architecture of the conquering English. While one cannot rule out the possibility that Maelgwn Gwynedd erected a wooden fortress in the sixth century, there is no clear evidence to support this. The castle that stands today was set out in stone at the behest of Llywelyn ap Iorwerth no earlier than the early 1220s. Construction appears to have succeeded that of nearby Castell y Bere, another made of stone, which places the date to no later than 1236.

After an initial period of work on the outer walls, which included two square towers, the second phase of construction was undertaken following the marriage of Llywelyn's son, Dafydd, and continued after the prince's death. An essential feature of the second phase was a circular keep: a mirror, many have argued, of the style of the Marcher lord. The tower at Dolbadarn remains mostly intact and has become celebrated for its architectural significance.

Reminiscent of other nearby fortresses such as Dinas Emrys, the castle is nestled in woodland and set against the stunning scenery of the twin glacial lakes of Llyn Padarn and Peris. Once completed, the combination of the imposing walls, round keep, and additional halls proved the perfect facility to monitor the entrance to the Snowdon and Glyderau mountain groups. The completion of the second phase was of particular importance. From the 1240s onward, Dolbadarn took over the running of the Is Gwyrfai district from Caernarfon. However, this would soon be threatened as Llywelyn's death saw Gwynedd's influence dwindle. By 1247 many of Llywelyn's eastern lands had fallen to Henry III.

The Welsh needed a hero and up stepped Llywelyn ap Gruffudd. On taking control of Gwynedd in 1255, Llywelyn imprisoned his brother

Owain Goch: a sentence that lasted twenty-two years. The poetry of Hywel Foel ap Griffri tells of Owain's imprisonment in a round tower, yet frustratingly Hywel was unclear of the location. Many historians believe that Owain was kept at Dolbadarn, as the round tower's characteristics fit his prison.

The lowest section of the keep has long been considered its most fascinating aspect, not least as there appears no clear record of its use. The underground chamber was only accessible via a trapdoor, which has led to speculation that it housed an oubliette – the little place of forgetting. As Owain, a brother of the prince of the realm and the son of royalty, survived for twenty-two years, it seems unthinkable he was kept in an underground dungeon. Nevertheless, one cannot discount the possibility that he and others frequented the tower.

After Llywelyn ap Gruffudd's mysterious death in 1282, the princedom of Gwynedd fell to his brother Dafydd. Such was the strength of Edward I's forces and the troublesome wintry conditions, Dafydd's retreat into the mountains saw Dolbadarn become his seat of government from May 1283 onwards. By October a force of 7,000 led to Dafydd's capture and Dolbadarn's fall to the English.

With Edward's conquest of Gwynedd complete, the imposing walls of the 'Iron Ring' soon materialised. As Caernarfon and its nearby siblings rose ever higher over the Welsh coast, Dolbadarn's significance as an administrative centre faded. Ignored by Longshanks, the castle was, by 1285, already being deprived of its raw materials. Among the relocations was the stripping of timber for use at Caernarfon. While the decision seems a strange one from a military and strategic perspective – Dolbadarn was one of the most impressive fortresses in Gwynedd – for Edward, the decision was likely also symbolic. Not for the first time, by eradicating the old Welsh structures and replacing them with new English ones, he sent a strong message that the age of the princes of Gwynedd was over.

While two native heroes would test the English regime's permanence, Dolbadarn never recovered. Used as a manorial dwelling for the remainder of the century, Owain Glyndŵr later captured the castle to house English prisoners. As fate would dictate, the rebellion's end would also end the castle's purpose, an episode that has been named 'Dolbadarn's last stand'. It is unclear whether the fortress was inhabited again after this point.

From the mid-eighteenth century onwards, the ruins became a favoured haunt of the romantic artists, most notably the ubiquitous Turner, whose painting from the turn of the nineteenth century is much cherished. During the Second World War, its final owner, Sir Michael Duff, entrusted the castle to the state and a future in the care of Cadw.

For the modern castle enthusiast, the small village of Llanberis, close to which the castle sits, is not the first place one would expect to find a native fortress. From here one can catch the train or hike the Llanberis Pass, renowned as the gentlest way up Snowdon. The area is, unsurprisingly, often overrun with tourists. The scars of slate mining do little to detract from the broader beauty of the craggy peaks, chilly lakes, and wooded hillocks.

One could argue that all of this is to Dolbadarn's benefit: a castle some have come to regard as one of the most overlooked in Wales. Some have also found a strange, poetic irony concerning it and the country's history: small but intimidating. A lack of contemporary sources and a past tendency to dismiss the previous regime's achievements has also contributed to Dolbadarn's lack of fame. It is due to this lack of information that many gaps remain in the castle's history. Regardless of whether the exact circumstances Owain Goch was forced to endure are ever revealed, there is little doubt that the castle witnessed many dark moments during its time as a prison. This is no less true of the area in general. While few stories exist of hauntings, the locality is famed for its legends.

One of the most famous stories concerns the Llanberis Pass. Halfway up the trail, close to an old stone bridge named Pont y Cromlech, a cannibal witch, Canrig Bwt, was once believed to lie in wait. A stone altar near the bridge is believed to date from the fifth century. Local lore tells that the witch set up home under the altar and fed on little children. In a bid to end her reign of terror, a young man set out to locate her. Sword in hand and blessed by a monk and a white witch, the young man sent her head rolling down the mountainside.

A second legend of the pass concerns the Tylwyth Tef: fairies who kidnapped unbaptised children. One of their bizarre traits was the kindness they bestowed upon the children. Some also left behind their own children as a gift for the parents whose children were taken. One story tells of a spot called Cwmglas Hollow, where a local woman would go on dark, misty mornings and leave a jug of sweet milk and a clean towel. On returning for it, she would always find an empty jar and a small gift of money. Some have concluded that the hollow equates with a climbers' cottage named Cwm Glas Mawr on the Llanberis, though no proof of its location has been found. Like the fairies themselves, its very existence remains elusive.

Harlech

Magnificent Harlech is the epitome of a great Welsh castle. Seated an imposing 61m above sea level, this coastal citadel sits on a rocky knoll, dubbed the Harlech Dome, that forms part of the Rhinogydd mountain range that runs to the east side of the town. The tall sandstone walls are incredibly eye-catching: a fact attributable to the depth of the sharp drop on the north and west sides and its concentric design.

How this came about is worthy of investigation. An oddity at first glance, one can find an explanation in the knowledge that the castle was initially set far closer to the sea. Taking advantage of the natural features, the double walls of defences, the outer of which was originally much taller, made conquest difficult, albeit not impossible. Behind the sturdy D-shaped gatehouse, three portcullises and two thick wooden doors guarded the interior. Within the outer walls, four large, circular towers overlook the inner ward, from which the views extend into eternity. Though little remains of the stone bridge towers, today's visitors can see the location close to the present entrance. Beyond the north-west tower, a water gate lies close to a dramatic stairway that connects the castle rock to the foot of the cliffs, where sea laps against the foundations. Reminiscent they may seem of a scene from Minas Morgul in the Lord of the Rings, their existence was vital during the Welsh rebellions in allowing the castle to take in supplies by sea.

A brightly shining jewel that stemmed from Edward I's conquest of Wales, many rightly regard the castle as master mason James of St George's finest achievement. There is little doubt that James took inspiration from his native Savoy, whose contemporary style also featured semi-circular door arches, corbelled towers, and similar types of windows.

There are many legends of Harlech's origins. Local lore has long associated the area with the myth of the beautiful Welsh princess, Branwen, King Brân the Blessed's sister. The story goes that Branwen was given in marriage to Matholwch, the king of Ireland. Bran's sinister half-brother, Evnissyen – or Efnysien – was furious at not being consulted on the festivities' planning and injured the Irish guests' horses in a fit of rage. Brân, however, remedied the situation by bestowing many fine gifts on his guests and had the steeds replaced. He also granted to the Irish a magical cauldron able to raise the dead.

The festivities complete, Branwen crossed the Irish Sea in the company of her royal husband. A son named Gwern soon followed. While most took the new queen to their heart, for some, Evnissyen's malice had sowed deep mistrust. On being threatened by a party of nobles, Matholwch capitulated and had Branwen banished to the kitchens. During her captivity, the kindly princess made friends with a raven – or starling – which carried a letter to her brother as thanks for feeding it. On hearing of his sister's plight, Brân amassed a large army and crossed the sea. On being delayed at a river crossing, the Irish having destroyed a bridge, Brân personally lowered himself down and allowed his men to cross over him.

Here, the story becomes even stranger. The warring kings made peace, but once again, Evnissyen's villainy threatened everything. No sooner had Gwern been made king of Ireland than Evnissyen threw the poor child into the fire. In the chaotic scenes that followed, Evnissyen was struck down attempting to destroy the magic cauldron, which the Irish used to replenish their flailing numbers, and a poisoned arrow wounded Brân. On their return, Brân succumbs to the poison, and Branwen dies of a broken heart. In one strange version, Brân ordered his head be cut off and even chatted merrily with the people of Harlech in a never-ending feast. The head was later taken to London and buried, later giving birth to the legend of the Tower of London's ravens.

That such outlandish myths have prevailed can undoubtedly be rationalised by the lack of historical sources regarding Harlech's early days. Evidence that the Welsh constructed a fortification before Edward's arrival remains elusive. On completing his conquest of North Wales in 1282, Edward began work on Harlech immediately. By the following winter, the inner walls were already at the height of 15ft. When construction was completed in 1289, a town had also been established. According to contemporary accounts, the cost came in at more than £8,000. On the death of Agnes, the widow and successor of John de Bonvillars, the castle's first constable, in 1290, a garrison of thirty-six was installed, and James of St George took over as constable.

A year after his departure, James's masterpiece encountered its first significant test. Throughout 1294 Welsh rebels rose in number under the flag of Madog ap Llywelyn. As the year progressed, several new English-inhabited towns were sacked. While Harlech's walls stood firm on being severely battered throughout the winter, the arrival of provisions via the watergate helped see the garrison through till spring. New defences were added to protect the outer stairway and extended down to the watergate to preserve the castle's walls. Additional work also took place following the Despenser War of the 1320s, with other towers added.

All was well for the remainder of the century. When a further revolt broke out at the turn of the fifteenth century, the reinforced walls faced their sternest test. By 1403, as the revolt of the charismatic patriot Owain Glyndŵr gathered strength, Harlech remained one of only a handful of castles still standing against the Welsh charges. Impressive though the walls remained, provisions dwindled. An illustration of the lack of preparation and resources comes with the arsenal listed at a mere three shields, eight helmets, four guns, twenty gloves and half a dozen lances. The garrison surrendered in the winter of 1404, overrun and undernourished.

Despite boasting the better numbers, the taking of Harlech was a significant coup for Owain. Just as Edward I had put down his coastal citadel as a mark of conquest, for Glyndŵr, the successful siege was equally symbolic. On capturing the fortress, he made it his principal residence. In August 1405, he held a Parliament there – his second as 'Prince of Gwynedd'.

By 1408, however, the tide began to turn. When forces under the command of Prince Hal – the future Henry V – reconquered Gwynedd, Glyndŵr's position was in peril. On reaching Harlech equipped with the latest marvel in siege warfare – the serpentine cannon – Hal's forces battered the late thirteenth-century walls. The castle stood firm despite seemingly much of the outer walls on the south and east sides being destroyed. Royalist perseverance under the command of John Talbot – relocated there by Prince Hal after raising the siege of Aberystwyth – failed to shift Owain's constable Edmund Mortimer. By February 1409, however, the long winter took its toll. Unable to arrange replenishments, the garrison was depleted by sickness and exhaustion, leaving Edmund no option but to surrender.

Throughout the remainder of the fifteenth century, the ebb and flow of the Wars of the Roses dictated Harlech's fortunes. Despite its isolated location, the castle remained important as a natural guard of the coast and the Irish Sea. In the aftermath of the Yorkist victory at the Battle of Northampton on 10 July 1460 – a battle remembered as the first in English history to feature heavy artillery – the defeated Queen Margaret of Anjou fled to Harlech. For the next eight years, the castle held out against the Yorkists under the command of her loyal Lancastrian ally, Dafydd ap Icuan. Just as it had in 1294, a combination of the impressive defences and ability to be supplied by sea ensured the garrison's longevity. By 1468 Harlech was the only Lancastrian castle Edward IV was yet to take.

Due to Margaret's early presence and sturdy defences, Harlech became something of a Welsh Lancastrian HQ. In 1466, Sir Richard Tunstall used the castle as his base to mount attacks. Two years later, Jasper Tudor landed there with reinforcements before raiding the Yorkist-dominated Denbigh – see also Denbigh Castle. On learning of Tudor's landing, Edward IV ordered William Herbert to besiege Harlech. On 14 August, after a month of ongoing damage, the garrison finally surrendered. Thus ended a campaign that lasted more than seven years and led to the garrison's immortalisation in the song, 'Men of Harlech'.

A combination of Yorkist dominance in 1468-85 and the lack of a serious pretender after Richard III's defeat at Bosworth spared Harlech further damage during the Wars of the Roses. As domestic stability throughout the Tudor period led to relative peace in the north of Wales, Harlech's position became relatively secure. This changed when the civil war broke out in 1642. Such had been the lack of perceived threat during that time, Harlech's walls had long been neglected. There is little evidence that any repairs had been carried out since the Yorkist success of 1468. Aside from the gatehouse, which had been used for local assizes, the fortress had become more or less redundant.

One of the few who realised this was Charles I's competent nephew, Prince Rupert. In 1644 Rupert installed the Royalist colonel William Owen as constable to patch up the damage. In June 1646, the Roundhead forces finally attacked Harlech. Owen's reinforcements must have been of high quality as it was not until 15 March the following year that the siege was successful. When the garrison of forty-four handed over possession to the Roundhead heavyweight, Major-General Thomas Mytton, Harlech became the final Royalist mainland fortress to change hands. With this, so ended the First War and Harlech's purpose as a key site to maintain the security of North Wales.

Like many Royalist fortresses, slighting awaited. Fortunately for heritage lovers, Parliament's orders were only partially carried out. Besides the destruction of the staircases within the gatehouse, Britain's government performed no extra damage to the walls. There is some evidence that the usual reuse of stones saw the building of local houses, albeit not significantly. At that time, the population was never more than a couple of thousand, if not merely hundreds.

A castle around which the history of Wales has often in some way revolved, Harlech has witnessed much blood and disaster. Built by the English Crown to defeat the Welsh, it also served the opposite purpose. A place of refuge for a foreign queen of England, the castle also witnessed a Welsh legend's defeat and kept out a Welsh-born future king of England. It is ironic, some might argue, that the fall of a castle used to symbolise English dominion briefly ensured English republicanism. It is perhaps more ironic that a castle built to subjugate the Welsh is now revered as a symbol of modern Wales.

That these walls have witnessed so much, it is perhaps a surprise that the castle is the source of so few paranormal happenings. Though fame was made in recent times for a photograph that allegedly captured a black-hooded monk – more likely a blacked-out window – Harlech has no other stories. Nevertheless, what the fortress lacks in intrigue, it is rightly celebrated for in its actual history. No castle in England or Wales performed better under siege: a feat attributed to its master design. Had the garrison of 1403 been better prepared, the fortress would likely never have fallen.

Thanks to a failure to fulfil Parliament's dreadful order to destroy the castle, this gem of a citadel still stands guard over the north-west coast. Following the usual pattern at the advent of tourism, the late Georgian and Victorian period saw many prominent artists, including John Varley, Henry Gastineau, Paul Sandby, and John Cotman, use the ruins in their paintings. Unsurprisingly, a work by the ever-busy Turner is nationally celebrated. Various restoration projects followed the castle being taken into state ownership at the beginning of the First World War. It was later handed over to Cadw. Thanks to such efforts, in 1986 UNESCO rightly classified the castle and town as a World Heritage Site. Along with nearby Caernarfon and Conwy, Harlech remains to this day one of 'the finest examples of late thirteenth century and early fourteenth century military architecture in Europe'.

Chapter 3

Cardiganshire, Montgomeryshire, and Radnorshire

Aberystwyth

The powerful Marcher lord Gilbert de Clare is recorded as having erected the first motte and bailey castle in Aberystwyth. Variously named Tan-y-castell, Aberrheidol Castle or Old Aberystwyth, the fortress was put down in 1110, about a mile south of the present castle. Like most, it served both a physical and symbolic role in the Norman augmentation of mid-Wales.

Just six years passed before the Welsh tested the first castle with a siege. The timber defences put up a stout resistance in the face of Gruffudd ap Rhys, Prince of Deheubarth. So much so that twenty years passed before Gruffudd's huffing and puffing finally blew the doors down. Complicit in his success were Owain Gwynedd and Cadwaladr ap Gruffudd, sons of Gruffudd ap Cynan, King of Gwynedd. Gruffudd was himself Gruffudd ap Cynan's son-in-law, having married the brave Gwenllian ferch Gruffydd: the same wretched princess who lost her life fighting so bravely earlier that same year (see Kidwelly Castle).

On capturing the castle in 1136, Rhys laid waste to the timber constructions. Owain Gwynedd initially presented Cadwaladr with the opportunity to rebuild the Norman fortress; however, the situation became complicated in 1143 when Cadwaladr attempted to murder Anarawd ap Gruffydd: Rhys's successor as ruler of Deheubarth. In retribution, Owain ordered his son, Hywel ab Owain Gwynedd, to raze the castle.

In keeping with the general trend of castle building during and following 'the Anarchy', the castle's third incarnation was of stone construction. After a series of short-term owners, the fortress became the property of Llywelyn ap Iorwerth, who torched it and started work on a fourth castle. The site's misfortune continued with the coming of Edward I, who flattened Llywelyn's building and began work at the new site to the north. The defences likely remained incomplete when the Welsh took Edward's castle in 1282, destroying it along with the town. When the war was over, work began on a sixth castle, overseen by James of St George. The castle was likely completed by 1290 and stood firm on being targeted by Madog in his revolt of 1294-95.

The end of the war brought better prospects for the town. Fifty years later, however, the castle's lousy luck returned. Owain Glyndŵr breached the walls in 1404 and put the castle to good use. He even hosted Charles VI of France to sign a treaty. By 1408 Owain's rebellion had lost momentum, and Aberystwyth returned to English hands. Over the coming centuries, the castle's fortunes would continue to wax and wane. A near wreck during Edward III's reign, it became an important seat of local government. As late as 1637, Charles I converted it into a royal mint, thus setting up a local monopoly on creating silver shillings. A Royalist regiment was stationed there during the civil war, at which time the mint was closed. From this time, the castle was used for storing precious metals, notably silver and lead, until its slighting in 1649 rendered it useless.

A ruin for more than 350 years, the castle takes on a different form at night. Although it appears lacking in hauntings, the area is rich in folklore, with tales ranging from mermaids and wild cats to Arthurian knights. The nearby Devil's Bridge was allegedly the work of the Prince of Darkness. After assisting an old lady in exchange for the soul of the first living thing that crossed the bridge, the woman sent her dog across. Local legend also claims that seven monks took the Holy Grail to the site of what is now a Georgian mansion for safekeeping during the Dissolution of the Monasteries in 1539. The so-called Nanteos Cup, named after the mansion, has long been an item of much intrigue for its alleged supernatural abilities. So much so, the cup was stolen in 2014, only to be recovered the following year. Like the stories of ghostly mine workers and the fate of a Second World War bomber, the cup's true origins remain a mystery. It is now on display at the National Library of Wales.

Cardigan

Seated on the banks of the River Teifi, the rugged remains of Cardigan Castle are a sadly uninspiring sight for the modern audience. True of most of its type, its earliest incarnation was timber motte and bailey, likely begun in 1093, when Norman nobleman Roger de Montgomery set about founding the town. The first castle was located about a mile from the present site and stood until shortly after Llywelyn ap Iorwerth's death.

Like many castles of the south, Cardigan's early history is inexorably intertwined with the powerful lords of Clare. While Roger de Montgomery is credited as the town's founder, the brains behind the castle appear to have been Gilbert Fitz Richard, styled Lord of Clare. The castle eventually entered the possession of his son, Gilbert de Clare, who was created Earl of Pembroke in 1138. Two years earlier, Owain Gwynedd, who became Prince of Gwynedd the following year, achieved something of a coup with the defeat of Cardigan's Norman overlords at the Battle of Crug Mawr. Despite Robert fitz Martin's sacking of the town, the castle initially held steady. Over the coming decades, Roger, Earl of Hertford held the fortress until its capture by Rhys ap Gruffudd in 1166. There is some evidence that Rhys upgraded the walls at this point. In so doing, Cardigan holds the rare distinction of being the first castle set in stone by the Welsh princes. It was also the setting of the first recorded eisteddfod: a cultural tournament that included bards and minstrels.

On Lord Rhys's death in 1197, his will split the inheritance between brothers Maelgwn and Gruffydd. A bitter dispute between the pair led to Maelgwn betraying Gruffydd, after which the castle was sold to King John and granted to the powerful William Marshal, 1st Earl of Pembroke. Throughout the remainder of John's reign and the early years of Henry III, during which Marshal served as regent, Llywelyn ap Iorwerth brought great terror to the lands of South Wales. In 1215 Llywelyn captured Cardigan, and in the Aberdyfi Parliament of the following year, his government ordered its transfer to the sons of Gruffydd ap Rhys II. In 1223, four years after Marshal's death, his son, namesake and successor as Earl of Pembroke, William Marshal II, recaptured the castle. After the younger Marshal's death in April 1231, the fortress again fell to the Welsh, courtesy of Llywelyn's supporter, Rhys Gryg, Prince of Deheubarth. On Llywelyn's death in 1240, Cardigan returned to the English Crown. Over the coming decade, relocation, rebuilding, and creation of the town's walls all followed.

Following Edward I's conquest, the threat to Cardigan's peace became much less severe. Due to its westerly location, the castle played no role in the Hundred Years' War, the Rose Wars, or any Tudor rebellions. After suffering damage in the English Civil War, any use appears to have been to incarcerate local felons. Around 1805, to make the castle properly habitable, John Bowen oversaw Castle Green House's construction within the walls. By 1827 the front range had also been added. The Wood family purchased the site in 1940 and remained there until 1996, despite its ever-worsening condition. In 2003 the Ceredigion County Council bought the castle and set about restoration. It was opened to the public in 2015.

A much-neglected site with a history of violence, it is something of a miracle that Cardigan survived at all. A mishmash of stone, dirt, greenery and possessed of a history that crosses several eras, it is no surprise that the castle is reputedly haunted. While any pre-1244 residents would have been confined to the former location – for which this author can find little evidence of ghost stories – no fewer than three spirits are said to return to the present site. A ghostly lady in a flowing white dress has been reported on several occasions. Paranormal activity has been witnessed in the Rainbow Room, including objects seemingly moving of their own accord. Past visitors have also claimed that the lift has a mind of its own in the early hours. When Castle Green House served as a military barracks in the First World War, two soldiers asked to be transferred after being unsettled by alleged hauntings.

For the medieval castle lover, Cardigan's modern revamp and Georgian epicentre has eroded any great connection with its former self. Frankly, it is difficult to shake the feeling that the heart of the castle has long ceased to exist.

A more encouraging glimmer, however, may be found in a series of discoveries from 2014. When an archaeological dig was carried out at the castle, more than 9,500 medieval artefacts were discovered, ranging from an arrowhead and original pottery to animal bones and part of a dolphin's skull. Work has also revealed part of the original castle. Who knows what future excavations could uncover on the back of such encouraging discoveries?

Montgomery

Little now remains of the original motte and bailey at Montgomery. Built at the behest of Roger de Montgomery, Earl of Shrewsbury, before 1076, the site, known as Hen Domen – meaning 'old mound' – sat for almost 150 years on a low hill a mile from the modern town and Offa's Dyke.

Much of the site's early history revolved around the descendants of its 'great' founder. Roger's son, Robert de Bellême, was a veteran of Robert Curthose's rebellion of 1088 and allegedly the origin of the famous medieval legend, Robert the Devil, about a Norman who discovered he was the son of Satan. When Robert de Bellême launched his own uprising against William Rufus's brother, Henry I, Bellême was deprived of his estates and banished to Normandy. The lucky recipient was Baldwin de Boulers, from whom Montgomery, in the native tongue, was named – the Welsh Trefaldwyn translates as 'Baldwin's Town'. From this point onwards, the family maintained the castle until Llywelyn ap Iorwerth destroyed it in 1215. Though the structure was refortified, it never served as anything more than an outpost. No mention of the castle exists beyond the reign of Edward I. The hill can still be seen and is a pleasant site, albeit somewhat sparse. The results of past excavations can be found in the Old Bell Museum in the town.

For the government of kings John and Henry III, Llywelyn's wrath brought both crisis and opportunity. The English viewed Montgomery as the 'key to Wales'; a reciprocal view was held by Llywelyn of England. Touring the area as part of his ongoing military campaign against Llywelyn in the summer of 1223, Henry III ordered the building in stone of a new castle at Montgomery, approximately a mile to the south-east. Commencement of the new castle occurred on 1 October, the king's sixteenth birthday. Henry entrusted the responsibility to his justiciar, Hubert de Burgh, the man to whom his father had previously granted custody of the three castles of Gwent (see the Three Castles of Gwent).

Should one visit the site today, the reasons for its construction are self-explanatory. On completing the steep climb from the charming modern town, the reward is a somewhat lonely site from which one can experience some of the most extensive views imaginable. The castle itself was an improvement on the original, not least because reaching the great rock above the town would have been highly energy sapping for any attacker. For the first five years, progress was swift. Work on the inner ward had seen the completion of an imposing gatehouse, two D-shaped towers and a sturdy curtain wall that meandered across the hill. Progress was halted in 1228 when trouble in the Middle March saw Llywelyn mount another attack. Fortunately for Henry III, the prince found the new castle a far tougher nut to crack. When the violence ended, Hubert commissioned the addition of the middle and outer wards. Henry had granted the town a royal charter the previous year, making Montgomery the oldest borough in Wales.

It was a state of near-completion that Llywelyn encountered in 1233 on attacking the castle a third time. A second failed attempt to breach the castle had occurred in 1231, although much damage was done to the town. On this latest occasion, the conflict was of direct consequence to the king's war against rebel baron Richard Marshal, 3rd Earl of Pembroke. A short time before the Marshal War, deteriorating relations between the king and Hubert de Burgh saw the latter sacked and relieved of his properties, including Montgomery. When two of Marshal's men – Gilbert Basset and Richard Siward – aided Hubert, who had entered sanctuary in a local chapel following his escape from Devizes Castle, the justiciar joined an alliance with Marshal and Llywelyn. Though Montgomery's walls again stood firm, the onslaught caused severe damage to the well tower, requiring a thorough repair and reroofing. The original had been of particular importance to Hubert, who brought in miners from the Forest of Dean to sink the well to ensure water always flowed.

Montgomery's existence was on a more peaceful footing for the next forty years. The one exception was Dafydd ap Llywelyn's sacking of the town in 1245 – he failed to conquer the castle. When the Second Barons' War ended in 1267, Henry III made peace with Llywelyn ap Gruffudd. The Treaty of Montgomery was sealed within the castle's walls, and Llywelyn was officially acknowledged as Prince of Wales. From those same walls in December 1282, Montgomery's soldiers set out to Builth Wells to ambush Llywelyn at the Battle of Orewin Bridge. It was a cruel twist that the same walls that witnessed peace should have also contributed to war.

When Edward I quelled Madog's rebellion in 1295, Montgomery's dwindling importance mirrored many Welsh and Marcher castles. Though work had taken place in 1282 on a new hall, kitchen, granary, and bakehouse, as well as stone town walls, it failed to find a settled purpose. By 1343 the castle was noted as in disrepair. In 1359 Roger Mortimer, 2nd Earl of March, oversaw much-needed refurbishment. As the fourteenth century continued, it found more use as a local prison and military outpost rather than a residence or a frontline garrison.

This changed with the outbreak of further rebellion in the early 1400s. Under the flag of Owain Glyndŵr, the town – now protected by strong walls – was sacked in 1402. Yet, thanks in part to Hubert de Burgh's slick design, the small garrison withstood the siege. Despite this, a cessation of hostilities and a lack of renewed threat of war was, ironically, bad news for the town. More than two centuries passed until it was rebuilt and repopulated, by which time the old town walls had fallen into ruin.

Records of the castle's status during the period 1405-1643 are sketchy. The available evidence indicates that a Royalist garrison was installed no later than the summer of 1644. In September, a Roundhead force led by Sir Thomas Myddelton accepted the garrison's surrender. On 18 September, the Royalists' attempt to recapture the castle culminated in the Battle of Montgomery to the south of the River Camlad. In May 1645, the Parliamentarian governor, Sir John Pryce, defected to the king; however, in June 1649, the castle was slighted. That the castle was in perfect condition by then is unlikely. Records suggest that it had enjoyed little work since the 1540s, which had included a new mansion in the middle ward. On Parliament's orders, it was destroyed in June 1649, despite the pleas of Richard Herbert, eldest son of Edward Herbert, 1st Baron Chirbury, who had held the castle for the Royalists prior to the surrender. The second baron, a local of the town if not the castle, was later buried there.

A site that has played host to war and peace, Montgomery has seen the good, bad, and ugly of Welsh history. A ruin since the civil war, the castle's military importance has long faded. Reports of paranormal activity appear to be nonexistent, not that there is a lack of candidates. The sieges that took place were among the toughest in history. Similarly, the loss of 500 Royalists in barely an hour ensured that the battle proved the bloodiest of the civil war in Wales.

A particularly bizarre story passed down involves one Maud Vras, a local widow. On arriving at the castle on 1 January 1288 to retrieve a saucepan from the assistant constable, William of St Albans, she was found dead from a rock to the head. Nine years later, her daughter Mabel pointed the finger at William at an inquest on 27 April 1297. The jury accepted William's story that a rock had fallen through the portcullis by accident as he tried on a new cloak.

Further to the above, the robber's grave story, or 'the grave of the man unjustly hanged', is a famous one. According to local historians, in 1821 a William Jones accused a plasterer named John Davies of Wrexham of assault and robbery. When Jones produced two witnesses to the assault but not the theft, Davies was brought before the autumn sessions and found guilty. In the 1820s, the act of highway robbery remained punishable by death. When brought to the gallows, witnesses heard Davies declare: 'If I am innocent, the grass, for one generation at least will not cover my grave!' As the noose was placed around his neck, the sky is said to have grown dark, and thunder rolled in from the deep. With his final breath, he cursed Jones's alleged witnesses and dropped through the trapdoor. Both witnesses died a short time later: one in a blasting accident and the other from disease. Even today, the grass around Davies's grave is somewhat patchy, though an improvement on the bare ground that lasted well into the 1900s. A sign, some have argued, that the cemetery at Montgomery holds the remains of an innocent man wrongly put to death.

Painscastle

Few will be familiar with the village of Painscastle. Situated three miles from the border with England, between Hay and Builth Wells, it is easy to miss if one is unaware of its existence. Less obvious still is the location of its former castle. Besides a typical motte that is best viewed from the air, only earthworks remain of the fortress itself.

The motte appears to date from the first half of the twelfth century at the behest of an Anglo-Norman lord named Payne FitzJohn. Payne is described in contemporary chronicles as one of Henry I's 'new men', a designation that separates him from the offspring of those involved in the conquest of 1066. The discovery of Roman artefacts both there and in the nearby fields probably confirms the long-held presumption that the castle was erected over a Roman fort. The choice would have made sense as it benefitted from several natural and pre-existing defences.

Over the coming centuries, ongoing war would test these defences on many occasions. In July 1137, Payne was murdered by Welsh raiders, after which the cantred of Elfael became the domain of Madog ap Idnerth. For half a century, the castle remained in Welsh hands until William de Braose, 4th Lord of Bramber, recaptured the area. A year or so later, in 1196, recent refortifications were tested by one of the bloodiest sieges in Welsh history. In 1198 a considerable force led by the ruler of Powys, Gwenwynwyn ab Owain, was defeated by Richard I's justiciar, Geoffrey Fitz Peter – later earl of Essex – whose charges occupied nearby Hay.

The de Braose occupancy of Painscastle ended with John's harassment of William in 1208. The exact reasons for the falling out are unclear. The official word that John was seeking payment of William's debts seems unlikely compared to the possibility that John wished to curb William's rising power. Regardless of John's true motive, the king's actions forced William to abscond. While he died in exile, the lot was far worse for his wife, Maud, and eldest son, another William, who starved in Corfe Castle's dungeons after being moved there from Windsor.

On William's deprival, John held the castle until it was taken by one of William's old allies, Iorwerth Clud, in the year of Magna Carta. A year later, Iorwerth relinquished it to John, who granted him the lordship of Elfael until he died in 1222. On Iorwerth's death, Welsh allegiance reverted to Llywelyn ap Iorwerth, who laid waste to much of the Marshal lands of the south-west and Welsh Marches during Henry III's minority (1216-27). The castle was destroyed during the conflict, seemingly by the Welsh.

A series of truces did little more than delay the recurring violence, which became a nightmare for Henry III. A particular low was Llywelyn's execution of William's grandson – also William – in 1230 after he was found alone in the chamber of Llywelyn's wife, Joan. As for the ruined castle, the site benefitted from a stone rebuild. During Henry's Welsh campaign of 1231, much business was concluded at the castle, most notably the return of the controversial Bishop of Winchester, Peter des Roches, from crusade. Also discussed was the fallout of the failed Poitou campaign of 1230 during a visit from Peter of Dreux, Duke of Brittany. The castle was also the destination of Simon de Montfort, 6th Earl of Leicester, and Richard Marshal, 3rd Earl of Pembroke, both of whom would play decisive roles in England's history.

The castle's rebuilding proved justiciar Hubert de Burgh's only success in his attempts to salvage the Gwent castellanship (see the Three Castles of Gwent). In 1233 the castle was granted to the Norman lord Ralph Tosny. Tosny's family stood guard over the locality for the next thirty years until Llywelyn ap Gruffudd conquered the castle in 1265. Eleven years later, Ralph's descendant and namesake recovered it. In time, it passed to the Beauchamp earls of Warwick. The site's final hurrah occurred during Owain Glyndŵr's rebellion of the early 1400s. Precisely what transpired here, if anything, is unclear. From this time onwards, the castle disappears from history.

A site of some importance, despite its small size, the castle is not without legends. On its refortification after its recovery by William de Braose in 1195, a story tells that his formidable wife, Maud, was responsible for much of the work, carrying large stones in her apron. A similar tale concerns the castle at nearby Hay, which she is reputed to have built in a single night (see Hay Castle). On firmer ground, she is recorded as having added a gateway to one of the towers.

Following the refortification, tradition also tells that Maud stoutly withstood constant Welsh siege, leading her troops in shining armour. Intriguingly, a year later, the imperious Prince of Deheubarth, Rhys ap Gruffudd, was victorious over the Marcher lords at Radnor, some eight miles north of Painscastle, before laying an unsuccessful siege that culminated in a truce. Regardless of the precise role she played, it is notable that many chroniclers dubbed Painscastle 'Maud's Castle'. The courageous lady's impact on the area remains worthy of note, even if the exact circumstances have since been forgotten.

Powis

Powis Castle is one of those rare breeds of fortress that means all things to all people. Established in the late-1200s by the Welsh prince Gruffydd ap Gwenwynwyn with Edward I's permission, Powis has since been upgraded into a sumptuous country mansion that sits at the heart of extensive parkland, deer park and formal gardens.

Unlike many of the great Welsh castles, Powis has survived mostly unblemished. Thanks to the business success of its owners, it has also avoided financial upheaval. Managed by the National Trust, yet still the seat of the Earl of Powis, the red sandstone walls provide modern-day visitors with a unique blend of a medieval military stronghold and post-medieval family home.

While Edward I established the Iron Ring to consolidate his victory over Llywelyn ap Gruffudd, Powis was begun as a reward for Gwenwynwyn's loyalty. In 1286 his son, Owain, renounced his claim to the kingdom of Powis in return for being made Baron de la Pole. On Owain's death, the barony and castle passed to his daughter, Hawise Gadarn, who married Sir John Charlton, 1st Baron Charlton, thus beginning the Charltons' 100-year tenure. In the 1400s, sisters

Joyce Tiptoft and Joan Grey inherited the castle and owned it equally. In 1578, one of the last baron's bastard sons leased the castle and lordship to Sir Edward Herbert, son of the Earl of Pembroke, a distant relative. Nine years later, Herbert purchased Powis outright and favoured the monarchy throughout the civil war. Fortunately, the castle fell peacefully to the Roundheads in October 1644 and was undamaged when it was returned at the restoration.

Deprived of high office under Cromwell due to his Catholicism, the third Lord Powis, created Marquess under James II, was made a key minister before following James into exile following the Glorious Revolution. After William III granted the castle to his nephew, Dutchman William Nassau de Zuylestein – styled 1st Earl of Rochford – the magnificent terrace garden was completed, as were many other improvements. In 1722 the second marquess, another William, was reinstated. When the third, also William, died in 1748, Henry Arthur Herbert, a distant cousin, was the beneficiary. In 1774 Sir John Cullum remarked that the castle's 'grand situation, its charming and magnificent prospccts, its extensive woody parks of many 100 acres [...] render it one of the first seats of the kingdom.'

This was the castle that Edward Clive, eldest son of Clive of India, inherited in 1784 on marrying Lord Powis's daughter, Lady Henrietta Herbert. The castle passed down through the family until they gifted it to the National Trust in 1952. Clive of India was estimated to be the richest self-made man in Europe – much of his fortune resulting from plunder following the Battle of Plassey – and the estate benefited greatly. Among its treasures, the interior boasts one of the most impressive art collections in Wales, including works by Sir Joshua Reynolds. A superb collection of other treasures ranges from fine sculptures and tapestries to furniture and carriages. The Clive Museum, opened in 1987, features many artefacts brought back from India, including precious metals, textiles, and armour. Another rarity is the survival of the state bedroom, which is contemporary to the restoration of the monarchy. The room is the only remaining example in Britain in which a balustrade separates the bed alcove from the remainder of the room. It is believed that Charles II visited the castle and may have enjoyed this room. The feather-shaped window latches were put in to honour the visit of Edward VII, at the time, Prince of Wales. The future George V, and his wife, Mary, also visited in 1909.

Surrounded by such an array of historical artefacts, a tour of this elegant stronghold could easily be compared with a trip back in time. Intriguingly, some have claimed that it is not just the keepsakes that create such an illusion. When the sun sets, a mighty shadow is cast, cloaking the mellow red walls in an eerie, blood colour. Although Powis has enjoyed a relatively peaceful history, many ghosts are said to haunt it.

One of the most common sightings is of a man. Said to haunt the ground floor, usually in the same place, the lonely figure appears briefly before disappearing without a trace. The 'Duke's room' is regarded by many as one of the castle's most haunted areas. Some staff members have reported a presence in one of the rooms at the end of the long gallery, even when it appears empty. Here visitors have witnessed the apparition of a woman in a black dress sitting quietly by the fireplace, only to vanish without a trace. Her ghost has also been seen standing by the door.

Music once reverberated softly throughout the ballroom wing. Since its transfer to the National Trust, the wing has become disused, though still well maintained. On one odd occasion, staff were disturbed by the inexplicable sound of piano music coming from the room, only to find the area was empty. The ballroom wing also includes an apartment once occupied by various members of staff. Although pleasant to look upon, it is often avoided due to its reputation as being haunted. Over the years, many former occupants have identified a woman wearing a mop hat sitting at the end of the bed. Another said to haunt Powis is a strange lady dressed in white who has been seen in one of the bedrooms.

The Clive Museum, as recently recalled, is one of the most fascinating features of the castle. In addition to its collection of rare items, the spirit of a young girl dressed in green has been seen. The well-kept grounds are a delightful location during the day, but when the moon casts an eerie shadow across the gardens, the spectre of a knight riding a black horse has been seen travelling at speed before vanishing into the darkness.

Of all the ghost stories and legends associated with the castles of Wales, one of the most intriguing must concern that of the hidden box. Recorded by a Methodist preacher named John Hampson, this curious tale from the eighteenth century was later passed on to a Mr Wright, who recorded the anomaly in his autobiography.

According to Wright's memoirs, the legend surrounds an unmarried seamstress who was given a room at the castle while carrying out repairs for the earl in 1778. The earl was absent, yet the steward agreed to take her on. On offering her board, the staff cruelly put her in a haunted room.

After a short time at the castle, she was settling down for bed one night, reading from her bible. As she warmed herself by the fire, the woman was unnerved by the visitation of an enigmatic figure wearing a gold-laced hat, a waistcoat, and matching clothing. The man proceeded towards the window before coming to a standstill. Remaining silent, he gazed across the countryside into the night. Though the entity's appearance startled the woman, she remained calm and watched in near disbelief as he left the room and slowly shut the door.

It was not until after the man had departed that the seamstress realised that the gentleman had entered and left without making a sound. Terrified by a growing belief that the inexplicable occurrence was not of this world, she began to pray. As she genuflected, the door opened for a second time without a sound. Again, the strange man came and went, after which she tried in vain to sleep. Finally, the apparition appeared for a third time and stood silently before her bed.

'Pray, sir, who arc you and what do you want?' the seamstress plucked up the courage to ask.

Clearly understanding the question, the apparition answered, 'Take up the candle and follow me, and I will show you.'

Although frightened, the woman reluctantly vacated her bed and followed the ghost along a passageway to a small chamber, where the spirit instructed her to lift the floorboards under which she would find a box. At this point, the apparition requested that 'Both casket and key must be taken out and sent to the earl in London. Do this, and I will trouble the house no more.'

A cleft on the wall housed a key, which fitted the box. The seamstress immediately went to find the steward and his wife and told them what the spirit had said. The steward sent the box to the earl, who was so rejoiced that he offered the woman a home at the castle for life.

To this day, the contents remain unknown to everybody except those connected to the incident. Also, the spectre that pointed out its existence has not reappeared. It would seem his purpose has been fulfilled, and his soul is now at peace.

Chapter 4

Pembrokeshire

Carew

The magnificent Celtic cross on the path to Carew Castle offers an atmospheric reminder of a darker time when ancient tribes roamed the land. Consisting of a combined wheel head and neck, fastened by a tenon on a tall shaft, the eleventh-century edifice is a rare one; indeed, only three similar features have been found throughout Wales. The inscription is in honour of Maredudd ap Edwin, the joint ruler of Deheubarth 1033-35, which may indicate he gave the land to the church. Although the Celtic era ended many centuries ago, such features offer a tangible connection with a mysterious people whose exact ways have become largely forgotten.

Enclosed by the Pembrokeshire Coast National Park, the ruined Norman castle lies on a limestone bank overlooking a 23-acre millpond, close to Carew Tidal Mill. The mill is itself a rarity. Now fully restored, it is the only remaining one in Wales. The remains of an early fort can be found close by, possibly dating back to the Iron Age. Most of what remained of the fort was converted into a Norman stronghold around 1095 under Gerald de Windsor. Carew was likely begun in the same carboniferous rock for which the castle is famous. It is equally likely that construction initially consisted of an imposing Norman keep before being revamped into a fine gentleman's residence in the Tudor era.

An elegant ruin whose 15-m-high walls have surrounded an empty interior for several centuries, the castle usually attracts more than 30,000 tourists a year. Be it medieval history lovers, Tudor enthusiasts, or those whose interest extends to the nearby mill, there is no shortage of reasons to become enthralled by Carew's colourful history. Nor are Carew's quirks limited to history. When the doors close and the moon rises, the much-loved ruins become the domain of a colony of bats. More than half the bat species in Britain are thought to reside within the walls.

Joining the nocturnal creatures as they fly throughout the empty halls, the ethereal likeness of a figure in white has been seen gliding across a long-forgotten walkway. Ending her journey before a void where a window once was, she gazes aimlessly across the landscape before disappearing. According to local lore, she is not the only entity believed to haunt this ancient fortress. A murderous pirate has also been heard lamenting his son. And most bizarrely of all, the eerie silence has been said to be disturbed by a demonic creature named Satan.

Few in Wales doubt the identity of the mysterious lady in white. When the castle was constructed, Gerald de Windsor lived there with his wife, Princess Nest ferch Rhys. Also appointed castellan of Pembroke Castle by Arnulf de Montgomery, Gerald built the first castle on a site that had formed part of Nest's dowry. The daughter of Rhys ap Tewdwr, Nest was regarded as one of the country's most sought-after women. After being brought to William Rufus's court as a prized captive, tradition states that she became Henry I's mistress while he was still a prince and bore him a child, Henry FitzHenry.

Despite the age gap, Gerald and Nest appear to have enjoyed a happy marriage. Her loins fruitful from her time with Henry, Nest bore Gerald no fewer than five children in their first nine years. Although she was devoted to her husband, things became complicated around 1109 after a chance meeting with her cousin, Owain ap Cadwgan, a prince of Powys. The pair had met several years earlier as children but had not seen each other since. Owain was said to have fallen for Nest's beauty at that first meeting and sought to take her for himself. On a cold dark Christmas night, Owain and fifteen men crept up to the castle. Assuming it to be an attack on him, Gerald escaped by hiding in the sewers, leaving Nest unguarded.

The princess's kidnapping sent shockwaves throughout Wales, resulting in a small-scale civil war. It may have been around this time that Nest was given her famous nickname 'Helen of Wales'. Despite her abduction, history records that Nest was a willing prisoner who may have born Owain two children. Owain's father, Cadwgan ap Bleddyn, lost much of his lands during the war, and Owain fled to Ireland. Motivated by Henry I's threats, he also returned Nest to Gerald.

Although reunited with his love, Gerald was tortured by his cowardly escape and plotted his revenge. Time passed, and by 1114 Owain had returned to Wales. Now in opposition to Henry I, he joined with the king's enemy, Gruffudd ap Cynan of Gwynedd. Two years later, after peace terms between the warring sides had been agreed, and the king had knighted Owain in Normandy, fate brought the two love rivals together as unlikely comrades in arms. Gerald, though, remained privately consumed by hatred towards the man who had taken his wife. During the fighting, as Henry I attempted to put down the rebellion of Gruffudd ap Rhys of Deheubarth – Nest's brother – Gerald caught Owain off-guard and killed him in cold blood.

Reestablished in their marriage, Gerald and Nest do not appear to have had any more children. The date of Gerald's death is also a mystery. Recording of it in one source as 1135 seems late. There is little or no mention of him after Owain's murder, which may indicate he died a short time later. Further evidence for Gerald's death can be found in the knowledge that Nest mothered one Robert FitzStephen on her marriage to Stephen, constable of Cardigan.

Despite her remarriage, Owain's death devastated Nest. Tradition tells that the beautiful princess continued to mourn her cousin and captor. For 900 years, Nest's ghost has been said to haunt Carew. She has been seen multiple times, usually looking out of one of the castle's windows, apparently longing for Owain's return. A notable appearance occurred in 1994 when one visitor stayed overnight to monitor the bat colony.

After initially serving as an impressive Norman stronghold, the castle was refurbished into an elegant home. The most notable of the early owners was Sir Nicholas de Carew, a descendant of Gerald and Nest, who lived there during the reign of Edward I. Chief among Nicholas's work were the lesser hall and chapel tower. Near the chapel's north-facing-window, the modern visitor can still see the faint remains of a Nine Men's Morris board. Legend from the time tells that should the Devil ever enter the chapel, he would get distracted and never disturb the mass. On his death in 1311, Nicholas was buried in the local church. His effigy can still be seen.

New ownership beckoned after the de Carew family, who had owned it after de Windsor, fell on hard times and mortgaged the fortress. Henry VII awarded Carew to Sir Rhys ap Thomas, a powerful landowner who came to prominence during the Wars of the Roses. Like many contemporary profiteers, Thomas had benefited from spurious allegiances, not least changing sides to support Tudor at Bosworth. One source even identifies him as the man who dealt the decisive blow to Richard III with a poleaxe.

A committed supporter of Henry Tudor from that time, Thomas extended the castle and revamped it with sumptuous apartments. A privy councillor and knight of the garter, he celebrated the latter with a five-day tournament at Carew in 1507. A coat of arms around an inner doorway in dedication of Henry VII, Prince Arthur, and his then-wife, Catherine of Aragon, dates from this time. Such allegiance would not continue into future generations. In 1531 Thomas's grandson, Rhys ap Gruffydd, was executed for treason against Henry VIII.

Owners of questionable temperament were by no means absent from Carew's later history. Of particular note was the man who became the castle's owner in 1558. Sir John Perrot was officially stepson of one Thomas Perrot but widely conjectured to have been the bastard of Henry VIII and his mistress, Mary Berkeley. Born in November 1528, John first appeared on the scene when Henry was negotiating his divorce from Catherine of Aragon. Artistic representations imply that he resembled Henry VIII in many ways.

During his time at Carew, Perrot's most impressive legacy was the north range, in which he housed several domestic rooms, including a Long Gallery. He also rerouted several roads and moved the village to improve the views. The castle was also the setting of one Bernard Jourdain, who Perrot imprisoned in May 1577. In league with an infamous pirate named Hicks, who waylaid a French merchant ship off the Cornish coast, Perrot chained Jourdain up in the Carew dungeons in exchange for a ransom and a share of the cargo.

Despite his corruption, Perrot performed well in Elizabethan society. Appointed Lord Deputy of Ireland by Queen Elizabeth in 1584 – apparently acknowledging that she had a half-brother – Perrot made many enemies. Having made the careless remark of Elizabeth that 'now she is ready to piss herself for fear of the Spaniard, I am once again one of her white boys,' news of his arrogance, plus embellishment of his plans by his enemies, saw Elizabeth send him to the Tower in 1588. At his trial three years later, a guilty verdict was returned, to which Perrot berated the lieutenant with the words, 'Will the Queen suffer her brother to be offered up as a sacrifice to the envy of my strutting adversary?' Her temper with Perrot cooled somewhat, Elizabeth retaliated by labelling the jury 'knaves' and refused to sign the warrant.

As fate had it, Perrot died from natural causes in November 1592. Intriguingly, one of his officers, Sir Thomas Williams, had been brought to the Tower and met a similar end a short time earlier. Similar was true of another of Perrot's number, Sir Thomas Fitzherbert, who had been transferred there in January 1591, under strict orders to remain in solitary confinement. Despite being allowed the freedom of the Tower, he perished three days before Perrot's funeral. A fourth, Sir Nicholas White, also followed in 1593.

Exactly what became of the luckless quartet has never been confirmed. Officially all four died of natural causes, yet this seems highly suspicious. It seems a slightly redundant yet fascinating sidenote that had Henry VIII followed in his ancestor John of Gaunt's footsteps and married his mistress, Perrot could well have reigned as John II. In that event, Anne Boleyn and Jane Seymour would never have been queen, and Edward VI and Elizabeth I never born.

On Perrot's death, Carew, like many properties, passed to the Crown. The de Carews repurchased it in 1607 and refortified it for the civil war. Later in James I's reign, Carew became the property of a character of particular ill repute. Sir Roland ap Rhys – alternatively spelt Rowland Rees – was an accomplished sailor and pirate. His fiery personality would later cause a bitter, long-lasting feud after he banished his son for falling in love with a Flemish merchant's daughter. Rhys lived a solitary life at the castle with his pet monkey, Satan, which he had acquired on one of his voyages to the Barbary Coast. Based on the limited information that survives, it is likely that the beast was a mandrill.

During his long bouts of loneliness, the tyrannical nobleman's personality became twisted. When people visited Carew, the strange pet became the bizarre centrepiece of entertainment, at which Sir Roland's mood often became volatile. One minute he would cry out for his beloved son; the next, he would curse him to hell. As time passed, most stayed away from the castle, knowing they would be the victims of the ageing man's wrath.

As his bitterness towards his son escalated, the developing feud culminated in an inevitable tragedy. One cold winter's night, the Flemish merchant visited the castle to pay his rent. Sir Roland reserved a special hatred for the merchant, having accused his daughter of bewitching his son. Worse for the merchant, trade was terrible that winter, and he had only part of what was due. On arrival at the rainswept castle, Sir Roland slated the merchant and mocked his daughter. Unable to shrug off the drunken man's ceaseless abuse, the merchant reportedly raised his hand to Sir Roland and knocked him down. In retaliation, the pirate blew on his whistle and unleashed the ape.

Barely escaping with his life, the merchant sought to leave Carew; however, to make amends, a kindly servant asked him to stay for a warm meal as the night was wet and windy. As they enjoyed each other's company, the piercing of Sir Roland's whistle again reverberated throughout the castle, after which the sounds of a struggle intensified. On climbing the stairs and entering his chambers, they witnessed the pirate dead on the floor, his throat slit, and the monkey's head burning in the fire with a sickly grin permanently frozen on its face.

Precisely what transpired that strange night has never been revealed. That Sir Roland blew the whistle to set the ape on himself in an apparent suicide mission is plausible. If so, what killed the ape? Did the poor creature accidentally burn itself in the fire, or did both succumb to a painful struggle, perhaps because of Sir Roland's drunken reflexes? Alternatively, in the absence of eyewitnesses, did the merchant, and maybe the servant, set upon the old pirate and his unique pet.

Whatever the exact circumstances, both master and ape perished that night. Since that time, loud footsteps have been heard throughout the otherwise empty chamber in the north-west tower. The same is true of hysterical laughter and piercing screams, all of which are thought to belong to Sir Roland. The ape has also reportedly been spotted running along one of the walls as well as in the long-abandoned fireplace. Of all the reputed apparitions concerning the castles of Wales, none are surely quite so bizarre. Nor so successfully struck fear into the hearts of those unfortunate to hear the piercing sounds.

Cilgerran

Standing on an outcrop above the River Teifi and overlooking the town of the same name, Cilgerran Castle encompasses much that there is to be loved in a medieval castle.

An older sibling of Edward I's Iron Ring, Cilgerran owes its appearance to Edward's father, Henry III, another keen builder. Prior to Henry's fortress, a more primitive motte and bailey is understood to have been erected around 1110 as Gerald of Windsor attempted to secure the area from the marauding Welsh. Though the early structure, consisting primarily of a timber palisade, proved useful in frustrating the natives, Gerald's efforts were by no means a permanent solution. By the time Rhys ap Gruffudd laid siege to the castle, the initial wooden defences had been upgraded in stone.

Within weeks of Rhys taking Cardigan (see Cardigan Castle), Cilgerran also fell. After razing the primitive structure, Rhys reassembled the fortress with a stone and lime mortar foundation. The new walls survived until an attack by William Marshal, 1st Earl of Pembroke, in 1204. With Rhys's son and heir, Maelgwn, ousted, Marshal set about further renovation. Sadly for Marshal, his efforts were in vain. When conflict with the Welsh resumed in 1215, Llywelyn ap Iorwerth took Cilgerran in a single day.

For the next eight years, the castle remained in Llywelyn's hands. In 1223, four years after Marshal's death, his son and heir encountered better luck. On retaking the fortress, William Marshal II, now 2nd Earl of Pembroke, began a substantial rebuild. Sadly, William never got to complete his father's earlier work. Nor would any of his four younger brothers. After passing away, from various causes, between 1231 and 1245 (according to one of the chroniclers, William was poisoned by the justiciar Hubert de Burgh and his brothers cursed by an Irish bishop), the finishing touches were added by the de Cantilupe family, proud and powerful Marcher lords.

At its height, the castle was impressive. Aided by the cliff's natural protection, the heavily fortified walls, gatehouse, and double drum towers proved an imposing combination. Eyebrows have been raised about the size of some of the stones, leading to suspicion that the castle was rushed. Try as they might, the Welsh never recaptured it. The worst onslaught occurred in 1258 after the Welsh defeated Henry III. Fortunately for the king, the sturdy walls held firm.

In 1272, the year of the king's death, the castle changed hands again. As the male de Cantilupe line died out, Cilgerran became the property of the Hastings family. Unlike their predecessors, the family's interest in the castle was fleeting. By 1387 it was already predominantly a ruin and probably deserted on Henry IV's accession. Still property, at least indirectly, of William Marshal's descendants, the castle remained part of the Pembroke estates until the Tudor period. In the following century, it was taken over by the Crown and abandoned. Due to its poor condition, it avoided involvement in the civil war and wasn't slighted. What remained became highly valued by the artists of the day. Especially revered is a collection of Turners that now hang in the Tate. Since 1938 it has been in the care of the National Trust, and in more recent times, in partnership with Cadw.

Since the early 1400s, historical reenactments are the nearest the ancient walls now see to renewed violence. Yet, while those days are gone, reminders of its past are easily found. A series of illegible graffiti and carvings can be found in some of the doorways. In contrast to many of Britain's castle dungeons, the markings appear to postdate the castle's habitation.

Further to the strange graffiti, Cilgerran's west tower is reputedly the haunt of a 'black-bearded wraith' who has been seen looking out through one of the windows. The strange being has been linked with Owain ap Cadwgan – see also Carew Castle. Owain was often in residence at the castle during the 1100s. Indeed, it was probably here where he held his glamorous cousin, Princess Nest, whom he abducted from Carew. Should Owain be the apparition in residence, his appearance would be particularly ironic as his beloved is famously believed to haunt Carew some twenty-five miles away. Past historians have conjectured that the story of Nest was the inspiration for the Arthurian tales involving the king, Guinevere, and Sir Galahad. An intriguing suggestion, albeit almost certainly false.

Haverfordwest

The medieval fortress in the centre of Haverfordwest is a rare survivor from the early Norman years. On the back of the castle's creation, an English-speaking market town grew due to the area's strategic importance at the lowest crossing point of the River Cleddau.

Pinpointing the exact time that construction began is challenging. The best evidence suggests that a stone keep and bailey fortress was established by Gilbert de Clare, Earl of Pembroke, around 1120. An Iron Age hill fort is recorded as having existed before that, though physical evidence is yet to be uncovered at the same location. The area was also reportedly frequented by Danish sea raiders, yet again there is no conclusive evidence.

Also influential in the area's development was the arrival of refugees from Flanders. After experiencing dreadful floods in their native Low Countries around 1108, hordes of Flemish arrived at Henry I's invitation to serve nearby Pembroke Castle in exchange for the usual privileges. Sources that contradict the de Clare accounts have also proposed that work on the fortress began just a couple of years after the Flemish arrival by Tancred the Fleming, uncle of Gerald of Wales through marriage. In future years, de Clare appointed Tancred's son, Richard fitz-Tancred, castellan. Regardless of the exact truth, a combination of Norman and Flemish influence seems likely.

Even before the birth of what is now the county town of Pembrokeshire, the castle served a vital purpose to the Normans. Within twenty years of its creation, the fortress faced its first significant test on becoming the target of Gruffydd ap Rhys. The exact dates of the Prince of Deheubarth's siege are sadly lost, though most estimates place it around 1135-36. In 1173, Henry II visited the castle on his way back from Ireland. Fifteen years later, Gerald of Wales noted a visit with Baldwin, Archbishop of Canterbury, who was touring the country in support of the third crusade. Gerald also recorded that part of the castle was being used as a local prison.

As usual with the castles of Wales, the thirteenth century brought significant upgrades. By the turn of the century, most of the castle was of stone construction, including a new keep. Its situation on a ridge also provided for abundant natural defences. In 1210, about ten years after the nearby priory was erected, King John sojourned at the castle on his way to Ireland. Sensing trouble ahead, three years later, he persuaded the Earl of Pembroke, William Marshal, to instal a garrison. Marshal oversaw significant rebuilding work throughout the next decade, which continued until his death in May 1219. The following year, Llywelyn carried out a threat from 1217 and razed the town's timber buildings. He failed, however, to breach the stone walls.

As fate transpired, Llywelyn's violence proved something of a blessing. When the wreckage was cleared, a comprehensive rebuilding programme led to the development of Haverfordwest as a hub for trading and commerce. When the male Marshal line died out in 1245, the castle passed to Humphrey II de Bohun. In 1257, Humphrey successfully quelled the forces of Llywelyn ap Gruffudd. Less effective, however, were the castle walls in withstanding the Royalist forces of William de Valence, Earl of Pembroke, who laid siege to the castle during the Second

Barons' War in 1265. In 1274, as Edward I returned from his crusade as king of England, the castle was granted to Humphrey's son and successor, Humphrey III. Ten years later, Edward and his queen made a personal visit during a pilgrimage to St David's. Eleanor was much enamoured with the fortress, and in 1288 she borrowed a considerable amount of money to purchase and develop it.

Though Edward would later make no effort to hide his grief at Eleanor's untimely death, it is less clear whether he shared his wife's love of the castle. Following Eleanor's passing in November 1290, it remained a royal property throughout the fourteenth century. During this time, many wealthy subjects tenanted and owned Haverfordwest, including Edward, the Black Prince. Restoration work in 1381-85, which included the town walls, proved invaluable in thwarting Owain Glyndŵr in 1405.

Despite passing its toughest test yet, the castle became typically redundant. Richard II's stay at the castle in August 1394 and the future Edward V's in 1473 were rare moments of intrigue. Cavalier troops briefly refortified and garrisoned it no later than 1644, until the apparent mistaking of a herd of cows for Roundheads saw it swiftly abandoned. A short time later, it was retaken and held until the Royalists' defeat at the Battle of Colby Moor on 1 August 1645.

It is unclear exactly how any remaining garrison responded to receiving letters from Cromwell in July 1648, ordering the castle's destruction, or else to ensure the locals' imprisonment in it. In 1778 the castle was described as derelict, around which time Eleanor's walls found a new use as the town prison. The governor's house, which guards the entrance to the inner ward, was also constructed around that time. In 1820 a new prison building was erected in the inner bailey and had the capacity for eighty-six prisoners. Its use continued until its closure in 1878, at which time the remaining inmates were transferred to Carmarthen. After the castle operated for a time as a police station and council offices, the governor's house was revamped to house a museum. The castle is now under the watch of the Pembrokeshire Coast National Park Authority and welcomes visitors.

Nothing now remains of the town walls – a shame considering their integral role in defending the town during the insurrection of 1405. Apart from the original keep, no reminders have survived from Gilbert de Clare's early castle. Whether the spirits of former soldiers or inmates still inhabit the remains is unclear. For many years the nearby A4076 has reputedly been the haunt of a shadowy female figure. A handful of reports even tell of baffled motorists stopping in the mistaken belief that they have accidentally run someone over.

Regardless of the facts behind the hauntings, there is no doubting the identity of the castle's heroine. Eleanor successfully raised funds to oversee mass rebuilding but, sadly, had little opportunity to enjoy it. She perished on 28 November 1290, a matter of months after the castle was completed. How she died is unrecorded. Longstanding conjecture has suggested that malaria was the cause. A family predisposition for cardiac problems has also been put forward. In the days following her death, the grieving king brought the government to a three-day halt. Plans were also put in place for her body to be interred at Westminster Abbey. Her husband's legacy for her can still be found in three of the twelve beautiful 'Eleanor's crosses' erected to mark parts of the journey to her rest. In her honour, Haverfordwest Castle also became known for a long time as 'the Queen's Castle at Haverford'. Both castle and queen deserve no less.

Manorbier

> [...] excellently well defended turrets and bulwarks, and is situated on the summit of a hill extending on the western side towards the seaport, having on the northern and southern sides a fine fish-pond under its walls, as conspicuous for its grand appearance, as for the depth of its waters, and a beautiful orchard on the same side, enclosed on one part by a vineyard, and on the other by a wood, remarkable for the projection of its rocks, and the height of its hazel trees. On the right hand of the promontory, between the castle and the church, near the site of a very large lake and mill, a rivulet of never-failing water flows through a valley, rendered sandy by the violence of the winds. Towards the west, the Severn sea, bending its course to Ireland, enters a hollow bay at some distance from the castle; and the southern rocks, extended a little further north, would render it a most excellent harbour for shipping [...] This country is well supplied with corn, sea-fish, and imported wines; and what is preferable to every other advantage, from its vicinity to Ireland, it is tempered by a salubrious air.

Such was the verdict of Gerald of Wales. Nestled in a heavenly part of the south Pembrokeshire countryside, overlooking a beach that remains almost as unspoilt today as it was in Gerald's day, it is easy to view the region as a taste of paradise. That Gerald considered it to be so is well known: 'In all the broad lands of Wales, Manorbier is the pleasantest place by far,' he recalled. The reason that the twelfth-century chronicler held Manorbier in such high esteem is no mystery. In addition to being an expert on the area, Gerald was born within the castle's walls. Today, a display in the north tower honours his place of birth and denotes his important contributions to Welsh life.

For modern-day visitors, it is easy to feel an affinity with Gerald's comments. Lying slightly off the beaten track, reached from the walled seaside town of Tenby or the equally historic town of Pembroke by narrow, often hedge-lined roads, the Norman castle possesses all the necessary ingredients of a genuine historical treasure. The Church of St James the Great that sits proudly on the opposite ridge is a rare contemporary of the fortress. Further traces of the feudal era also survive lower down the valley, itself chiselled from the timeless flow of two small streams that enter the sea at Manorbier Bay. Perhaps most intriguing of all, a Neolithic burial chamber known as King's Quoit offers a connection back to around 3000BC.

Few castles fit the definition of a residential fortress better than Manorbier. Its pretty façade and verdant surroundings, coupled with an efficient layout and thick-walled-defences, make the castle lavish and defendable. Abundant vegetation cocoons the outer ward like an extra layer of defence, while beyond the gatehouse, the inner ward's beauty and functionality encapsulate the site's duality perfectly. The bright flowers and the immaculate lawns, around which the sturdy curtain wall connects imposing corner towers that offer seemingly endless views of the surroundings, still convey much of Gerald's paradise. It is extraordinary how within this flowery setting sit two industrial hearths on the west and south walls below impressive Flemish chimneys. At no other place in Britain can this author recall the picturesque and the fires of industry seated side-by-side so seamlessly.

The nearby Neolithic burial chamber confirms prehistoric settlement in the area; however, if a more primitive fortress predated the castle, its foundations are now lost. Like most Welsh castles, the fortress itself owes its origins to the post-Conquest period. The beneficiary of the first estate was Odo de Barri. A busy participant in the Norman Conquest, Odo was rewarded by William the Conqueror with the Manorbier estates, including the manors at Begelly, Penally, Jameston and Manorbier Newton. Odo's castle does not appear to have been much more than a standard motte and bailey, which was rebuilt in stone the following century.

The brains behind the stone castle was Odo's son, William de Barri, Gerald's father. William put down a hall-block within the inner ward, which served as the principal residence throughout the castle's history. A rarity among Britain's castles was the creation of a hall-keep as part of the curtain wall – usually, the keep was a separate structure around which the curtain wall was constructed. Further along the south-western border, the equally impressive great hall dates from the 1130s and is locally celebrated among the earliest stone buildings in west Wales. Like the keep, the great hall's walls were thick and integrated among daily functional areas, such as the kitchen and buttery. In addition to Gerald, Manorbier was also the birthplace of Angharad, the daughter of Gerald de Windsor and Princess Nest of Carew Castle.

As building technology developed, so did Manorbier. Revered for its ornately vaulted interior, the chapel was put in around 1260 south of the great hall. Remarkably, elements of the medieval wall painting have survived, which is a rarity in Europe. Close by, the spur tower – where the latrines were located – and watergate that allowed delivery of supplies from the nearby bay all added to the castle's functionality and prestige.

By comparison to many British castles, Manorbier's history was mostly uneventful. Aided by its obscure location and solid defences, only twice was the castle subjected to military onslaught. In 1327 it was the setting of a family feud, which saw its storming by rightful owner Richard de Barri. The de Barris maintained ownership of Odo's original estates until 1359. From this point on, the toing and froing of ownership became the norm until the castle became a royal possession under Henry VII. Its royal tenure ended when Elizabeth I sold it to the Bowen family. At this time, the fortress was lamented as 'ruynous [...] quite decayed'.

Manorbier's involvement in the civil war would appear to confirm that the castle remained of some strategic or military value. At the very least, the family must have been efficient in refortifying it. For the modern visitor, reminders of the period still litter the outer ward, including earthen embankments that delayed Cromwell's progress. For the Bowens, slowing the Roundheads down was all that was achieved, and in 1645 the castle was taken and slighted.

As was usual at that time, the Parliamentarians' vandalism ended Manorbier's existence as a property of some importance. In 1670 the family sold it to the Philips family – also the owners of Picton Castle – for 6,000 marks, approximately £400,000. The new owners used the estate for farmland before leasing it in 1880 to J.R. Cobb, who was instrumental in the castle's salvation. The southern section of the inner ward was renovated and converted into caretaker's lodgings. The so-called 'modern' house was Cobb's doing in the late 1800s. Thanks to his efforts, Manorbier – along with many others in Pembrokeshire – is safe to visit, and the lawns a pleasant place for a sandwich or a cup of tea on a nice day.

A site that has witnessed the birth of a great writer, family feuds and civil war, Manorbier has no shortage of hidden treasures for the castle hunter to enjoy. Coupled with the nearby church, the beach, and the neolithic settlement in the valley below, Manorbier is a perfect site to gain an insight into the old feudal system. The former area of orchards, crops and a deer park can still be found in the lands below, albeit now plagued by bracken and marshland. A short walk from the castle, the remains of the old mill, pond, fishpond, and dovecote all offer a fascinating glimpse into its former life. In the early 1900s, the renowned author Virginia Woolf paid a visit and set her 1908 novel *The Voyages Out* there. The famous playwright George Bernard Shaw also often stayed here, and the poet Siegfried Sassoon wrote a poem about Manorbier in 1924.

According to local lore, the castle is residence to many ghosts. A lady in black has been seen on many occasions, commonly in September. The castle is also reputedly the haunt of more minor spirits. Besides poltergeist activity, the nearby tower-like dovecote is said to be somewhat doleful in ambience. Formerly the store for the castle's winter meat, it has been alleged that many locals were executed for stealing from it. Whether they were killed there or the vicinity was used as a place of execution is unrecorded.

A little haven in an area dominated by war, it is no surprise that Gerald of Wales regarded the castle with such affection. If local legend is true, the great chronicler's spirit remains bound to his former home; ironically, Gerald wrote that poltergeists were common in Pembrokeshire.

Though such tales seem to be more in terms of presence than sightings, it is a nice thought that even after an absence of more than 800 years, a part of him remains ever tied to what he regarded as 'the pleasantest place by far' in all of Wales.

Narberth

It was recalled in an old chronicle found in the Cotton Library that a fortress of Arberth was destroyed in 1116 by the forces of Gruffudd ap Rhys. The library is a revered one in the United Kingdom, and with good reason. What began with works collected by the antiquarian and MP Sir Robert Bruce Cotton eventually led to establishing the world-renowned British Library.

It is possible that the castle at Arberth is not the same ruined Norman fortress that sits in the pleasant market town of Narberth. An alternative theory has been put forward that Sentence Castle, located in the nearby village of Templeton, was the site in question. Unlike Narberth, this never developed beyond ring work and would have proved unable to withstand the Prince of Gwynedd. It was never rebuilt and likely made way for the stone fortress at nearby Narberth.

Narberth is an interesting one in Welsh history. The castle was situated along what is now known as the Landsker Line, a crudely identified border that separated the English-speaking invaders from the native Welsh. The present ruins are mainly from the 1200s and were created at the behest of one Andrew Perrot to guard a strategic routeway and river ford. The original structure was rectangular with an outer and inner bailey, corner towers and a gatehouse surrounded by a defensive ditch. The inner bailey was rebuilt in stone by Roger Mortimer in the late 1200s; the outer was likely always timber. Based on what remains, a great chamber once stood over a vaulted storeroom or chapel. For the next two centuries, the castle enjoyed a relatively stable existence, its south-westerly location placing it mostly out of the way of the chaos of the two Barons' Wars.

When Owain Glyndŵr's rebellion reached Pembrokeshire, the castle was targeted but never conquered. In 1404 Henry IV granted Narberth to Thomas Carrewe in gratitude for his role in withstanding Glyndŵr. Carrewe's achievement is even more astounding considering that it was done with a small garrison. The castle had only entered royal hands two years earlier when Sir Edmund Mortimer, younger brother of Roger, 4th Earl of March, forfeited it because of his alliance with Glyndŵr on being captured in 1402. The castle eventually reverted to Mortimer during Henry V's reign, but Edmund's successor, his nephew of the same name, died childless in 1425. Consequently, the castle returned to royal control under Edward IV.

For the next two centuries, Narberth seems to have endured a slow decline. Despite substantial investment by the Welsh hero Sir Rhys ap Thomas in the early 1500s, a source in 1603 described the area as one of nine Pembrokeshire boroughs in decay. When the civil war came to town, the Parliamentarians slighted it, and by the 1740s, its condition was perilous. Only in the twentieth century did the castle rediscover any form of purpose. Early that century, the townsfolk held an annual procession that ended with dancing and singing in the castle grounds. The council-owned ruins were reopened in 2005.

A relatively low-key player in Welsh history, Narberth continues to throw up surprises. An engraving on an information board at the nearby train station implies the former presence of Flemish-style chimneys, in keeping with those at Manorbier. Archaeological excavations have found at least twenty graves on the north side dating from the 1200s, indicating that a church was once on the site. The stonework has also contributed to the construction of many local houses.

Narberth is not without legends. A story contained in the *Mabinogion* – a selection of tales recorded in Middle Welsh in the twelfth and thirteenth centuries from earlier oral traditions – cites Castell Arberth as the location in which the heroine Rhiannon was imprisoned and forced to carry travellers through the gates as penance for killing her son. Two nearby earthworks, including Sentence, may suggest Narberth was not the site in question; however, the Norman tendency to build over older ruins may have eradicated the evidence in any case. In the *Mabinogion*, the castle was the palace of Pwyll, Prince of Dyfed.

Early Welsh literature aside, the area is also associated with other legends. A beast with red eyes has long been reputed to plague a nearby stream. The strange being has been identified with Yr Hwch Ddu Gwta, usually a bobtailed black pig. The author Wirt Sykes, writing *British Goblins* in 1881, recalled the water beast: 'A black calf, which haunted a Pembrokeshire brook early in the present century, was believed to be the

Devil in familiar guise. It appeared at a certain spot near the village of Narberth – a village which has figured actively in mythic story since the earliest ages of which there is any record. One night two peasants caught the terrible calf and took it home, locking it up safely in a stable with some other cattle, but it had vanished when morning came.'

Sykes also referred to a strange local ceremony aimed at courting the Devil. The local conjurer was one John Jenkin, who brought the group together to solve a mystery concerning money stolen from the school and reputedly summoned several spirits. The consequences of this saw a young boy in attendance become emotionally scarred. Of the extraordinary occurrence, Sykes wrote: 'But when he did call, there came out of the wood a spirit dressed in white, and went about the circle. "Ah," said the schoolmaster, "we shall now hear something from this." And sure enough "this" told the conjuror (in a language the boy could not understand) where the money was, and all about it. Then it vanished in red fire; and that boy 'has never been well since, the effect of the great fright still cleaving to him."'

Pembroke

When Arnulf de Montgomery set to work in 1094 to establish a primitive motte and bailey castle on a natural outcrop close to the southwestern tip of Wales, it was unlikely he could have envisioned the great citadel that would eventually follow. On witnessing the castle for the first time in the modern day, either looming above the main street or from across the murky waters of the adjacent millpond, it is difficult to subdue the initial feelings of awe and astonishment. Coupled with the walled town, Pembroke is not only one of Wales's largest castles but also one of Britain's most impressive double acts. With so much to see, a visit to the castle is unlikely to disappoint.

Even before the Montgomerys, the area was not devoid of history. Indeed, Pembroke Castle sits on a site that has been occupied for nearly 12,000 years. The discovery of Roman coins also offers persuasive evidence that the site was of some importance at that time. The castle's sheltered position nestled between two arms of the river also leads to the likelihood that an Iron Age fort once existed there. The inner ward is about the correct size for a fort of that age and may have influenced the

Norman designs. It has also been speculated that a Dark Ages palace was located there. The fact that the Normans made for Pembroke following the death of Rhys ap Tewdwr in 1093 also suggests the area was already in use.

Shortly after Tewdwr died at the Battle of Brecon, Roger de Montgomery, 1st Earl of Shrewsbury established his base at Pembroke. A cousin of William the Conqueror, Roger had provided 60 vessels for the invasion of 1066 before commanding the right flank at Hastings. The site chosen was a limestone headland close to the coast. Further to any abandoned Roman settlement, its lofty position offered uninterrupted views of the Bristol Channel to the south and what is now Milford Haven to the north. On Roger's death, the responsibility fell to Arnulf. The fifth and youngest son of the imposing Norman warlord, Arnulf excelled himself in the Norman subjugation of Wales. William Rufus may have rewarded him with the earldom of Pembroke, though no documentation has survived.

No account exists of the timber palisade being breached – not that records from that period are necessarily complete. The sturdy ramparts and outer defences were still largely intact when Arnulf joined his elder brother, Robert de Bellême, in his unsuccessful rebellion against Henry I in 1102. In so doing, the pair forfeited their lands in Britain and Henry I held Pembroke for the remainder of his reign. In 1138, Henry's successor, Stephen of Blois, granted Gilbert de Clare the Earldom of Pembroke, which his son Richard 'Strongbow' maintained on paying homage to Henry II. The king's patience was tested when Strongbow assembled an invasion fleet of 1,200 men at Pembroke to sail to Ireland in 1171. The king stayed at Pembroke on his trip to and back from Ireland to dampen Strongbow's rebellion.

The timber ramparts appear to have still been intact when Richard the Lionheart granted the castle to a new beneficiary in 1189, by which time the male de Clare line had died out. That man was William Marshal, later 1st Earl of Pembroke. The minor son of a minor lord, Marshal's story was very much one of rags to riches. On relocating to the continent and the household of William de Tancarville, from where he became an expert competitor on the European tournament circuit and knighted, William later became a trusted attendant of Eleanor of Aquitaine and tutor to Henry the Young King. After finding favour in the king's circle, Marshal avoided the temptation to kill the Lionheart on unhorsing him in battle. The pair came to peace on Richard's accession, and Richard entrusted him the Pembroke estates along with the hand of the late Strongbow's daughter, Isabel de Clare. On the death of his elder brother, he also inherited the ancestral title: lord-marshal of England, which his family had held since Henry I's reign.

On finally taking possession of Pembroke, the Earl Marshal set up his new power base. On upgrading the early Norman defences, the castle that followed was among the most impressive in Wales. At the heart of the inner ward, the domed roof crowned a circular keep whose twenty-three-metre-high interior spanned four storeys. A horseshoe-shaped gateway also punctured the curtain wall above which an observation turret offered the watchman views of the coastline. Complementary to the defences, a great hall and apartment block provided luxurious fixtures for his entourage. The outline may also have been set out for the outer ward.

Marshal was instrumental in the castle's development but was never granted the opportunity to enjoy it fully. Entrusted by John as regent for his young son, Henry III, Marshal ended his life at the highest rung of English government – a king in all but name. On William's death in May 1219, the man dubbed 'the greatest knight' by the archbishop of Canterbury Stephen Langton was succeeded by his eldest son and namesake. Over the next twelve years, the younger William's life was dominated by the ongoing war with Llywelyn ap Iorwerth. On William's unexpected death in 1231, according to the chronicler Matthew Paris, poisoned by the justiciar Hubert de Burgh, the mantle passed to his next brother, Richard, the 3rd earl, who engaged in a rebellion against the king in 1233-34 before being killed in Ireland. The chronicler Roger of Wendover also recorded that Richard was forced to besiege Pembroke to gain entry. On his death, the regent's third son, Gilbert, successfully strengthened Pembroke's defences before his death in 1241 during a tournament accident.

Such was the pattern for the remainder of the great regent's line – at least on the male side. On the death of William's fifth son, Anselm, in 1245, the castle endured two years in limbo before Henry III granted it to his half-brother William de Valence from his mother Isabella's marriage to Hugh de Lusignan, Count of la Marche. To cement William's receiving of the Pembroke earldom, Henry oversaw William's wedding to Marshal's granddaughter, Joan de Munchensi.

For the next seventy years, Valence and his descendants thrived in the role. Beyond Marshal's inner curtain wall, the building of a stone twin-towered gatehouse and barbican connected to a clutch of circular towers positioned along the outer wall, construction of which continues to define the castle's appearance. Unique to Pembroke, a wooden platform known as a hoard was erected for extra defence. Due to its location close to the millpond, the wall was weakest on the waterside, while a trebuchet was also set up facing the sea. Work on the castle briefly ceased following Henry III's capture at Lewes in May 1264, at which point Valence fled abroad. He returned by ship to Pembroke a year later in time for the Battle of Evesham.

As Valence mellowed in later years, his love of Pembroke extended. The suite of domestic and chancery buildings also date from his time. At some point during the reigns of Edward I and Edward II, the town itself benefitted from the construction of mighty town walls, the east gate of which was based on the castle's barbican. Valence fought for Edward I's cause against Llywelyn ap Gruffudd and the subsequent rebellions 1277-95.

When William's son, Aymer, the second earl, died without issue in 1324, the castle passed to the Hastings family through his sister's grandson, Lawrence, who excelled himself in the Hundred Years' War. His son and namesake enjoyed worse luck, being murdered by his captors after suffering defeat at La Rochelle in 1375. His seventeen-year-old son, another John Hastings, succumbed to a similar fate to Gilbert Marshal in 1389, after which the castle once again became a royal possession.

It is unclear how much the Hastings clan saw of the castle. During this time, the inattention of its stewards saw it fall into disrepair. Among the greatest crimes, one custodian, William Beauchamp, stripped the roof of lead. After eleven years of short-term leases, including the unscrupulous Beauchamp, rebellion by Owain Glyndŵr placed it on the Welsh radar. Though a French invasion, in league with Owain, captured the constable Thomas Roche, a substantial financial offering from the leaseholder, Sir Francis Court, ensured the French left the walls unharmed.

For the next fifty years, Pembroke enjoyed a relatively calm existence. After the ineffectual tenures of Humphrey of Lancaster, Duke of Gloucester, and his successor, William de la Pole, Duke of Suffolk, Henry VI created the seventh line of Pembroke earls. The lucky beneficiary was Jasper Tudor, his half-brother through the widow of Henry V, Catherine of Valois, and the minor knight, Sir Owen Tudor. It was to Pembroke that Tudor brought his sister-in-law Margaret Beaufort in 1457 to give birth to her son, the future Henry VII. Jasper retreated to Pembroke in 1471 and was reputedly besieged by the Yorkists. Henry VII returned the castle to Jasper on his accession. Unlike many previous earls, Jasper spent much time there and carried out significant refurbishment, including a fine oriel window in the private chambers. On Jasper's death in 1495, it passed to the marchioness, Anne Boleyn.

For the next century and a half, the peace the Tudors had enjoyed continued for Pembroke's residents. This ended, however, with the emergence of Oliver Cromwell. Due to James I's sale to the Pryses of Gogerddan, Pembroke was an oddity in being the one castle in South Wales to support Parliament. As such, it was a siege by Royalist troops that Pembroke was forced to endure. Despite being forced to undergo a significant fight, a Roundhead dispatch at Milford Haven saw not only the castle's salvation but the taking of Tenby, Carew and Haverfordwest.

In 1648, conspiracy by the commander, Colonel Rowland Laugharne, local mayor John Poyer, Colonel Powell of Tenby and Sir Nicholas Kemeys of Chepstow forced Cromwell to besiege his lost castle. The catalyst for the defection, as was common at the time, was the soldiers going unpaid. Seven weeks of brutal onslaught followed until it was returned. On the garrison's surrender in July on the arrival of heavy guns, the quartet was charged with treason, and the castle's destruction was ordered. Though the order was never thoroughly followed, on being abandoned, it was left to decay. The trend continued until 1880, when brief efforts, notably by J.R. Cobb, were made at restoration. In 1928, the castle's fortunes truly improved under the ownership of Indian army vet and Liberal politician Major-General Sir Ivor Philipps. On his death, a trust was established that exists to this day.

A castle that has long served as the major power base in the south of Wales, it is no surprise that stories abound. Ominous shadows, the feeling of being nauseous and the clinking of armour or weapons have all been reported.

Ghosts aside, the castle is unique for more tangible reasons. A fifty-step stairway exists beneath it, leading down to what's locally known as Wogan Cavern. A natural creation formed from the limestone's erosion, the cave was later protected with a wall that contained a gateway and arrow slits. Of its exact purpose, conjecture has been rife. The cavern was almost certainly a shelter during the Ice Age. Available evidence suggests the garrison probably used it as a sally port. Roman coins have been found there, while discoveries dating back to the Stone Age have been made by archaeologists in similar locations.

Yet of all the stories associated with the castle, one quickly rises in prominence. How did all five sons of the great regent die so young and childless? An intriguing legend, brought down by the chroniclers, tells that the misfortune William's heirs endured resulted from a curse put on the family by the Irish bishop of Ferns, Albin O'Molloy. The story tells that the act was performed as a punishment for William's seizure of two of the bishop's manors between 1207 and 1213. After excommunicating Marshal, to which Marshal argued the confiscation had occurred during a time of conflict, their feud became bitter in April 1218 when Henry III's government banned the bishop from prosecuting. Two months later, Pope Honorius III's intercession saw requests of the archbishop of Dublin and Pandulf, the papal legate, to attempt a reconciliation failed.

On William's death in 1219, Albin's petition of Henry's government for the manors came to nothing. Equally unsuccessful in having Marshal's excommunication overturned, O'Molloy is alleged to have predicted the family's end. In April 1231, Marshal's eldest son – William Marshal II – was laid to rest alongside his father in the Templar church in London. When told of the younger William's death, the king is reported to have lamented his grandfather's role in the murder of Becket, 'Woe, woe is me! Is not the blood of the blessed martyr Thomas fully avenged yet?'

Similar, alas, would be true of William's brothers. After Richard was laid to rest in Ireland, the third brother Gilbert suffered his fate at a tournament in 1241 – ironically, an event Henry had explicitly forbidden due to fears he might lose a prime warrior. The fifth earl, Walter, followed, dying at Goodrich Castle in November 1245. Within a month, Anselm also died. How five seemingly fit men could all endure such misfortune still seems beyond coincidence. Whether foul play was involved in all five or not, their fate was sealed. The Marshal Curse, it would seem, had been fulfilled.

Picton

Like most castles in the south-west of Wales, Picton has experienced something of a chequered history. The Norman victory over Rhys ap Tewdwr, Prince of Deheubarth, at the Battle of Brecon in 1093 paved the way for the first onset of castle building in the area. In 1102, Henry I created the Marcher lordship of Pembroke after withstanding rebellion by his brother, Robert Curthose. Six years later, severe flooding in Flanders, the land of his mother, Matilda, prompted Henry to offer many of the affected a home under the jurisdiction of the new lordship.

Such trends would play a significant role in the development of the Norman feudal system. The king's charitable action had offered a home to those afflicted yet also boosted the garrison at Pembroke Castle with many loyal retainers. Around this time, Picton was built close to Haverfordwest – where many refugees were housed – at the behest of a Flemish knight. Little is known of the man other than he was a follower of a lord named Wizo; the nearby Wiston Castle originated from his endeavours. Picton was among the estates granted to his followers, located three miles to the south. Equally unknown is the castle's exact site. Though the second castle might well have been built atop the first, the presence of a mount a few hundred yards to the east brings that into question. Equally unclear is how the family died out.

While many questions concerning the first castle remain unanswered, the history of the second is better recorded. The present structure, whose imposing grey walls rise over well-maintained lawns, was created on Sir John de Wogan's instructions around 1280. Unlike the unnamed Fleming, Wogan served as Justiciar of Ireland 1295-1313 and Lord of Wiston. Through marriage, the family were also descended from the lords of Dyfed.

It was mainly due to Wogan's impressive work that Picton became the family's principal residence. The building was probably completed by 1308, around which time, Wiston was abandoned, leaving the sparse yet pleasant ruins that litter the local greenery. Picton's style has correctly been remarked as being separate from many of its Welsh contemporaries. In addition to the absence of a keep, there is no inner courtyard. For modern visitors, the castle has more in common with a stately home and would appear to illustrate an Irish influence, most likely developed during Wogan's time in the justiciary.

Early the following century, a series of cosmetic alterations preceded the arrival of French mercenaries conscripted to Owain Glyndŵr's rebellion in 1405. For a time, Owain took the castle, though it was later returned to the Wogans. When the male line died out, a marriage between Owain Dwnn and Katherine Wogan saw Picton enter a new line. Two generations later, the death of Sir Henry Dunn, who fathered no male heir, saw the castle's transfer to his 'golden daughter' Joan. In 1491, she married Sir Thomas ap Philipps, who hailed from Cilsant in Carmarthenshire.

As the family flourished, so too did the castle. Under the watchful eye of Sir John Philipps, Picton underwent significant redevelopment. Capping the family's era of prominence was the £1095 purchase of the baronetcy from James I in 1611, which went to help the king's war in Ireland. The family enjoyed the trimmings of grandeur for the next thirty-four years before the Parliamentarians briefly seized the castle.

Fortunately, the castle was never slighted or destroyed, and in 1697, Sir John Philipps, 4th Baronet, extended it. A member of the Society for Promoting Christian Knowledge, Sir John remains renowned for his influence on more than fifty new London churches. From 1749 onwards, Sir John's son, heir and namesake, the 6th baronet, oversaw further work, including the redevelopment of the Great Hall and chapel in the Georgian style. His son, Richard Philipps, 1st Baron Milford, sadly tore down the medieval tower and added a new block to the west. The castle remained in the same line until the baron died in 1823. In the absence of a living heir, Picton passed to his cousin, Richard Grant, who changed his surname and later assumed the baronetcy. In 1987, the castle was granted to the Picton Castle Trust, which now manages the site as a visitor attraction. With this, more than five centuries of Philipps affiliation finally came to an end.

Today, Picton is a real treasure trove of history, lovely gardens, revamped towers, and medieval vaults. Among its many curiosities, in the 1930s, the Philipps family purchased a fascinating artwork called 'The Picton Renoir'. Family lore tells how Pierre-Auguste Renoir gifted the painting to Claude Monet; however, it is unsigned, and authenticity remains highly contentious.

The castle has a reputation for paranormal activity. Close by, a hatted man in breeches reputedly haunts the road. Exactly who he is or why he appears remains a mystery. A strange sighting was recorded in 1904 involving a party that included one Brigadier-General Harris. Journeying to the castle, the party moved to one side to avoid impact, only to find that the figure had dissolved into thin air.

Roch

Constructed in the second half of the twelfth century on an isolated rocky projection two miles inland from the Pembrokeshire coast, Roch Castle owes its existence to one Lord Adam de Rupe, who played a vital role in setting up the English community in Pembrokeshire. The stone tower house that stands today was likely begun atop an earlier timber fortress, yet this cannot be proved. The site was a contemporary of Pill Priory near Milford Haven and was one of the first fortresses built on the unmarked Pembrokeshire border that separated the English and Welsh.

According to legend, it was not geographical prominence alone that persuaded Lord de Rupe to construct his castle. A short time after he arrived in South Wales, a soothsayer foretold that the powerful lord was destined to die from the venom of a viper's bite within twelve months. However, if he were to evade the sting for an entire year, he would break the curse and live to old age. Taking heed of this grim advice, de Rupe set to work on building a sanctuary in which he was unlikely to encounter such a threat. After choosing a rocky area off the coast, he set up home in the highest storey of his new tower.

For eleven months, the Norman lord is said to have led a reclusive life. Then, with the year almost over, fate struck the cruellest of blows. As the wintry weather became ever more unforgiving, de Rupe instructed his servant to gather firewood from the nearby woodland. Little did servant or lord realise that concealed within the firewood was an adder.

Although the legend is regarded as superstition, a lack of sources for de Rupe's life and death makes it difficult to confirm the reasons for the location. The name itself translates from the French for 'rock'. A similar word, *rupestre*, refers more specifically to plants among the rocks.

Regardless of the exact reasons for its creation, Roch Castle has long stood tall on this remote outcrop, enjoying the coast's natural protection. Around 1420 the de Rupe line ended, and the castle was acquired in the 1600s by the Walter family. The chief magnate, Lord Walter, was loyal to Charles I and installed a Royalist garrison at the beginning of the English Civil War. In 1644 it briefly fell to the Roundheads, only to be recaptured. It fell again a second time and was razed by the predominantly Puritan army.

Such was the castle's wretched condition, Walter never returned to Roch. His daughter, Lucy, born there in 1630, remained in London and famously became Charles II's mistress after meeting him in the Netherlands. Charles later acknowledged the paternity of Lucy's son, James Scott, 1st Duke of Monmouth, who led a doomed rebellion against his uncle, James II. On his return to England after being banished to the Netherlands, Monmouth appears to have claimed the castle before being captured after suffering defeat at Sedgemoor. Roch was left to decay until around 1900 when John Philipps, 1st Viscount St Davids, purchased it and embarked on a period of restoration. In more recent times, the castle was converted into a luxury hotel.

Though Monmouth would endure the bloodier death – being condemned to the block and requiring at least five strokes of the axe at the hands of the infamously incompetent Jack Ketch – it is his mother who haunts the castle. Neglected by Charles, Lucy died in poverty at the tender age of twenty-eight. Modern-day guests have seen her ghost, appearing as a misty figure floating through locked doors and vanishing inside the rooms. Whether she is responsible for the reports of guests being awoken in the dead of night by the sounds of footsteps echoing along the corridors remains unclear. The sounds of a person roaming the halls are familiar at Roch, echoing softly before ending with an eerie silence. A room is named in her honour.

Chapter 5

Brecknockshire and Carmarthenshire

Brecon

Situated in the town of the same name at the heart of the glorious Brecon Beacons, Brecon Castle owes its origins to the late eleventh century. On exploring the area after conquering Brycheiniog in the Easter of 1093, a campaign that culminated in the killing of Deheubarth royal Rhys ap Tewdwr, Bernard de Neufmarché identified a site in the shadow of Pen-y-Fan to establish a fortress. Few characters have aroused greater intrigue in this era than Bernard. Unquestionably one of Wales's original 'conquerors', claims that he was William's half-brother is almost certainly false. That he was a distant cousin is possible. Better evidence concerns his title as 'Lord of Brecon.'

Dubbed by some the Snowdon of South Wales, a combination of the Pen and the Beacons' natural defences provided the new fortress with a perfect protective shield. In addition to establishing a presence in the heart of old Brecknockshire – a vital route to Ireland – the Norman settlers were also blessed with hydropower for the local mills. As the following years would show, being at the confluence of the Usk and Honddu would be of prime importance to the future town.

Like many early Norman fortresses, the original castle was a motte and bailey. Yet, unlike most, it was of stone construction. Some previous commentators believe that the castle was the first in Wales to be erected in stone from the offset; however, Chepstow most likely beats it. The stone appears to have come from Norman pillaging of the Roman town of Caer Baddon.

In the following century, the castle passed to the de Braose clan. Initially firm supporters of King John, relations between William de Braose and the king deteriorated. On taking Brecon in 1207 after William rebelled, John forced him into exile. A worse fate awaited his wife, Maud, and eldest son, also William, who were confined to Corfe

Castle's dungeons (see also Painscastle). Following William's death in France in 1211, his family took up arms for the barons in the First Barons' War and retook the castle in 1215.

Conquered once already by the combined forces of Reginald de Braose and Llywelyn ap Iorwerth, the castle faced renewed onslaught in 1231 and the Marshal War of 1233-34. For the latter, a new curtain wall was created around the shell keep. The walls were already in need of a refurbishment when Henry III granted Brecon to new owners in 1241. The beneficiaries were the powerful de Bohun family, whose number were earls of Hereford. The garrison fell to the Welsh during the Second Barons' War of 1263-67. Further significant damage also occurred in 1273, when Llywelyn ap Gruffudd's power was rising, and Edward I remained uncrowned and on crusade.

The castle remained a de Bohun property until 1373, when the seventh earl, Humphrey, died without fathering a son. The castle passed to the Staffords, the chief magnate of whom, Edmund, 5th Earl of Stafford, owned Stafford Castle. Among Edmund's claims to fame was his marriage to Anne of Gloucester, granddaughter of Edward III through the king's youngest son, Thomas of Woodstock, 1st Duke of Gloucester. Anne's mother was Eleanor de Bohun, herself the eldest daughter of Humphrey de Bohun, thus his *de facto* heiress. A further battering of the walls was repelled, albeit at a high cost, in 1403 when Owain Glyndŵr brought his rebellion to Brecknockshire. In February 1478, the controversial Edward Stafford, 3rd Duke of Buckingham, was born at Brecon. Henry VIII executed him in 1521, and posthumous attainment saw his estates taken over by the Crown.

For the family, the legal process of reclaiming the lost lands would be long and arduous, but eventually, somewhat successful. As for Brecon Castle, the best years were behind it. Battered by the Welsh and English at various times, the castle endured one last assault in the English Civil War. A pounding on the command of the Roundhead Major-General Rowland Laugharne saw it fall in 1645. By the end of the Hanoverian era, the castle was a total wreck. Renovations by one Sir Charles Morgan began in 1809, after which the castle was converted into a hotel. Today, travellers can enjoy the alluring mix of a modern hotel in the shadow of the ruined walls for themselves.

An excellent location for modern-day guests, the castle retains its historic atmosphere with lots of rooms worthy of exploration. Over the years, tales of the paranormal have also been uttered, and strange photographs noted. Whether or not William the Conqueror's key supporter or the controversial Buckingham are behind the sightings is a matter for conjecture. The anomalies remain unexplained.

Builth

Little is known of the first castle at Builth Wells. Located at the junction of many important roads and designed to include a double bailey to complement the usual motte, the original fortress was frequently a site of conflict. By the mid-1200s, the castle had paid host to both Norman and Welsh garrisons, during which the future spa town of Builth Wells began to take shape. In 1260 the castle was the brutal victim of Llywelyn ap Gruffudd. Whether it was destroyed during the onslaught or already damaged is unclear. Available evidence suggests the site lay dormant for about seventeen years before Edward I rebuilt it in stone.

The second castle at Builth earned the distinction of being Edward I's first such attempt in Wales. While work remained ongoing between May 1277 and August 1282, the king's need for funds and, quite possibly, reallocation of the labour force to work on his mighty bastions in the north saw the project grind to a halt. Another possibility is that Edward deliberately changed strategy after learning that Llywelyn had been killed. Nevertheless, early progress still left the king with a total bill of £1,666.

As the following years would show, Edward's decision to halt construction proved somewhat costly. In 1294 the incomplete castle was besieged by Madog ap Llywelyn's forces and only narrowly survived. On 7 February 1301, Edward gifted it to his son and heir, the future Edward II. In 1310, three years following his accession, Edward II entrusted the castle to Roger Mortimer, his future usurper and possible cuckolder. After five years, however, Edward gifted the castle to his queen, Isabella, who rented it back to Mortimer for 340 marks a year. An agreement was also struck that the castle would revert to him on her death; however, Mortimer's execution in 1330 ensured he predeceased his royal partner.

In the aftermath of Mortimer's treason, the Crown seized his properties, including Builth. The castle passed to Gilbert, 1st Baron Talbot, who served

Edward as justiciar of South Wales. As such, he was also responsible for the legal reassignment of property. Edward III later granted Builth to the noblewoman Alice de Lacy and her second husband, Eubulus le Strange, in thanks for her assistance in snaring Mortimer into captivity at Nottingham in 1330. Alice's third husband, Hugh de Freyne, later became lord of Builth. Bizarrely, Hugh had earlier abducted Alice, then in her fifties, and reputedly raped her. As typical of rape in medieval England, the pair later married.

By 1359 both Alice and her husband had died without issue. Having no credible family claimants, Edward granted the castle to his son and heir, Edward, the Black Prince. The move proved beneficial for Mortimer's heirs. After the Mortimers agreed to contribute to the garrison in times of war, the Black Prince rented them the property on identical terms to those enjoyed by their forebear. When further rebellion broke out under the flag of Owain Glyndŵr, Builth was refortified. The garrison's command rested with Sir John Oldcastle – reputedly a loose inspiration for Shakespeare's Falstaff. Oldcastle served Henry IV and V loyally before falling out with the latter after involving himself with the new wave of Lollardy – a precursor to Protestantism. His heresy led to a minor insurrection against King Hal and his eventual martyrdom. He is a rare example of a man hanged and burned at the stake simultaneously.

Relations between the Crown and Mortimers remained constructive until the Wars of the Roses. Richard, 3rd Duke of York – a Mortimer heir – became the Yorkists' leader until his forces were massacred at the Battle of Wakefield on 30 December 1460. In 1493, eight years after Richard III's defeat at Bosworth, the area was again established as a Marcher lordship. The initial beneficiary was Prince Arthur, Henry VII's heir. On his death in April 1502, the heirdom passed to his younger brother, later Henry VIII. During his reign, the castle may have suffered fire damage. A more violent inferno – the great fire of Builth – struck the town in December 1690, destroying large parts of the masonry. Constant plundering then caused its gradual disappearance. Today, the only signs of earlier fortifications are the mound, embankment, and ditches.

A scenic yet often lonely area in daylight hours, the castle could be defined more by the rustic charms of the surrounding countryside than mighty walls. A happy place for dog walkers, hikers and nature lovers, the motte is an area of relaxation. Yet when night falls, and the iconic shape is cloaked in darkness, it is not difficult to imagine the ghosts of Llywelyn ap Gruffudd, Roger Mortimer or any of the other legendary figures from the castle's heyday strolling the former battlements. Should one take the nearby lane between the castle and modern spa town, the noise of the traffic vanishes as though one has entered a time slip. The views from the summit of the river and surrounding rooftops are charming. Even in the stonework's absence, one cannot escape the earthworks' simple magic. Nor should one forget the castle's important role in augmenting English authority over Powys. Local tradition has long maintained that large parts of the masonry were used to construct the nearby White House. Either way, in the surviving motte, history can at least show appreciation for the memory of Edward I's lost fortress.

Carmarthen

Dating from between 1104 and 1109, the origins of the first castle at Carmarthen are uncertain. The castle may have been created at the behest of Walter, Sheriff of Gloucester, to defend the town from the marauding Welsh. William Rufus had earlier ordered the erection of a more primitive fort, which does not appear in the records again after 1106.

A more elegant fortress than its predecessor, Walter's castle was also a simple motte and bailey. It was this castle that Gruffudd ap Rhys conquered in a well-planned night attack in 1116. In the following weeks, Gruffydd flattened the timber earthworks and plundered the local community. The subsequent rebuild was also primarily wood-based, thus rendering the fortress susceptible to renewed attack. Among the bloodiest was Owain Gwynedd's sacking in 1137. Further carnage followed in 1143, leading to a year of Welsh rule. After being briefly recaptured the following year, the castle was taken by Gruffydd's son, Cadell, in 1146 and retained for the next half-century.

In 1195, the late Cadell's famous half-brother, Rhys ap Gruffudd, destroyed the wooden defences. On taking the castle after a five-day siege in 1215, Llywelyn ap Iorwerth invested heavily before losing it to William Marshal, 2nd Earl of Pembroke. After this, sieges from Richard, 3rd Earl of Pembroke in 1233 and Owain Glyndŵr in 1405 failed to breach the newer stonework. The fortress would serve as the final destination of Edmund Tudor: a son of Owain Tudor and Catherine de Valois. A staunch Lancastrian throughout the Wars of the Roses, Edmund took the castle on Henry VI's behalf. As momentum swayed to the Yorkists, a force led by William Herbert took Carmarthen in August 1456. In early November, the imprisoned Edmund died. The following January, his thirteen-year-old wife gave birth to a boy. Her name was Margaret Beaufort. Their son, Henry Tudor.

Like many a British castle, Carmarthen met its destiny at the hands of Oliver Cromwell. On capturing the castle, the Roundheads largely dismantled the defences. From the restoration of the monarchy onwards, the castle's sole purpose was to keep local felons in its eight cells, and in 1789 it was officially made the new county gaol. In the early 1860s, a police station was also added between the castle's outer and inner walls. It was there that prisoners were held in transit between the prison and the courthouse. The process continued until three years before the Second World War when the prison was relocated beyond the walls and the newer cells destroyed. Eleven years later, in 1947, the police station was closed and set up in new premises. On purchasing the gaol in 1925, the local council built a new County Hall on the site in 1938.

For the typical castle lover, the view of Carmarthen Castle from across the chilly waters of the Towy is far from a fairy-tale image. Indeed, dwarfed by the twentieth-century colossal extremity, it is easy to miss the walls and mistake the 'chateau' hall for a Victorian warehouse. Nevertheless, the outer walls' survival has ensured a substantial part of the original castle remains. Within them, Castle House, which once contained the police station, houses a museum and information centre.

In many ways, Carmarthen has always been a castle of contrasts. A relic of medieval violence juxtaposed with Dickensian-style squalor, it is difficult to avoid comparisons with the likes of Rochester Castle, if not the Tower of London, albeit on a far smaller scale. For the castle purist, a moment outside the original gatehouse will undoubtedly offer a delight that the interior can never live up to. Yet neither, in this author's opinion, should be overlooked. Indeed, to stare deeply into the heart of the imposing twin-towered gatehouse is to catch a glimpse of the castle in its heyday. As well as offer an insight into the terror experienced by those forced to suffer incarceration within its walls.

Carreg Cennen

Towering high over the village of Trapp in the heart of the Brecon Beacons National Park, magnificent Carreg Cennen Castle is another rare breed of fortress whose story encompasses everything from the ancient to the modern. Set upon a massive limestone outcrop, from which the reward for the modern-day visitor is among the most spectacular views in all of Wales, the six-towered, strong-walled structure is one of the most distinctive in Britain.

Many questions remain over its formation. The discovery of ancient bones at the site confirms some form of prehistoric settlement, while the presence of an Iron Age hillfort can also not be discounted. Coins from the Roman era also indicate at least a temporary dwelling before the Norman invasion. On more solid ground is the history of the stone castle. The man behind the initial process was almost certainly the Lord Rhys (Rhys ap Gruffudd), who ruled the kingdom of Deheubarth from 1155 until 1197. After his death, the castle remained in the family's possession for the next fifty years.

In 1248 came the castle's first significant turning point. Inspired by enmity against her son, Rhys Fychan ap Rhys Mechyll, Matilda de Braose made the controversial decision to enter a pact with England's rulers over Carreg Cennen's transfer. On learning of his mother's plan, Rhys swiftly captured the castle. Over the next thirty years, possession of the fortress would be subject to an ongoing tussle between Rhys and his uncle, Maredudd ap Rhys Gryg, whose feud extended to the command of Deheubarth itself.

By 1277 the family had a far more formidable foe with which to deal. On his march deep into enemy territory, Edward I conquered the castle and installed an English garrison. The Welsh briefly recaptured the castle in 1282; however, Edward reestablished control the following year, at which time he granted Carreg Cennen to one of his barons, John Giffard. It was likely under Giffard's command that Llywelyn ap Gruffudd had been killed at Cilmeri a year earlier.

For the next century, the castle appears to have enjoyed a more peaceful existence. This changed in July 1403 when a force of 800 under the flag of Owain Glyndŵr laid siege to the castle. Despite a persistent campaign led primarily by Sir John Scudamore, a future son-in-law of Glyndŵr, several months of bombardment failed to breach the walls. By 1409 Henry IV's garrison had repaired the damage before the castle fell into Lancastrian hands during the Rose Wars.

The Lancastrians' failure to hold the fortress ensured its decline. A Yorkist force of 500 – 300 fewer troops than Owain sixty years earlier – took the castle in 1461 and subsequently destroyed it. It was later owned by the Vaughan and Cawdor families whose work on the castle was limited. Redevelopment began in the nineteenth century under the direction of the 2nd Earl Cawdor. Thanks to the family lawyers' incredible stupidity, the Morris family of next-door Castell Farm acquired the castle after the deeds were mistakenly included as part of the farm. Though still privately owned, Cadw maintains the site.

For the modern castle hunter, Carreg Cennen is easily among the most striking fortresses one will see in the British Isles. It was most likely under Giffard's watchful eye that the castle was remodelled. When viewed from a distance, the building bears an unmistakable resemblance to the mighty citadels of the Languedoc and the Holy Land. The natural protection of the limestone cliffs, especially the sheer-sided gorge over the River Cennen, only intensifies this feel. It seems probable that a crusader was involved in the architecture. Regardless of the reasons, it is no surprise that the castle became beloved by sightseers. Among the most famous was the artist J.M.W. Turner, who sketched it in 1798.

Unlike many castles of the medieval age, its towers and walls vary in size and style: a product of nature and siege damage as much as the original architect's intention. Six imposing towers and interconnected walls are arranged around a square court before which one must pass the great twin-towered gatehouse on the north side. The alluring 'King's Chamber' complements the usual facilities; within it, an ornate stone fireplace and traceried windows remain genuine treasures. A series of ditches were cut into the rocks to the west of the cliffs for additional protection. The outer ward, barbican, and gatehouse all surround the inner ward, around which deep pits were also dug. Among the natural defences, the cliff ledges have long been resting places for birds and rare plants. The surrounding wooded slopes are also natural habitats and include species such as ravens, red kites, buzzards, and the Spotted Woodpecker.

Beneath the walls, Carreg Cennen conceals one particularly unique feature. A set of stone steps in the south-east corner lead down to a vaulted passage and a natural cave that encroaches deep into the hillside. From a distance, the windows of the passage are visible. Under normal circumstances, one can also enjoy the views from the interior. Within the cave rises a freshwater spring, which, legend told, could grant wishes. Whether the Lancastrian garrison ever thought to wish for protection against the Yorkists is unclear. In times of drought, the spring would have proved a valuable complement to the cistern that collected rainwater.

For the modern visitor, Carreg Cennen is a genuine delight. A strenuous journey up from Castell Farm is not unlike completing a pilgrimage; however, the reward is evident from the moment of arrival. Though stories surrounding the spring are the most alluring of its legends, a warm atmosphere possesses the lonely citadel. That the ghosts of the castle's violent past still inhabit the ruins, reports are inconsistent. Even so, it is difficult to shake the feeling that the past remains very much alive. As night falls and shafts of moonlight filter down on the hillside, a mystical glow pervades, as though one is caught in a permanent time slip. And when the visitor departs, one can never be sure if they have experienced the real thing or merely a door to the past briefly reopened, only to vanish again as inexplicably as it arrived.

Dinefwr

At its prime, the commanders of south-west Wales regarded no fortress in Wales more highly than Dinefwr. Perched on a rocky ridge 100 feet above the north bank of the Towy, the natural defences were among the most extensive of any Welsh castle. Coupled with commanding views across the surrounding valley, it is no surprise the rulers of Deheubarth felt it the ideal place to conduct affairs. Even today, everything about the castle presents the allegory of being seated on a throne.

One should not doubt Dinefwr's vast importance in the context of Welsh history. Over the years, Roman artefacts have been uncovered around Dinefwr Park. Surveys have also revealed the former presence of two forts. It was most likely at nearby Llandeilo where St David's sixth-century contemporary, St Teilo, founded his famous monastery. Legend tells that the castle was built during the ninth century by the Welsh king Rhodri Mawr – Rhodri the Great. While no evidence has yet been found to confirm this, it does not rule out the possibility that a timber structure once existed.

On firmer ground is evidence for its condition the following century. Before 950, the castle was the principal court of Mawr's grandson, Hywel Dda, who established himself as the first king of Deheubarth, ruled much of Wales and created its first legal system. That the area merited inclusion in the Welsh law codes – known in Welsh as the *Cyfraith Hywel*, which held sway until the Statute of Rhuddlan in 1284 – has rightly convinced many historians that the castle should be regarded among the most important possessions of Welsh royalty. Hywel's laws were among the most liberal in Europe and included the rights of women.

By 1163 the castle was the main HQ of Rhys ap Gruffudd, the Lord of Deheubarth. Rhys's reign brought a time of rare stability, both locally and throughout the nation, in which Wales enjoyed something of a cultural renaissance. At least two religious houses – Talley Abbey and Llanllyr – were created at Rhys's behest. He also supported the Cistercian order at Strata Florida.

Rhys recognised the importance of the castle in withstanding the Marcher lords. It was during his reign that Dinefwr was rebuilt. The same was true of nearby Carreg Cennen and Dryslwyn – the latter of which can just be seen from Dinefwr. A story recorded by Gerald of Wales tells that on planning an assault on the castle, Henry II sent ahead one of his followers, who sought out a local cleric's assistance. On failing to live up to his promise to lead the Englishman by the most straightforward route, the holy man rounded off his detour by grazing the local grass, explaining that this was the local custom. Interestingly, the king never mounted his intended attack.

Rhys's death proved a watershed moment in Welsh history, not least concerning his sons' succession. His fourth son was Rhys Gryg, who oversaw new work at Dinefwr. Progress would be reversed, however, when Gryg had the castle dismantled to evade the wrath of Llywelyn ap Iorwerth. On taking the site, Llywelyn was impressed with the natural vantage point and restored the castle. Its distinctive circular keep most likely dates from the 1230s.

In 1255, fifteen years after Llywelyn's death, his grandson, Llywelyn ap Gruffudd, entrusted ownership to Rhys Fychan ap Rhys Mechyll: Rhys Gryg's grandson, and hence a prince of the house of Dinefwr. He, in turn, passed it on briefly to his uncle Maredudd ap Rhys – another son of Rhys Gryg – before it was returned to Fychan. The decision may well have concerned Maredudd's loyalty.

Any suspicions Llywelyn had were confirmed when Maredudd entered an alliance with Prince Edward, later Edward I. During Rhys Fychan ap Rhys Mechyll's tenure, Llywelyn inflicted a devastating defeat on the English at Coed Llanthan – the Battle of Cadfan – in 1257. On Fychan's death in 1271, the castle was inherited by his son, Rhys Wedrod. With Edward's help, Maredudd's son, Rhys ap Maredudd, attempted to conquer Dinefwr under the impression that the fortress would be his as a mark of gratitude. However, when Wedrod placed the castle in Edward's hands around 1276, the move benefitted only Edward. Rhys retook the castle in 1287, only to be countered almost immediately by a substantial English force. In 1291 Edward captured Rhys and executed him in York the following year on charges of treason.

From the 1290s onwards, the castle largely remained an English possession. Throughout the final decade of the thirteenth century, an English settlement developed in Dinefwr Park near modern Newton House. This 'New Towne' offset the Welsh settlement around the castle and was filled with English families and later granted privileges by Edward, the Black Prince. After suffering damage during the Llywelyn Bren rebellion of 1316, the castle was repaired and granted by Edward II to the controversial Hugh le Despenser the Elder. Repairs were undertaken on Hugh's arrival, then again in 1326. Despite this, according to a document dated 1343, the great tower was already on the verge of collapse. Further repairs must have been made in the following years as the castle was clearly in good enough condition to resist Owain Glyndŵr's rebellion of the early 1400s.

By the end of the century, Dinefwr had become severely dated. So ambitious was the rebuilding project that the castle underwent a complete renaissance. Gruffydd ap Nicholas became deputy justiciar on being granted the lordship of Dinefwr in 1439. The former gained him control of the South Welsh government. Henry VI is said to have addressed him as a 'right trusty and well-beloved friend'. He also acted as a patron and judge at the Carmarthen Eisteddfod, from which came the modern rules of poetic metre.

The family's importance to Welsh history should also not be understated. According to legend, the family descended from the early-medieval king Urien Rheged, who ruled Northern Britain. The same was true of the Ravens of Urien, which protected the king's son, Owain. The coat of arms of Gruffydd's descendants – the Dynevor family – features ravens. Marriage between Thomas, the son of Gruffydd ap Nicholas, and Elizabeth, a daughter of Sir John Gruffydd – himself a descendant of Lord Rhys – brought both lines together. Gruffydd ap Nicholas's grandson, Sir Rhys ap Thomas, and Henry Tudor were both descended from Lord Rhys. When Tudor landed at Milford Haven, Rhys raised troops in support. Tudor knighted him after Bosworth and appointed him Chamberlain of the Principality of South Wales, which included possession of Dinefwr. He was later granted the justiciarship of Wales – a similar role held by his ancestor.

Like many of his forebears, Rhys ap Thomas oversaw extensive rebuilding of Dinefwr. For three generations, the fortress remained in the family, ending with his grandson, Rhys ap Gruffudd, being executed for treason in 1531. Though the Crown requisitioned the castle, the family later reclaimed it. It was abandoned in the 1660s for nearby Newton House, after which the upper storeys of the keep were revamped as a summerhouse. The keep was gutted by fire in the eighteenth century and fell into ruin.

An important citadel of past rulers, Dinefwr has all the hallmarks of a mighty fortress. Exploring the area – care of which is a joint effort of the Wildlife Trust, Cadw and the National Trust – the round keep reveals a trapdoor that covers a dark basement, with slabs laid over bedrock. A narrow spiral staircase also leads to one of the towers, which conjures up images of mystery. Another rarity is the nearby White Park Cattle. The modern herd that one can find grazing in the nearby fields are believed to be descendants of earlier stock kept at the site. Cattle was a measure of wealth in the time of the Welsh princes and would have kept the area well stocked with meat.

Even if the ghosts of the princes of Deheubarth or any of the castle's other famed residents no longer wander the ruins, there is more than enough magic in Dinefwr for the castle enthusiast to enjoy. The illusion of timelessness is powerful here. Sandwiched between a deer park, river and lush valley, one can't help feel that medieval Dinefwr was itself a tiny bit of Eden, in which humanity was never meant to remain.

Hay

There is an old legend that the Devil himself was behind the medieval walls of Hay Castle. On sitting down to deal with the Prince of Darkness, the Norman lord of the time cemented the unholy agreement, which culminated in the castle shooting up in the space of one night.

The truth behind the castle's early years is indeed subject to a degree of mystery. The reasons, of course, has more to do with the lack of contemporary documents – somewhat ironic considering Hay's modern reputation as a literary town. In 1091, the Norman warlord Bernard de Neufmarché completed a violent conquest of Brecknock – modern-day Brecon – and granted the first manor of Hay to his follower, Philip Walwyn. That the native Welsh, dedicated Christians, considered the coming of the Norman overlords as something of a judgment of biblical proportions seems particularly fitting.

Construction of the original wooden structure most likely began on Walwyn's watch. This basic castle appears to have been established either late in the reign of William Rufus or early in that of his younger brother and successor, and possible murderer, Henry I. The design was probably oval and lay close to the church of St Mary's outside the early settlement. To this day, a motte known as 'Hay Tump' stands at the spot.

As the twelfth century progressed, the lordship of Hay Anglicana became increasingly wealthy. After Walwyn, the lordship passed to Miles Fitzwalter of Gloucester, 1st Earl of Hereford, through marriage. It was most likely on Miles's watch that stone walls were erected around the town. A second fortification was also constructed within the walls, some 200m from Hay Tump. Complementing an earth ringwork – a bailey castle with no motte – a stone gatehouse protected the interior. By no later than the turn of the thirteenth century, the manor became the property of William de Braose. Under William, the castle benefitted from a period of rebuilding and expansion: a curtain wall, buttressed by timbers, was put up around the gate-tower, which was converted into a keep. The Chapel of St John in the town also found use among the garrison.

Around 1207 William's tenure was cut short. As previously recalled, his feud with John ultimately culminated in William fleeing to Ireland and France, while his wife and son died sad and lonely deaths in Corfe Castle's dungeons. William's improvements were nevertheless critical in the context of the chaos that followed. During the First Barons' War, John struggled to withstand the Welsh, and the castle fell. Particularly important was an alliance between William and Maud's son, Reginald de Braose, and his father-in-law, Llywelyn ap Iorwerth – Reginald was married to Gwladus Ddu. In 1231, when the area was back in English hands, Llywelyn sacked the town and briefly took the castle. Two years later, Henry III rebuilt the fortress for his next military engagement with Llywelyn, who entered an alliance with rebel baron Richard Marshal, 3rd Earl of Pembroke for the Marshal War of 1233-34.

History repeated itself in the Second Barons' War. In 1263 Prince Edward – the future Edward I – captured the castle. Yet merely a year passed before an alliance between Simon de Montfort, 6th Earl of Leicester, and Llywelyn ap Gruffudd saw it razed. After Edward became king and Wales fell under English rule, the rebuilt Hay Castle enjoyed a century of relative peace. This ended in 1401 when the forces of Owain Glyndŵr inflicted considerable damage attempting to storm the walls. In 1460 more of the same followed in the Wars of the Roses; however, in neither case did the castle fall. When the Tudor antiquarian John Leland visited Hay around 1540, he perceived the castle as 'bene right stately', though the town itself was 'wonderfully decaied'.

In the century that followed, Hay's prospects improved. Work on the two-storey Jacobean mansion that stands within the ruined walls was undertaken in the 1600s. Formal gardens were added around the keep and were still in place when the house passed to the Wellingtons around 1700. Between 1700 and 1812, the keep's basement became an annexe of the town gaol. Three years earlier, the industrialist Sir Joseph Bailey leased the property before buying it outright in 1844. Further to regular maintenance of the terraced gardens and the planting of several trees, the addition of a walled kitchen garden, dubbed Castle Gardens, was undoubtedly a jewel in the crown. For a time from 1825, when Bailey was still leasing the property, the castle served as a vicarage.

A series of owners followed up to 1910 when the architect W.D. Caroe embarked on a period of restoration. Such efforts suffered a setback in 1939 when a fire gutted the east section. In 1961, the bookseller Richard Booth acquired the castle and opened a bookstore. It was sold again in 2011, after which time another fire had devoured the western section, and most of the walled garden had been sold. Thanks to the purchase by Hay Castle Trust, whose intention was to convert it into an arts and education centre, the castle's future is potentially bright.

Today, Hay-on-Wye is very much renowned as a literary town. There is no doubt that Hay Castle played an indispensable role in the transition. It is also ironic that a castle that allegedly began life at the Devil's will has now found a purpose as a site where tales of magic are stored. In such ways, it is only fitting that at least one ghost story complements those found on the bookshelves. Famed in the annals of British history for her spat with King John, the spirit of Maud de Braose is said to return to her former home.

Maud is another candidate who, according to legend, made a deal with the Devil. Though the suggestion that she lost her soul in the building of Hay can perhaps be interpreted as a compliment to her unwavering spirit, the legend is also a sad one. Fortunately, in more recent times, her courage in the face of adversity is becoming rightly celebrated as that of a truly 'formidable woman'.

Kidwelly

Built on a steep ridge overlooking the River Gwendraeth near its tidal limit, Kidwelly is one of the truly great Norman castles of South Wales. Established as a timber motte and bailey by Roger le Poer, Bishop of Salisbury, early in the reign of Henry I, Kidwelly was one of several strongholds designed to enforce Norman dominance. Today, the castle is well integrated within the modern town.

Visitors to the town will instantly see that the solid outer curtain wall bears the scars of past sieges – some of which proved successful. The castle's ownership changed hands regularly until Edward I's subjugation of the country in 1282. Conquest by Rhys ap Gruffudd in 1190 saw the timber castle upgraded. Twenty-five years later, its retaking by Rhys's son, Rhys Gryg, caused fresh headaches for King John. In 1220, a frustrated Gryg was forced to release the castle on Llywelyn ap Iorwerth's orders to Hawise de Londres, which lasted three years before William Marshal II, in alliance with two of Rhys's grandsons, liberated it. Llywelyn retook it in 1231 before it was eventually returned to Hawise.

Following Hawise's marriage to Patrick de Chaworth, the castle became the property of the de Chaworth family. Much of the timber castle was completed in 1257 and thwarted the Welsh after they razed the town. Six years later, Llywelyn ap Gruffudd captured the castle for the Welsh, after which the Chaworths returned. On returning from crusade with Edward I around 1274, Pain de Chaworth began to rebuild the castle in stone. On the death of Pain and his brother Patrick in 1279 and 1283, Patrick's infant daughter, Matilda, inherited the castle. In 1297, Edward I granted the fifteen-year-old Matilda in marriage to his nephew, Henry, Earl of Lancaster, son of Edmund 'Crouchback', Earl of Lancaster. When their son, Henry of Grosmont, died without issue, Kidwelly passed to Grosmont's successor as Duke of Lancaster, John of Gaunt.

While the oldest parts of the castle date back to Bishop Roger in the early twelfth century, the latest dates from the second reign of Edward IV, c.1476. Back in 1403, it was the subject of a further siege by Owain Glyndŵr in alliance with soldiers from France and the duchy of Brittany. Despite taking the town and burning a gatehouse, the castle stood firm. Three weeks later, a Norman relief force put paid to any lingering hopes of Welsh success. Further attempts by Owain two years later would also prove fruitless. On Henry VII's victory at Bosworth, Sir Rhys ap Thomas took over ownership. In keeping with the other family properties, it reverted to the Crown on the execution of Rhys's grandson, Rhys ap Gruffydd, for treason in 1531.

As fate had it, the siege of 1403 was the last major onslaught the old walls faced. Being in the south of Carmarthenshire, its position was of little strategic importance in the civil war. Thanks to this, Kidwelly survived as one of the best-preserved castles of the age. Strengthened by the construction of a new gatehouse, the four round towers that defend the inner baileys still stand tall, their appearance reminiscent of mythical lookout guards in constant vigil. From across the river, its square interior aided by the semi-circular outer wall that clutches the riverside hill like a grappling hook looks particularly imperious. It is no surprise that many regard Kidwelly as the best example of a defensive castle in Wales.

Though the present ruins would look at home on a movie set, behind the walls, the memory of its turbulent past refuses to sleep. A ghostly medieval sentry has been seen patrolling the battlements. Two ladies are also said to haunt the interior. One of them may be the famous lady of the castle Hawise de Londres. The area is also chock full of legends. According to a local nursery rhyme, Hen Fenwy Fach was a kindly lady who gave sweets to children. Local legend also tells that a black cat was found alive in the burning rubble of the town and later became the town's symbol. Other versions suggest that the cat was the first sign of life after the plague or that one was seen on the church roof after a great flood in 1607. The possibility that cats were seen in all circumstances seems likely. As does the possibility that the cat is a corruption of the town's archaic name, Catweli.

Following many assaults on the castle in the early twelfth century, the Normans were defeated by Gruffudd ap Rhys, Prince of Deheubarth, in 1136. After successfully claiming the fortress, the prince took up residence within the walls with his sons and his wife, Gwenllian.

Henry II, Richard I, John and Henry III.
(Matthew Paris, *Historia Anglorum*)

Right: Bodelwyddan.

Below: The West Prospect of Chirk 1733–47. (William Henry Toms, National Library of Wales)

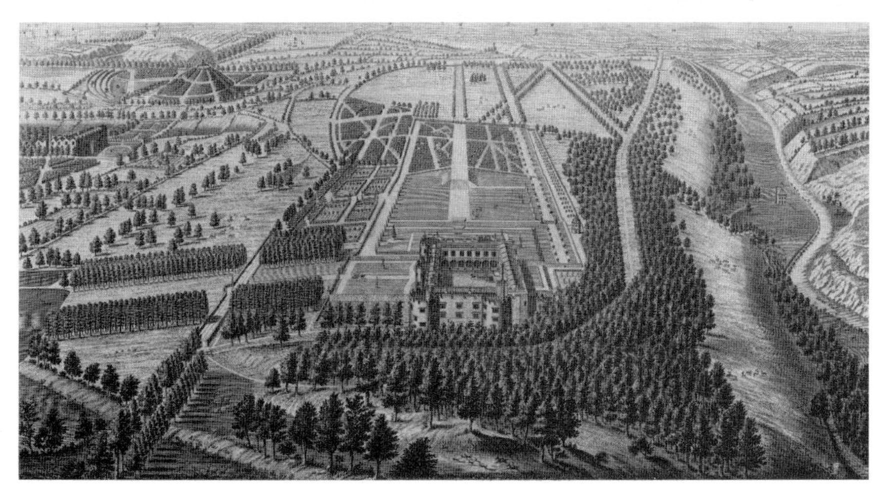

Above: Denbigh.

Below left: Llywelyn ap Iorwerth and his sons, Gruffydd and Dafydd. (Matthew Paris, *Chronica Majora*)

Below right: The Death of Llywelyn ap Gruffudd. (*Flame Bearers of Welsh History*, 1905, National Library of Wales)

Right: Gwrych.
(Circa 1920s)

Below: Rhuddlan.
(Mike Davis)

Bottom:
Beaumaris.
(Mike Davis)

Caernarfon. (Mike Davis)

Conwy. (Mike Davis)

Conwy Town Walls.

Right: King John, Henry III and Edward I as they appear before the west front of Lichfield Cathedral. (Mike Davis)

Below: Criccieth. (Mike Davis)

The discovery of two dragons below Dinas Emrys, as prophesised by a young Merlin. (Lambeth Palace Library MS 6 folio 43v illustrating an episode in *Historia Regum Britanniae,* circa 1136)

Left: Harlech. (Mike Davis)

Below: Carew.

Owain Glyndŵr. (From his great seal, circa 1800s)

Above left: Edward I. (John Cassell's, *Illustrated History of England*, 1864)

Above right: Edward I and Eleanor of Castile. (*The Rochester Chronicle*, British Library)

Manorbier.

Above: Pembroke.

Left: Carreg Cennen.

Below: Kidwelly.

Laugharne.

Right: Caerphilly. (Mike Davis)

Below: Cardiff from the north-west. (From an engraving by Samuel and Nathaniel Buck, circa 1700s)

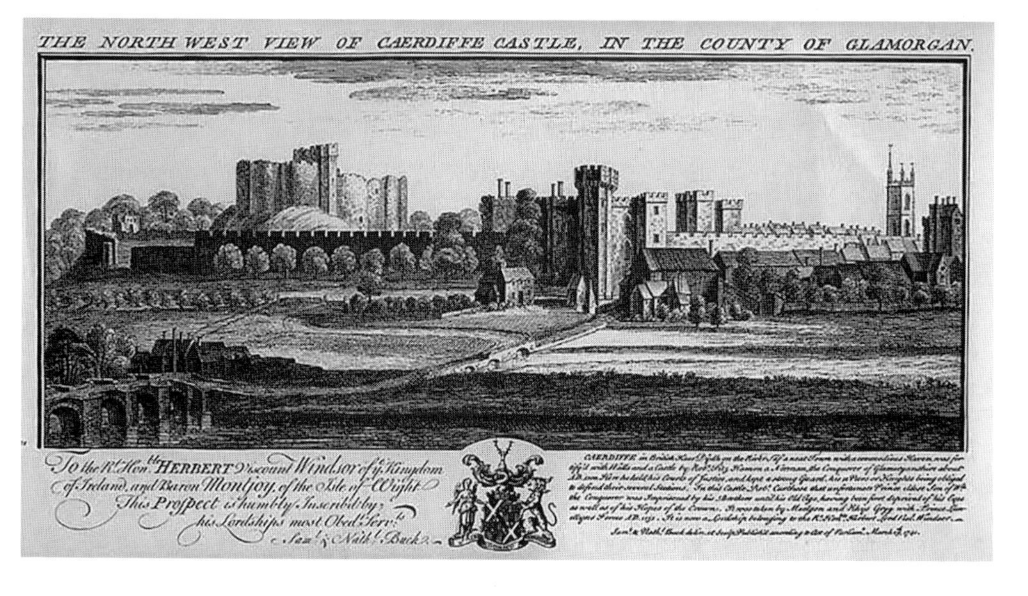

Castell Coch. (Mike Davis)

Above: Oystermouth.

Left: Oxwich.

Dinas Brân.

St Donat's. (From the watch tower, Charles Latham, circa 1900)

Caerleon Amphitheatre.

Chepstow. (Mike Davis)

Grosmont.

Above left: Whitecastle. (Mike Davis)

Above right: Monmouth.

Montgomery.

Raglan. (Mike Davis)

Goodrich.

Whittington. (Mike Davis)

Hopton.

Stokesay. (Mike Davis)

Above left: Dolwyddelan. (Mike Davis)

Above right: Usk.

Predictably, Norman retribution was swift. Later that year, while Gruffudd was seeking an alliance with his wife's father, Gruffudd ap Cynan, in Gwynedd, the ferocious Maurice de Londres, in league with other Norman commanders, conducted a series of raids throughout Deheubarth. When they attacked Kidwelly in Gruffudd's absence, Gwenllian and her sons faced the arduous task of raising an army to withstand the Norman assault. Despite her best efforts, the courageous lady was defeated. Among the slain was her son, Morgan. Another son, Maelgwyn, was also executed after being taken prisoner. The most significant loss was Gwenllian herself, beheaded at de Londres's behest.

Gwenllian may have been defeated, but word of her bravery soon spread. Over the coming years, the princess's determination inspired many in South Wales to stand tall against the invaders from the east. In Gwent, revolt by Iorwerth ab Owain, grandson of Caradog ap Gruffydd, led to the death of the Marcher lord Richard fitz Gilbert de Clare, whose control stretched across Ceredigion. On hearing of Gwenllian's death, her brothers, Owain Gwynedd and Cadwaladr ap Gruffudd, laid waste to Ceredigion, taking Llanfihangel, Aberystwyth and Llanbadarn Fawr. Spared death in the battle was the princess's youngest son, Rhys, who would grow up to be remembered as Lord Rhys ap Gruffudd. In 1190, Rhys would return and capture Kidwelly.

More than eight centuries have passed since Gwenllian was unjustly put to the sword. Yet even today, her story has not been forgotten. Comparisons with Boadicea and other female warlords have, of course, followed. Indeed, the princess remains the only confirmed Welshwoman of the Middle Ages to have led an army into battle. In the centuries since 'Revenge for Gwenllian' became something of a national battle cry. Before her death, a reputation for despoiling English, Norman and Flemish merchants of their property and redistributing it among the people of Deheubarth earned Owain and Cadwaladr something of a Robin Hood legacy.

Perhaps appropriate for the magnitude of her legend, local lore has long claimed that her spirit continues to haunt the location of her last stand. During the eighteenth and nineteenth centuries, Gwenllian's ghost was seen on many occasions, wandering the field where she eventually met her end. The reputed battlefield to the north of the town was named Maes Gwenllian – the field of Gwenllian. Local legend tells that the spring in that same field runs from the point where she died. A tribute, one might argue, to her courage, or else the area's eternal weeping for its lost daughter. A memorial to Gwenllian stands outside the castle.

Joining Gwenllian in her haunting of Kidwelly is thought to be Lady Nest, the daughter of Sir Elidir Ddu, the castle's lord during the reign of Richard I. Although of Welsh birth, unlike Gwenllian, Nest welcomed one Norman named Sir Walter Mansel. Soon, the setting became the scene of a complicated love triangle. Also vying for Mansel's affection was Nest's cousin, Gwladys, Elidir's niece. To complicate matters further, Nest's brother, Gruffydd, had been spurned in his fondness for Gwladys.

When Sir Elidir departed Kidwelly on crusade, he placed Gruffydd in charge of the castle. Chief among his duties was the wellbeing of those in residence, including Nest. Ever jealous of Nest's increasing involvement with Mansel, Gwladys sought to end their affair by manipulating Gruffydd's loyalty to his father. After learning that his sister and Mansel had been meeting in secret, Gruffydd employed a mercenary, Merig Maneg, to murder the Norman. Maneg waited for his victim in a bed of reeds near a bridge where Gwladys claimed the lovers met. As night fell, Nest finally came and was followed a short time later by Mansel. Overjoyed at being together again, the sudden sight of an arrow piercing her lover's side sent her into a torrent of anguish. As the Norman battled in vain to stem the bleeding, Maneg emerged for the first time and threw him into the River Gwendraeth. Heartbroken, Nest made a fateful decision to follow her lover into the river.

Many centuries have passed since the dramatic event that cost both lovers their lives, but it is said that Nest's spirit refuses to rest. Local legend tells that, prohibited from passing the gates of heaven due to her suicide, she is condemned to walk the earth until a member of her family marries a Mansel. Over the years, she has been seen on many occasions, usually on the modern bridge where the fateful event happened. In her honour, the bridge has become known as Pont-yr-Yspryd-Gwyn, the 'bridge of the white spirit'.

Laugharne

The year 1172 was an important one for relations between England and Wales. Distracted by concerns that the Earl of Pembroke, Richard de Clare's recent marriage to the daughter of Diarmait, King of Leinster, could establish a separate Norman dynasty in Ireland, Henry II planned to cross the Irish Sea and deal with the problems.

Aware that a visit to Ireland involved passing through South Wales – an area caught up in the Welsh uprisings of 1164-70 – Henry planned to first make peace with Rhys ap Gruffudd. The pair held extensive talks in October 1171 at Pembroke Castle on the king's way to the coast. They met again in 1172, at which point Rhys was appointed 'Justice on his behalf in all Deheubarth'. Though the exact dates are subject to conflicting sources, on one thing most agree: the diplomatic royals of England and Wales agreed to peace at Laugharne Castle.

The castle's story begins some sixty years earlier, in 1116, with the Norman Robert Courtemain. Laugharne was one of many fortresses built to defend important river crossings along the south coast. At some point in those early years, Courtemain is recorded as having entrusted Laugharne to one Bleddyn ap Cedifor. Bleddyn's name implies that he was a Welshman, which may indicate that relations between native and Norman were amicable at that time. Along with nearby Pembroke, this would explain Henry II's reasons for choosing Laugharne for his meetings with Rhys. A notoriously careful and wise administrator, Henry would have taken security extra seriously.

Good relations between the King of England and the Prince of Deheubarth continued until Henry died in 1189. As soon as news of Richard's intention to ignore the earlier treaty on his father's demise reached Rhys, the prince acted swiftly to seize control of Laugharne, as well as nearby St Clears and Llansteffan. It has been alleged that Rhys razed the early structure. Though little remains of the original earthworks or stone hall, it is challenging to prove Rhys's exact actions. Following its recapture, the Plantagenets rebuilt the castle in stone.

Whatever its exact condition in the early 1200s, it is doubtful that Laugharne was entirely able to defend itself when Llywelyn ap Iorwerth laid siege to it in 1215. How long it took for Llywelyn to take the castle and by what means he achieved victory sadly lacks contemporary sources. By 1217 William Marshal, 1st Earl of Pembroke's heroics while acting as regent to the young Henry III concluded the First Barons' War and the castle's return to English hands. In 1247 it was granted to the de Brian family, among whose number Guy de Brian modernised parts of the castle. Guy was captured at Laugharne ten years later when Llywelyn ap Gruffudd razed it to the ground.

Once again, Laugharne needed rebuilding. The north-west and south-west towers date from the thirteenth century, most likely in the years following its destruction. The same is true of the curtain walls and outer ward. It is possible that the north-west tower was already in use as a keep and guarding the entrance. In the mid-fourteenth century, the curtain walling at the south-western corner of the inner ward was raised in height. The same was true of the nearest tower and inner gatehouse. A change in colour from the usual red sandstone to a murky green denotes the timing in both cases. The man behind the work was Guy de Brian VII, a close ally of Edward III. Such improvements would soon prove vital. On reaching Laugharne in 1403, Owain Glyndŵr was caught unawares by a Royalist ambush and lost a staggering 700 men. On the warnings of a local mystic, the prince retreated.

For the next 150 years, the castle enjoyed a relatively settled existence in royal hands. In 1584 Elizabeth granted the castle to the controversial courtier Sir John Perrot, who, according to contemporary gossip, was her illegitimate half-brother (see Carew Castle). Though undoubtedly the offspring of Mary Berkeley, a known mistress of Henry VIII, confirmation that he was of Tudor descent remains a dubious topic. Based on a portrait of him by George Powle, a facial resemblance with the king who married six times is visible. Contemporary documents also attest to his referring to himself as the queen's brother. That Elizabeth held Perrot in some regard appears evident from her appointing him Lord Deputy of Ireland. However, this did not save him from time in the Tower of London and a mysterious death.

Under Perrot, Laugharne received something of a facelift. Coming at a time when many of Britain's castles were remodelled into country estates, Laugharne was similarly converted. Further to the addition of more luxurious accommodation, counterfeit battlements atop the curtain walls and a cobbled courtyard were also added. The work remained incomplete at Perrot's death, and the mock battlements did not fare well when the civil war came to Laugharne. The Royalists secured the castle in 1644, yet less than a year passed before a Roundhead force led by Major-General Rowland Laugharne arrived before the walls. Though by no means the longest of sieges, the week-long onslaught was sufficient in ensuring Roundhead cannon fire culminated in severe damage. When the Royalists surrendered, the castle was slighted and left to rot.

For eighty years, Laugharne's existence was a wretched one. This changed, however, when moves were made to bring new life to the site. In the 1730s, the pink-fronted Castle House was erected close by. A century later, the outer ward was being used as formal gardens. In the 1930s and 40s, the building was leased to the author Richard Hughes, whose 1938 novel, *In Hazard*, was inspired by his gazebo's river views. His famous visitor, Dylan Thomas, enjoyed the same winning formula two years later when he wrote his short prose collection, *Portrait of the Artist as a Young Dog*. The visit inspired Thomas's permanent stay in Laugharne, during which he wrote some of his most significant works. Among them, his 1944 work *Poem in October* lays clear his love for the area. Dylan's so-called 'Birthday Walk', which lies at the poem's heart, is also popular among locals and visitors. The famous boathouse, in which the family set up home in 1949, lies just a short walk up the estuary from the castle. Visitors can still see his writing shed, which remains mostly unchanged since his occupation.

A place of war, literature and natural beauty, there is a unique charm about Laugharne that is difficult to appreciate without visiting it. At certain times of the day, especially in the months of summer, the sun setting over the river has a beautiful, timeless quality, as though one is witnessing the estuary as it had been in the distant past. Nearby, to the west of the castle's gatehouse, there was a large pit, in which the Gwyglli – known in English as the 'dog of darkness' – reputedly dwelt. In Welsh mythology, the sight of the dog, with its large red eyes, was equated with misfortune and death. The rattling of a chain was also regarded as a terrible sign for the unfortunate witness. It was almost certainly the dog of death that inspired J.K. Rowling's 'The Grim' in the third Harry Potter novel.

Llansteffan

A short jump across the mouth of the Towy estuary from Laugharne, close to both Kidwelly and Carmarthen, the small village of Llansteffan is another genuine jewel in Carmarthenshire's crown. Translating into English as 'the church of Stephen', rolling hills, sandy beaches, pleasant homes, and quaint Norman churches are just some of the delights one can find on visiting the area. As a bonus, the village also hosts one of the prettiest ruined castles in Wales.

Enthroned on a steep grassy hillock overlooking the chilly waters and bright sands on which cockles abound, the ruins of Llansteffan Castle rise imperiously into the heavens. The climb is a steep one but well worth it. On reaching the castle, evidence of Llansteffan's history oozes from every nook and cranny. Outside the mighty gatehouse, the sparse remnants of an Iron Age hillfort tell the tale of the time before the Normans. Before the usual stone upgrade, the castle undoubtedly consisted of timber ringworks, many of which now lie forgotten beneath the upper ward. The present fortress originates from around the turn of the twelfth century, at which time Henry I granted it to the powerful Marmion family. In 1146 the Prince of Deheubarth, Maredudd ap Gruffydd, conquered the area and held it for twelve years. On Henry II's death, the castle fell a second time to the marauding Rhys ap Gruffudd, but as with nearby Laugharne, his holding of it was brief.

Following its return to English hands, the castle passed by marriage to the de Camvilles. The timber earthworks were upgraded in stone in 1192 with two towers and thick stone walls between the upper and lower baileys. Nevertheless, it would be taken twice. The first was the castle's razing by Llywelyn ap Iorwerth in 1215. On retrieving the castle around 1223, the de Camvilles created a new inner gatehouse and a circular keep. They also improved other parts, including the upper ward.

In 1257 a similar pattern followed under Llywelyn ap Gruffudd on his stunning victory at nearby Coed Llathen. When the de Camvilles regained control in the 1260s, they extended the boundaries by adding the lower ward. The great gatehouse, the west and north towers, the east bastion, great hall, and further walls were all added. The towers may have also provided quarters for the garrison and offered further reconnaissance.

The castle's defensive capability was understandably of prime concern to the family. Instead of incorporating a comfortable residence with countless fireplaces and airy windows, they prioritised the covering of the entrance with two imposing portcullises, thick double doors, and a series of murder holes. The narrowness of the arrow slits also adds to the likelihood that not getting hit was considered the greater priority. The views from the south section of the curtain wall are especially far-reaching and provided for natural surveillance to protect against siege.

In 1338 the male de Camville line died out. The castle subsequently passed in marriage to Robert Penrees. It is likely that the fortress had already suffered a period of neglect before their departure, as by 1367 sources describe it as ruined. It was in little better condition when Owain Glyndŵr launched his assault on Carmarthenshire. In contrast to his setback at Laugharne, Glyndŵr captured the castle twice, firstly in 1403 and again two years later. In 1408 the failing rebellion saw it recaptured by Sir John Penrees. The castle had already entered the Crown's possession in 1377, but the family retained permission to live there.

With this, Llansteffan's time in the spotlight gradually faded. At the Crown's granting, the three-storey D-shaped gatehouse was converted into a residence. On being given the castle in 1495, modifications to the gatehouse became the preserve of Henry VII's uncle, Jasper Tudor. Somewhat bafflingly, the castle fell into a state of disrepair soon after. By the late-Tudor era, the great hall appears to have been either used as, or replaced by, a barn. By the 1700s, the ruins formed part of a private farm. In the following century, the romantic ambience brought the artists and tourists. In more recent times a combination of Cadw and private ownership has seen the castle become a treat for visitors.

A site that boasts more than 2,000 years of history, it is somewhat surprising that the castle is the home of so few legends. Located so close to Laugharne, the pair unsurprisingly share the tale of the Gwyglli, or 'dog of darkness' (see above). In this, we are offered a reminder that walls were often built to keep out the same enemies: be they human or the creation of our darkest fears.

Tretower

Erected to guard the road from Mid Wales into and out of England, the ruined fortress in the Powys village of Tretower is a fine example of an early Norman citadel.

Sources are typically scant about the castle's early years. Begun as a humble motte and bailey, perhaps as early as 1081, it was held in 1103 by Roger, the first baron Picard, a follower of Bernard de Neufmarché whose descendants owned the fortress for at least six generations. As the

Anarchy brought ruin to many timber structures, the castle was rebuilt in stone by the second Picard, often remembered as Roger I. Among Roger I's additions was a stone tower, possibly a shell keep. The new build appears to have continued along the same lines as its predecessor with the motte and keep remaining at the western corner. A circular three-storey keep was added the following century, most likely 1235-50 under Roger II, Roger I's great-grandson, when the castle was rebuilt following the Marshal War of 1233-34. Though limited records of Tretower's role in the skirmish survive, Richard Marshal, 3rd Earl of Pembroke, appears to have conquered the castle in alliance with Llywelyn ap Iorwerth no later than 1233.

Adjacent to the castle stands Tretower Court, a fine fourteenth-century fortified manor house. The court's existence is rare and provides a valuable example of the castle's evolution. The manor was likely possessed of private quarters and chambers.

It is unclear whether any of the new building was in place when the Picard line died out by the early-1400s. At the time of Owain Glyndŵr's rebellion, the castle is listed as a defensive fortification of Henry IV. Less clear is whether this distinction concerned the development of the residence next door. Under Sir James Berkeley's guidance, the castle withstood a Welsh siege and remained in royal hands throughout Owain's rebellion. In 1429, William ap Thomas acquired both castle and court. While Willian's son, William Herbert, became Earl of Pembroke and built Raglan – see Raglan Castle – Tretower became the property of his half-brother, Roger Vaughan, regarded by some as the wealthiest commoner in Wales.

Under Vaughan, Tretower Court developed into a rare example of a substantial late medieval country residence. Indeed, in certain quarters the name itself was described as a 'byword for magnificence'. Certain questions remain unsolved regarding Vaughan's background. William appears to have gifted Roger Tretower no later than 1450. Roger also changed sides at least once during the Rose Wars. Ironically considering his family had been staunch Lancastrians, it was the Yorkists who knighted him. After being beheaded at Chepstow when his mission to capture Jasper Tudor ended in disaster, his son, Sir Thomas, inherited both properties, following which the court benefited from further developments. Limited records specify the castle's continued use, which may indicate that it was abandoned in favour of the newer building. On visiting in 1540, Leland wrote of a 'pretty castle belonging now to the king, and thereby also in the village is a fair place of Henry Vaughan esquire'. Neither the castle nor manor saw action in the civil war.

While the castle deteriorated, progress at the court continued under Vaughan's descendants. Their number included the writer and poet Henry Vaughan, a grandson of the former owner, William, mentioned by Leland. The court remained a Vaughan property until 1786. After they sold up, the building was used as a farmhouse, and the surrounding acres were cultivated as farmland. The tenants reused parts of it for animal husbandry, including as a piggery. Both buildings are now open to the public.

The story of Tretower Castle and Court is indeed a unique one in Wales's history. Both in their respective ways stand as relics of different eras of Wales's past. There also is no denying a sense of magic encapsulates both places. As regularly discussed in my previous work, *Castles of England*, the fourteenth century saw a transition in castle design. Such trends were evident in many fortresses, such as Bodiam and Herstmonceux. In Wales's case, the site's development would be crucial to the flourishing of the country estates of the Tudor era and beyond. Today, the two buildings stand side by side, uninhabited yet possessed of very different fabrics. When viewed together, the evolution is crystal clear.

It is surely no surprise that two buildings that have lived through more than 900 years of Welsh history are reputedly hubs for paranormal activity. Especially prominent at the court is a lady wearing a white dress. She has been seen pacing the main bedroom, as well as the gallery. A woman has also been spotted sitting by the windowsill. Described by some as being of an anxious disposition, others have suggested that she appears calm and peaceful. It is unclear if they are the same ghost.

Similar is true of the second bedroom, in which the spirit of another woman dressed in white has been seen. Possessed of intense green eyes, her demeanour nervous but not aggressive, the apparition has much in common with the first lady and might be the same. While the hauntings have been so upsetting to several staff members that they refuse to set foot in certain areas unescorted, the spirit had such an effect on one female visitor that she returned multiple times as she was worried about her. Intriguingly, another woman of identical appearance and temperament has been spotted pacing the gallery and battlements of the castle. Over the years, she has appeared with her gaze on the horizon as though longing for someone to return. Speculation has long been rife that at least one of these women was a Vaughan wife.

Outside the courtroom, a bricked-up door once led to the lord of the manor's court. The door was the public entrance, presumably bricked up when the estate ceased to be used for public trials. The area has been described as possessed of an oppressive atmosphere. Sightings of a little boy close by have also been reported. In contrast to the room's former legal purpose, the boy appears dressed in smithy's clothing. At various times, the room also served as a judge's chambers and as a farrier's – a smith who made horseshoes.

Chapter 6

Glamorgan

Caerphilly

Commonly mislabelled as one of Edward I's 'Iron Ring', work on Caerphilly was already underway during the final years of Edward's father, Henry III, when Edward was planning his expedition to the Holy Land. The castle was commissioned in 1268 by Gilbert de Clare: initially the husband of Edward's half-cousin, and later his son-in-law following his second marriage.

Though one can easily argue that Caerphilly helped lay the foundations for Edward's future success, many features distinguish it from the other thirteenth-century Welsh castles. One of the first things people notice is its layout. Concentric in design, the castle was the first in Britain to be deliberately built this way. Only Kenilworth can be regarded as of similar design following its significant redevelopment under John and Henry III. Equally in keeping with Kenilworth was the inclusion of defensive lakes. The castle measures 12ha (30 acres), making it the largest in Britain after Windsor. Its heavily fortified walls are unquestionably among the greatest of its type. Only the Tower of London can lay claim to being more substantial.

Situated in the town of the same name in the Rhymney Valley, Gilbert's masterpiece continues to dominate the landscape. The chosen location was close to the remains of a Roman fort on land Gilbert inherited in 1263. The initial structure was completed by 1272, despite Llywelyn ap Gruffudd's attempts to raze the area two years earlier. The finished defences proved particularly important to Gilbert's descendants in withstanding attacks from the Welsh.

The revolt of Madog ap Llywelyn in 1294 proved the first real test. In 1316 this was followed by an onslaught of some 10,000 men led by Llywelyn Bren. Particularly influential in the castle's defence was the resourceful Eleanor de Clare, daughter of Gilbert de Clare and his second wife, Joan of Acre – a daughter of Edward I and Eleanor of Castile – who held firm for six weeks. In 1326, Caerphilly proved equally crucial in the usurpation of the first English Prince of Wales, later Edward II of England. Edward stayed at the fortress between late October and early November before abandoning £14,000 of coin and extensive provisions in his attempts to flee Isabella's forces.

An improvement in the nation's fortunes paradoxically saw Caerphilly enter a period of decline. The castle appears to have survived Owain Glyndŵr's rebellion unscathed – if it was even used. After a time owned by the le Despenser family, it passed in marriage to Isabella le Despenser's husbands: Richard de Beauchamp, Earl of Worcester, followed by his similarly named cousin, Richard Beauchamp, Earl of Warwick. Future owners included Richard Neville, 16th Earl of Warwick (the Kingmaker), and Jasper Tudor, Earl of Pembroke.

By the sixteenth century, the defensive lakes had been drained and the walls depleted. The renowned Tudor antiquarian John Leland lamented on visiting the castle no later than 1540 that while it had 'walles of a wonderful thiknes', they were surrounded by marshland and that only a tower used to hold prisoners remained habitable. It later appears to have acted as a Royalist garrison during the English Civil War, though a second fort was also established on the old Roman one. It is no longer clear whether the nominal damage incurred from the Roundhead soldiers was intended as a deliberate slighting or simply a result of the fighting. Nevertheless, when the war ended, the castle became redundant and was abandoned.

For the next century, the great fortress was left to its fate. In 1776 the Marquess of Bute, John Stuart, acquired the property, after which steps were made to ensure its longevity. The third marquess, Stuart's grandson, John Crichton-Stuart, showed great passion for the castle, his reroofing of the great hall among his legacies. Progress continued under his successor and namesake before the fifth marquess, another John Crichton-Stuart, presented the castle to the state in 1950. Like many of its type, it is now looked after by Cadw.

Despite its desertion more than three centuries ago, many believe Caerphilly is a castle that refuses to sleep. The site of numerous battles and bloody sieges, the well-preserved defences were never conquered by force. Instead, like the great empires of old, the castle's road to ruin lay in the greed of its owners. In such ways, the story of Caerphilly greets us with a cautionary tale reminiscent of a Shakespearian tragedy.

As appropriate for such a fortress, the stories of ghosts are plentiful. Caerphilly's first ghost story concerns the castle's early days. Known as 'the red' due to his fiery personality and the colour of his hair, Gilbert de Clare inherited the Gloucester earldom in 1262 on the death of his father, Richard. Throughout the 1260s, Wales remained a site of turmoil, and like many a Marcher lord, Gilbert sought to capitalise. Successful in claiming suzerainty over large parts of South Wales, he took up residence at Caerphilly, whose walls locals described as 'the finest any of them had ever seen'. The 'red' lived there with his wife, Princess Alice de Lusignan of Angoulême, whom he had wed in 1253. Famous for her beauty, Alice was equally revered as a great hostess and entertainer. Throughout their early tenure, Caerphilly's great hall was the setting of many a fine banquet.

Although devoted to Gilbert and accustomed to the delights that his wealth and status could bestow, Alice longed for affection. While such things were not forthcoming from the red lord, during one of his many periods of absence, Caerphilly is said to have played host to the handsome Prince of Brithdir, 'Gruffydd the fair'. Like many in her presence, Gruffydd was instantly besotted by Alice's beauty and became a frequent visitor to the castle.

Like many a forbidden romance, the affair was doomed from the start. Smitten by his new love, Gruffydd entrusted his feelings to a local monk, most likely under the sanctity of confession. Unbeknown to Gruffydd, the monk was in Gilbert's employ and revealed the secret. In his fury, Gilbert sent Alice back to France, disgraced by the scandal. When the prince learned of the monk's betrayal, he tracked him down and hung him from a tree – now known as 'Monk's Vale'. A similar fate awaited Gruffydd. On hearing of the sad turn of events, Alice supposedly died from shock. In reality, records confirm she died in 1290, aged 54, after a long separation from her husband.

More than 700 years have passed since the tragic love affair. Yet, according to local lore, the ghost of the beautiful princess returns to the castle. Dressed in an ethereal shade of green, thought to represent the envy of her husband, her apparition has been seen pacing the ramparts and even floating from turret to turret. On one occasion, she was apparently nearly caught by some local boys from the town.

Throughout its period of occupation, soldiers vigilantly patrolled the battlements. For such reasons, it is perhaps unsurprising their ghosts are said to continue to do so at night. Some personnel refuse to enter parts of the castle amid claims that a mysterious fragrance occasionally lingers. South Wales was synonymous with mining for many years, which led to the development of many superstitions. The strange smell has long been regarded as invisible 'death flowers' and viewed as an omen of disaster.

The double moat is another unique feature of the castle's defences. Being protected on three sides by water, the front entrance was the only option for potential intruders. The renowned castle author R. Allen Brown wrote glowingly of 'the most elaborate water defences in all Britain'. However, according to legend, the moat carried its own threat. Sightings of a foul and hideous apparition – known in Welsh as Gwrach y Rhibyn, the 'hag of the moat' – have long been associated with gross misfortune.

Though the hag is not a typical haunting among the castles of Great Britain and Ireland, she is famed in Welsh folklore as a spectre of death and is often associated with the Irish Banshee or the Scottish Glaistig. She has reputedly been seen when the rain pours down, her cries an ominous premonition of death. Tradition states that the spirit would howl the name of the family member before disappearing into the moat. It may also connect with the dreadful wraith once believed to haunt St Donat's (see St Donat's). Although stories of this spirit have become inseparable from ancient Welsh mythology, the hag's affiliation with Caerphilly probably dates to Gilbert de Clare's tenure. The legend is popular in the Middle East: a land where Gilbert spent many years on crusade.

Enjoyed by tens of thousands of visitors every year, there is no doubt that Caerphilly is a deserving candidate for the crown of Wales's most splendid castle. As the historian Norman Pounds rightly stated, Caerphilly was a 'turning point in the history of the castle of Britain'. It was this design that later inspired Edward I's castles in the north. Nevertheless, it is somewhat sad that this magnificent castle was ever allowed to become a crumbling shell. It may lie empty, yet the spirits of this magnificent fortress seem destined to resonate throughout its forsaken walls, an ethereal testament to an empire that collapsed under the crippling weight of greed and desire.

Cardiff

General Aulus Didius Gallus's establishment of a fort in 55AD is believed to have marked the first Roman settlement in Wales. The antiquarian William Camden recorded the city's original name as

Caer-Didi, which he believed to have developed from a corruption of caer (fort) and Didius. Whatever the exact truth behind the fort's origins, over the next 2,000 years, consistent additions to this simple farming settlement would see the area blossom into the largest city in Wales.

There is much to love about the capital of Wales. Granted city status in 1905, modern Cardiff contains a unique blend of refined architecture that encapsulates the city's past, present, and short-term future. Renowned for hosting the Welsh Assembly, the construction of many luxury homes, shops, hotels, and other modern facilities such as the Millennium Stadium marks a city's changing face as it takes on life in the twenty-first century.

As usual, the first step in Cardiff's evolution was the construction of a castle. The original was a typical motte and bailey situated on top of the old Roman walls. The third-century defence was most likely a successor of the original, both of which had stood guard over the Roman road and defended the coast from pirates. Though the walls were in poor condition by the Normans' arrival, they provided a good beginning for the castle perimeter. At the time, the motte was the largest in Wales.

Whether this occurred on William the Conqueror's orders following a pilgrimage to St David's in 1081, or Robert Fitzhamon, feudal baron of Gloucester, around 1091 is unclear. When Fitzhamon died in 1107, still carrying his battle wounds from Tinchebray, Henry I granted the castle to Robert FitzRoy, 1st Earl of Gloucester, husband to Fitzhamon's daughter, Mabel, and one of the king's many bastards. Most likely on Gloucester's guidance, the castle was rebuilt in stone the following century. A shell keep and strong walls were erected in place of the timber assemblies, some of which survive. Such things were in place by the 1130s when Robert Curthose was moved there from Devizes. Son of William the Conqueror and brother of Henry I, Curthose had been imprisoned since 1106 on the back of his failed insurrection.

Further developments followed during the Anarchy on the watch of William Fitz Robert, 2nd Earl of Gloucester. In 1158 the castle was subjected to a raid from Ifor Bach, Lord of Senghenydd, who took William hostage. By William's death in 1183, new town walls had been erected to offer extra security around the castle. In the absence of a son, Henry II declared William's daughter, Isabella, Countess of Gloucester, sole heiress to the estate. She later became the first wife of John, later King of England, only to divorce in 1199.

On Isabella's death in October 1217, control of the castle passed through her sister to Gilbert de Clare and thus formed part of the Honour of Clare. As a Marcher lord territory, Cardiff enjoyed special privileges and a degree of independence from the Crown. Due to this combination, the castle became central to the family's power and inspired a series of significant upgrades. Among the most important were those undertaken by Richard de Clare, 6th Earl of Gloucester, in the second half of the thirteenth century. With this, Cardiff was a perfect citadel to withstand the Marcher wars and later rebellions, including those of the two Llywelyns. When the final de Clare, Gilbert, died at Bannockburn in 1314, Edward II granted the castle to his controversial favourite, Hugh le Despenser the Younger.

A combination of bad weather, which led to dreadful harvests and food shortages, and Despenser's general tyranny inspired the unsuccessful insurrection of Llywelyn Bren in 1316. On Hugh's orders, Llywelyn was hanged, drawn and quartered at Cardiff two years later. In response to the widespread condemnation of Llywelyn's treatment, Hugh arrested and executed Sir William Fleminge as a scapegoat three years later. The Marcher lords' dismay soon culminated in the Despenser War, during which Cardiff was sacked. Though Hugh swiftly recovered the castle and town, his downfall led to his execution for treason in 1326.

Despite Hugh's death, the castle remained in Despenser hands for the remainder of the century. As the family made more use of nearby Caerphilly, Cardiff's importance dwindled. In 1400 the Ricardian loyalist, Thomas le Despenser, was executed for conspiring against Henry IV. Four years later, the castle fell to Owain Glyndŵr, whose rebellion caused severe damage, especially to the Black Tower. Though the castle was later recovered, on the marriage of Thomas's daughter Isabel following the deaths of Thomas and his son, Richard, Cardiff passed to the de Beauchamp family.

Having not gained Caerphilly as part of the marriage settlement, Isabel's second husband, Richard de Beauchamp, Earl of Warwick, set about making Cardiff his perfect home. This included the addition of a new tower in 1430 alongside the Black Tower. Also of note was a range of new buildings comparable with Edward III's great work at Windsor the previous century. The castle remained in de Beauchamp hands until it passed in marriage to the infamous 'kingmaker' Richard Neville, 16th Earl of Warwick.

Reflecting the toing and froing of circumstances in England during the Rose Wars, the owners following Warwick's death included Edward IV's brothers (George, Duke of Clarence and Richard III), Jasper Tudor, Anne Beauchamp (Neville's widow) and the future Henry VIII. In 1495, ten years after Henry Tudor's accession, the king officially revoked Cardiff's Marcher territory status. In 1536, Henry VIII abolished the remainder: a somewhat inevitable move as many of the lordships had been swallowed by the Crown since Henry IV's usurpation. Consequently, Cardiff's purpose as a defensive castle diminished. In 1513, the Crown leased it to Henry Beaufort's legitimised bastard, Charles Somerset, 1st Earl of Worcester and Edward VI sold it to William Herbert, later Earl of Pembroke, in 1550.

The following years would mark a real turning point in the castle's future. On visiting Cardiff around 1540, John Leland spoke of the keep as 'a great thing and strong, but now in some ruine'. Greater encouragement was offered of the Black Tower, which had found renewed use as a prison. Among those incarcerated was the controversial Thomas Capper, who Henry VIII burned as a heretic. In 1610 the cartographer John Speed produced a more encouraging report of the castle, describing it as 'large and in good repair'. Throughout this time, the castle also became renowned for its pleasant orchards and gardens.

Such would be the way until the civil war. Due to Philip Herbert's Parliamentary sympathies, the Roundheads quickly overcame the Royalist garrison – something that local tradition blames on a secret passageway. A surprise attack from the Royalist Marquess of Hertford, William Seymour – later 2nd Duke of Somerset – met with success. This, in turn, inspired a Parliamentary siege, which lasted a mere five hours. Early in 1645, the town itself was taken following a rebellion by the high sheriff, backed by Cavaliers from Oxford. Despite being aided by a naval squadron deployed to assist the garrison, the Royalists retook the castle.

For Charles I, control of Cardiff would be a minor blessing. After travelling there in July to parley with local leaders, a small army of locals – self-dubbed the 'Peaceable Army' – demanded they be granted the castle. In the end, a compromise saw the Royalist garrison give way to a local force. However, in September, Charles went back on his word, and the garrison was forced to surrender. Less than a month later, a combined force of the defected locals and Roundheads took the castle.

Further fighting broke out in 1648 when a Royalist force of 8,000 was assembled against some 3,000 at St Fagans. The Royalists were defeated, but the castle survived slighting. Due to the threat of a pro-Royalist Scottish invasion, the Roundheads maintained a garrison. Throughout the Interregnum and the reign of Charles II, the castle remained the property of the Herbert earls of Pembroke, during which time the constable doubled up as the local mayor.

Herbert control of Cardiff Castle continued until Lady Charlotte Herbert's marriage to her second husband, Thomas, Viscount Windsor. On her death in 1733, possession passed to their son Herbert, whose daughter, Charlotte Jane Windsor, married John, Lord Mount Stuart in 1766. It was Stuart who, in 1794, became the first Marquess of Bute.

Under Bute's ownership, renovation work on the castle began in earnest. Gone were the bedraggled and dilapidated buildings in the castle's orbit: notably the knights' houses, Shire Hall and a stone wall that separated the baileys. Cardiff was blessed with magnificent gardens in their place, a proud legacy of Lancelot 'Capability' Brown and his son in law, Henry Holland. Further work was carried out on the main lodgings, including two new wings, at the expense of previous additions. The moat was filled, and pathways added, along with a summerhouse. In the following century, Bute's grandson and heir embarked on a mission to revitalise the local docks. With this, the value of the family's mining and land interests skyrocketed.

Such success would not be mirrored within the castle's walls. Though Cardiff remained the centre of the family's political power, the second marquess's love of the Isle of Bute in Scotland saw the castle's importance diminish. In 1831, throughout the Merthyr Rising – a violent protest which broke out to address local working-class rights – Bute based himself at the castle. Local reform followed by Act of Parliament four years later, at last severing the link between the city council and the castle's constable.

This would not be the only link severed. The 3rd marquess inherited the castle in 1848 before celebrating his first birthday and developed a longstanding hatred for his surroundings. While still a young man, he employed architect William Burges to revive its fortunes, as he did at Castell Coch (see below). What resulted was the substitution of a dated and botched mesh of styles for a masterpiece of gothic revivalism. Aided by the family's enormous financial clout, Burges brought in his trusted team of experts. A combination of his respect for the castle's history and rare imagination culminated in the unique creation one can see today. In 1868 work was completed on the new 150-foot-high clock tower, complemented by several lavish chambers. Interestingly, the exterior was born of an unsuccessful design Burges had made for London's Royal Courts of Justice.

As the century progressed, so too did other work on the castle. With this, the conversion of the tired mishmash to Victorian country house was complete. The clock tower was undoubtedly the crowning glory of Burges's dream. Praise was also offered of the Octagon Tower's roof. No better tribute can be found of Cardiff's gilded interiors than the words of historian Megan Aldrich that they are 'the most magnificent that the gothic revival ever achieved'.

Although work on Cardiff Castle continued into the next century, it is to Bute and Burges that this superb house owes the most generous acknowledgement. While work by Capability Brown and others sadly destroyed much of ancient and medieval consequence, the fortuitous discovery in 1889 of the old Roman forts led to an archaeological investigation the following year. Forty years earlier, 434 acres of castle grounds were opened to form Bute Park.

While the faltering coal trade convinced John Crichton-Stuart, the fourth marquess, to sell many of the family's local holdings, work on the castle continued. Development included restoring medieval masonry in 1921 and rebuilding the South Gate, West Gate, barbican tower, and town walls. In 1927 the Swiss Bridge was also moved, allowing for new archaeological work in the early 1920s. The gatehouse was also redesigned, while the 1930s saw the end of the grand staircase.

Like most cities, Cardiff played a central role in the local war effort during the twentieth century, almost three centuries since it last experienced combat. The famous tunnels were reused as Anderson shelters, and the exterior was often the anchor to tether barrage balloons. Two years after World War Two ended, death duties led the fifth marquess to sell his interests in the city and gift the castle and park to the state. A lowering of the family flag marked a handover ceremony, thus ending the castle's long history as a powerbase and beginning its tenure as a tourist attraction.

Though much has changed since the Norman era, the city harbours many reminders of its colourful past. The medieval market is still a popular area. Many churches and two other castles also offer visual reminders of its former glories. The city's official population surpasses 300,000, yet some claim the true number may be vastly more. According to locals, Cardiff is a haven for the supernatural.

Famed the castle may be as a mark of the wealth and ambition of the 3rd marquess, it is possibly due to the circumstances of his father's untimely passing that it is plagued by paranormal activity. After a spectacular banquet in 1848, the 2nd marquess died suddenly in a small drawing-room behind the library. The room where he perished was later converted into a chapel, and a bust commemorates the site. His apparition has been seen there and in the library, uncannily reminiscent of a nearby portrait.

The marquess is not alone in his ghostly endeavours. His wife, Sophia, is also thought to haunt the castle. The lady, dressed in an ethereal shade of white, has been seen floating through the neighbouring passageways. The main dining room, although magnificent in appearance, is a particularly intriguing area. Popular with visitors in the day, many avoid it at night. At 03:45 am, the room frequently reverberates to banging sounds, as if the main doors were suddenly opened and forcefully shut again. Lights have also been seen flickering. The ominous happenings are thought to mark the marquess's passing.

It is not only the Butes that are said to haunt the castle. An apparition described as a 'faceless vision in a flowing greyish-white skirt' has been seen near the stockroom. Over the years, staff have often entered to find objects misplaced, despite the doors being locked. In 1975 the castle's custodian was also the surprise witness of a strange man standing at the far end of the hallway. When he approached the mysterious figure, it faded out of sight. The man was also seen in one of the bedrooms and has been blamed for locking doors. Throughout the last two centuries, reports circulated of a phantom coach crossing the courtyard and exiting through the main gates. Intriguingly, the sounds of a horse and carriage have been heard as the vision crosses the concrete floor before fading to silence. The third marquess also recorded hearing a horse and carriage.

The Roman fort may have largely vanished, and parts of the medieval masonry have been swept away by previous owners' brash efforts, yet Cardiff Castle remains a jewel in Wales's crown. Both a historic castle and a fine country home, like Windsor and Warwick, Cardiff incorporates many eras. While the gilded interiors, to quote Joseph Mordaunt Crook, can be considered 'three dimensional passports to fairy kingdoms and realms of gold', one may be pleasantly surprised by the nuggets hidden among the nooks and crannies. As the architectural historian John Newman was only too correct to point out, Cardiff is undoubtedly one of the 'most successful of all the fantasy castles of the nineteenth century'.

Castell Coch

Few castles in Britain divide opinion like Castell Coch. The Victorian folly that now stands on the site of a medieval ruin has been decried as an illustration of the 3rd Marquess of Bute's extravagance as well as a romantic legacy to honour the wife he adored.

Sited on a wooded hillside five miles north-west of Cardiff, close to the village ofTongwynlais, the present castle was completed around 1891 atop the ruins of a far older structure destroyed during the Middle Ages. Of the original castle's exact form, creation and destruction, records are frustratingly scattered. Some form of construction, most likely a motte and bailey, was built by the Normans sometime after 1081. Its purpose was almost certainly to protect Cardiff and the Taff Gorge; however, it was soon abandoned.

What happened next remains a mystery. The twelfth-century Welsh lord Ifor Bach – also known as Ifor ap Meurig or Ivor the Little – may have been responsible for the castle around 1158. Though he famously attacked Cardiff Castle and captured Richard of Gloucester, there is no conclusive evidence he built the castle. The motte was reused and upgraded sometime between 1267 and 1285 by Gilbert de Clare, 7th Earl of Gloucester, who held the lordship of Glamorgan. On Gilbert's death, his wife, Joan, took over ownership. Their son, also Gilbert, inherited the castle before he fought and died at Bannockburn in June 1314. Around this time, the term *Castrum Rubeum* or 'red castle' came into use, most likely in honour of the sandstone defences.

Of the second castle's appearance, history is no more revealing. The design is believed to have been triangular with smoothly sloping curtain walls joining together the three large stone towers. In contrast with the well-fortified structures of the time, the castle was probably used as a hunting lodge. Like the present one, thick beech trees surrounded it. Again, there is no documentary evidence to confirm what became of it. Logical explanations are that it was gutted in the Welsh rebellion of 1316 or Owain Glyndŵr's of the early 1400s. On being visited in 1536 by the ubiquitous Tudor antiquarian John Leland, the site was described as 'all in ruin, no big thing but high'. Evidence of Leland's recordings can still be found in the lower parts of the modern castle.

Little changed until John Stuart, 3rd Earl of Bute – later 1st Marquess – acquired the remains in 1760 as part of a marriage settlement. In 1848 John's grandson, John Crichton-Stuart, 3rd Marquess of Bute – the owner of nearby Caerphilly and reputedly the world's wealthiest man – inherited the castle and later employed the renowned architect William Burges to rebuild Castell Coch as a country residence. Though possessed of very different personalities, a close bond formed between the pair.

Such tastes lay at the heart of the castle's resurgence. So much so Bute spent a great deal of time researching medieval castles throughout Europe, including the thirteenth-century remains at Castell Coch. During a four-year period that commenced in 1875, work took place on the exterior. The interior was eventually completed in 1891, ten years after Burges had passed away. A vineyard was planted nearby and remained until the First World War. After being little used by the family, the fifth marquess bequeathed it to the state in 1950.

On visiting Castell Coch, it is easy to see why the structure inspires differences of opinion. The nineteenth-century Gothic Revival design is broadly comparable with the tower houses of Scotland. A better comparison still can be made with the mighty fortress of Chillon on Lake Geneva and the King Ludwig castles of Bavaria (the most famous of which, Schloss Neuschwanstein, inspired Disney).

Beautiful as Castell Coch's interior may appear, behind the glamorous façade, a darker side is said to dwell. At least two spirits are said to call this fairy-tale fortress home. The first of these was reputedly seen by the 3rd marquess's wife, Gwendolen Fitzalan-Howard. Of noble stock herself as the granddaughter of the 13th Duke of Norfolk, Gwendolen and Bute were dedicated to one another and often wrote when they were apart. A fiercely independent woman, Gwendolen lived at the castle for a short time in her servants' company following her husband's death. During this time, the ghostly visitations of one figure from the castle's past are believed to have become so frequent that she decided to leave for good.

The ghost in question is thought to be Dame Griffiths, a resident of Gilbert de Clare's castle. Wearing a long, white dress, she has been described as possessed of a sad and distant manner, which may be explainable by an event that supposedly occurred during her employment. According to the legend, her young son drowned in a pool of water somewhere in the nearby woodland. This tragedy may also explain why she reputedly haunts the nearby woods.

The lady in white is by no means the castle's only curiosity. Of Scottish heritage, Bute considered himself of Celtic ancestry and was learned in Welsh culture and mythology. Throughout the rooms, many baffling features abound. Countless Green Men adorn the drawing room, which is also rich in pictures of wildlife, supposedly denoting the fragility of the food chain. In the chapel, several stained-glass windows honour the lives of saints. Arguably the most striking is Bute's bedroom, in which animals, birds and creatures from mythology are just a handful of the figures carved around the fireplace. Though the decorations are believed to offer an insight into Bute's personality, many are in keeping with the castle's character and seem to be connected to its oldest legends.

At the heart of the castle, twisting spiral staircases lead to a wooden balcony with stunning views over the Welsh countryside and the cobbled courtyard where the ghost of a cavalier has been seen. Local legend connects the cavalier's spirit with one of the red castle's most intriguing tales. The story tells that the cavalier buried a hoard of jewels, money and plates in an iron chest and hid it. What became of him afterwards is a mystery. As a supporter of the king, it is plausible he died in the English Civil War. The tale is especially curious as his death occurred before Bute's castle was restructured. The original fortress may have been destroyed before that time; however, one cannot rule out that the ruins were briefly used as a lookout post. Over the years, passages into the mountain have also been proposed.

Another story concerning the cavalier's treasure occurred early in the eighteenth century when a gamekeeper lived here with his wife. Though they initially enjoyed the natural charm and serenity, the couple were consistently disturbed by frequent sounds of tapping, scraping and intolerable whisperings. One night, the wife awoke to find a man standing in the room, dressed in a Royalist soldier's uniform. His face a deathly pale, his expression mournful, he recoiled to the door and disappeared into the darkness.

Intriguingly, the phantom cavalier and his hoard is not the only treasure tale associated with the castle. A second, even more outlandish story dates to Ifor Bach, who developed a fearsome reputation throughout Wales. He once boasted that an army of 1,200 of his men could defeat ten times that number from any opponent. During his alleged time at Castell Coch, he reputedly constructed an underground passage to connect the fortress to nearby Cardiff Castle. At the head of the route, a gigantic cavern existed within the mountainside, in which Ifor deposited a large iron chest. Upon doing so, the prince used his magic to turn his three most loyal servants into eagles. According to local lore, the great creatures are described as possessed of dark grey plumage, their eyes red like the fires of hell, and capable of flashing a brilliant light throughout the darkness of their lair. They are reputedly most likely to make their presence known between October and March, with thunderous cries that puncture the winter bleakness.

Despite the eagles' fearsome reputation, attempts have been made to locate the treasure. In the seventeenth century, a group of armed men apparently set out on a Jules Verne-style mission to discover the cavern, only to retreat at the horrific sight of the demonic trio. After hearing of the unsuccessful mission, a different group followed suit. On this occasion, they had weapons blessed by a priest and enlisted a devout friar. Despite their sharp blades and extra firepower, they, too, were driven out by the monstrous beasts.

Attempts to locate the treasure did not stop there. Another group of gentlemen descended on the cavern in the eighteenth century, armed to the teeth with pistols and cutlasses. After a relentless tussle with the eagles, they were forced to admit defeat and exited the cavern to the ecstatic screams and thunderous clapping of their wings. For more than eight centuries, Ifor Bach's treasure is said to have remained in the darkness, waiting to be claimed by one who is genuinely deserving.

Due to the third marquess's death in 1900, Castell Coch never lived up to its potential. As such, the elegant turrets that crown the thick towers and personal illustrations that decorate the castle's interior are very much a legacy to a unique man. From the outside, it is easy to see the fairy-tale-esque structure, delicately poised on the wooded slopes, as a somewhat sad reminder of a dream that was never quite realised. Nevertheless, it remains an exceptional feat of architectural engineering and design: one the historian David McLees hailed as 'one of the greatest

Victorian triumphs of architectural composition'. Further to Burges's attempts to replicate the style at Chillon, it was designed to create a dramatic silhouette that merges imposingly with the landscape.

While critics rightly point the finger at the extravagant costs, not least in the context of the poverty endured by Cardiff's miners, the castle also offers a unique insight into the mindset of the world's richest man. As the architectural historian Joseph Mordaunt Crook recalled, Castell Coch was 'the learned dream world of a great patron and his favourite architect, recreating from a heap of rubble a fairy-tale castle which seems almost to have materialised from the margins of a medieval manuscript.'

Loughor

Around 75AD, the Romans erected the military fort of *Leucarum* to overlook the River Loughor. The word itself originates from the river's name in Celtic.

That anything more primitive predated the fort is unlikely. Archaeological evidence from the time has confirmed that the Romans embarked on an extensive building project across the country's south-west. Located seven miles north-west of modern-day Swansea, *Leucarum*'s position was vital in protecting the road to Gower and offering support to its navies as they crossed the Bristol Channel. The fort was also deliberately sited close to a ford, which appears to have been crossable most times. The fort was likely abandoned during the second century and reoccupied by the Romans in the late third. The reasons for the brief absence remain unclear.

Somewhat predictably, Loughor's history then enters a period of limited sources. When the Normans made their intrusion across Offa's Dyke, their progress was cemented with the erection of a series of timber castles on top of several abandoned Roman forts. Loughor was among the newly constructed motte and baileys established on the western edge of the Gower Peninsula. The exact date for construction is no longer known. Henry I's granting of the Gower to Henry de Beaumont, Earl of Warwick, around 1106 appears to tally with the castle's emergence. The possibility cannot be ruled out a temporary structure preceded it; however, if so, no trace has survived.

As the Norman grip on South Wales tightened, the Gower developed in importance. With it, Warwick enjoyed the usual Marcher perks of local independence. The castle's purpose, meanwhile, mirrored that of *Leucarum*. As well as standing guard over the river, which offered access to the Bristol Channel, its location on the road that led through the Gower from Beaumont's chief residence at Swansea Castle was of clear benefit. It was from the fort that the castle was named. On the south side, the castle had the advantage of a steep slope and the natural marshiness of the riverbanks. What remained of the fort was incorporated into one of the corners. Parts of the old building were likely reused to establish the twelfth-century oval-shaped ringwork.

The defensive structure would come in particularly handy throughout the twelfth century. Although the south-west of Wales was largely spared the onslaught of the Anarchy, it proved a familiar battleground between Norman and Welsh. The Welsh rebellion of 1151 was most likely the reason for the castle's razing. When talks between Henry II and Rhys ap Gruffudd, Prince of Deheubarth (see Laugharne Castle) culminated in a peace treaty, Loughor was rebuilt in stone. The original bank of ringwork was widened from its original size, which allowed for new buildings on the site. The filling of the middle section of the ringwork developed a mound. By the end of the century, two new stone buildings had been erected at the castle's heart. It was most likely around this time that the latest earl's debts saw the castle repossessed by the Crown.

On Henry II's death, Loughor became one of many areas targeted by Rhys ap Gruffudd. In 1203 King John granted the castle to his key ally, William de Braose; however, this became complicated when William's familial links with Rhys contributed to the pair's feud later that decade. While John ordered the confiscation of William's lands, including Loughor, resistance by William and his alliance with Llywelyn ap Iorwerth ultimately led to his absconding to Ireland and the imprisonment and death of his wife and eldest son. Though William died in exile in France in 1211, the pact with Llywelyn allowed his son, Reginald, to marry Llywelyn's daughter, Gwladus Ddu. In 1215 Llywelyn conquered Loughor and granted Reginald control of the Gower. This ended when Reginald made peace with the young Henry III's government after hostilities in 1217. Llywelyn subsequently removed Reginald and replaced him with the late Rhys ap Gruffudd's hot-headed son, Rhys Gryg.

Gryg's rash behaviour would be bad news for the castles of the Gower. At least one of the chroniclers recorded that Gryg had the English-built fortresses destroyed to eradicate all foreign influences. Another of Llywelyn's daughters, Margaret, was married to Reginald's nephew John. This prompted Llywelyn to entrust him Loughor no later than 1220.

Reports are sketchy of Loughor's fate at that time. While John set about a series of improvements, less clear is whether Llywelyn's attack of 1215 or Gryg's of 1217-18 resulted in its destruction. A curtain wall was built in stone, which included a sally port on the north side to allow easy access to the river. John's death in July 1232 saw the castle pass to his son, William, a lad of just eight. Nearly two decades later, in 1251, William was forced to withstand renewed Welsh violence. In the aftermath, a square tower consisting of three chambers was constructed in stone. William also inserted a gateway into the curtain wall to the south of the new tower and created two stone buildings within the walls.

In 1291 William's death saw the rise of his son, William, who, in 1302, now about forty-two, granted the castle to his seneschal, John Yweyn, for life. When Yweyn died in 1322, William's powerful son-in-law, John de Mowbray, took advantage of William's old age and seized the lands. Mowbray was later heavily involved in Thomas, Earl of Lancaster's rebellion, leading to his execution. The grievances of Yweyn's next of kin, one Alice Roculf, culminated in her being granted his lands. However, this would be reversed on Edward II's abdication in 1327 to the benefit of John de Mowbray's son and namesake.

True to the pattern that surrounded the castles of Wales, the coming of Edward I brought centuries of violence to a close. As such, Loughor's importance dwindled. The castle was seemingly unused in the rebellions of the early 1400s. Its geographical position also ensured the same was true of the Wars of the Roses and the English Civil War. By the Victorian period, the castle was rich in ivy but lacking purpose. The attractive coverings were to the benefit of the artist William Butler, who captured the ruins alongside the modern industries. By this time, a new railway line had damaged the site of the old fort. It seems likely that this contributed to the collapse of the south-east tower in the 1940s. Bizarrely, it fell intact and remains at an angle. At the end of the war, the castle was taken over by the state and sits within the grounds of what is now Loughor Castle Park.

Pummelled by violence and later depleted by thieves, only a small part of the castle still stands. Nevertheless, its attractive façade, coupled with its historic location, makes it a worthwhile stop.

Ogmore

The contemporary cleric Caradoc of Llancarfan recorded that possession of the manor and castle at Ogmore was granted to William de Londres. William was a somewhat mysterious figure in the twelfth century and is listed as one of the legendary Twelve Knights of Glamorgan. His surname offers a clue to his origin: Londres being the gallicisation of London.

The castle, which dates from around 1106, was one of three in the area built at that time – the others being Coity and Newcastle (not to be confused with Newcastle Emlyn in Pembrokeshire). Located on the south bank of the River Ewenny beside a key fording area, the castle was of crucial strategic importance. Contemporary records tell that William was granted the fortress by Glamorgan's Norman conqueror, Robert Fitzhamon, himself responsible for building several other castles in the vicinity, including Newport.

A decade after taking ownership of Ogmore, de Londres was forced to flee a substantial Welsh force. Despite the worrying numbers, his butler, Arnold, stayed on and ensured its protection. In gratitude, he was granted ownership, along with the manor of Dunraven. In 1141 one of William's kin or descendants, John, also put down the Benedictine Ewenny Priory, a mile or two away. The castle remained in family hands until the male line died out around 1298 when the final heiress married into the Chaworths of Kidwelly.

Through Maud Chaworth, wife of Henry, 3rd Earl of Lancaster, the castle became the property of the Duchy of Lancaster. No later than 1345, the fortress passed to their son Henry of Grosmont, 1st Duke of Lancaster. After Grosmont's death, his replacement, John of Gaunt, the third son of Edward III, inherited his properties. It is from Gaunt's line that the House of Windsor claim descent. Seven centuries later, the castle remains a Lancastrian property.

Initially constructed as a typical oval ringwork, the castle was later upgraded in stone. The rectangular keep, which dates from the 1120s, was likely at the behest of William's son, Maurice, and is reputed to be the oldest Norman one in Glamorgan. Around the turn of the century, Thomas de Londres upgraded the original palisade with a curtain wall, while a second storey was also added as private apartments.

Throughout 1120-1400, the castle appears to have managed to stay free of trouble. This probably changed with the arrival of Owain Glyndŵr; however, records are unclear. A fourteenth-century rectangular courthouse flanked by two chambers was rebuilt in 1454, most likely due to damage sustained at Glyndŵr's hands. Evidence suggests that the courthouse remained in use until the mid-1600s. Due to the lack of evidence that the castle was involved in the civil war, it seems likely it was no longer in a fit state to be garrisoned.

For the modern-day visitor, Ogmore Castle is not without its charm. The surrounding sandhills make for picturesque views. The ditch that surrounds the grounds floods at high tide to create an ad hoc moat. An embedded stone wall was erected to dam the waters from the inner ward, while a series of stepping stones protrude above the river's waterline and act as a convenient walkway.

Other intriguing novelties can be found nearby. The village of Merthyr Mawr, reachable by an ancient footpath, is home to several rare medieval sculptured stone crosses, the oldest of which was carved in the fifth century. The nearby ruined fortified manor house of Candleston Castle is home to the 'Goblin Stone': a Celtic cross that reputedly bewitches passers-by until they become entangled. Tradition also tells that a local village vanished mysteriously. If there is any truth in the tale, it seems plausible that it sank into the shifting dunes.

Though the castle's history is less eventful than some, there is a strange story that a local was awoken one night by the apparition of a lady in white, known in the native tongue as Y Ladi Wen. On being coaxed into following her, the man found himself among the moonlit castle ruins, where he was directed to a particular stone under which a cauldron was filled with gold coins. He was then instructed by the lady in white, 'take half for yourself and replace the stone over the rest.' On replacing the stone, he realised that the lady was already gone.

His fortune inevitably became the talk of the village. Yet, no matter how badly the locals pestered him, he refused to acknowledge the source. Rich beyond measure, the spectre of greed nevertheless soon reared its ugly head. On returning to the castle one dark night, he sensed a disturbance in the atmosphere and looked up to see the familiar apparition looking down on him.

'Foolish man,' the apparition cried, 'You have all you could ever need, and yet you still want more. From this night forth your fortunes shall be reversed.'

Fearing the ghostly lady's words, he replaced the gold under the stone and hurried home. A short time later, he was beset with a fever and deteriorated. Before his death, he revealed his doings, but the location of the gold remains a mystery.

An exciting yarn, many would agree, and not without value. The story has a ring of Geoffrey Chaucer's *The Pardoner's Tale* about it – albeit without the murdering of accomplices. Alternative versions of the story tell of the ghost wandering the area until a man approached her. Some versions also claim that the apparition's fingers turned to claws and attacked him on returning for the second half of the gold. It was also only after the man confessed his greed that he perished.

For many years, Y Ladi Wen stories have been famous in Glamorgan. Some local historians believe they are related to the tradition that the river contains the spirits of those who died without disclosing the treasure's location. Strangely, a nearby inn had a reputation for travellers going missing and their bodies turning up in the river. Bones were reputedly discovered in the inn's cellar when it was demolished. 'Y Ladi Wen's Revenge' supposedly became the name for the death of any person close to disclosing the whereabouts of a treasure. It has also been claimed that their spirits would only find peace when the treasure was found and thrown into the water.

A similar story tells of a strange occurrence in nearby Ewenny, known as 'White Lady's Meadow'. Here, the lady in white is said to walk around, always pointing in the same direction. A man once offered his assistance, to which she asked him to take her hand. They walked on for a time before she disappeared.

Similar sightings of the lady have been noted within the castle. One interesting theory put forward is that her haunting is a Jacob Marley-style penance: perhaps that the treasure was stolen from innocent travellers who were murdered. Should this be the case, the real-life connection with *The Pardoner's Tale* would seem complete.

Oxwich

Much mystery surrounds the castle at Oxwich. An undeniably grand structure seated in a prominent position, it is caught in that grey area between an early castle and a converted comfortable coastal residence.

The fortress started life on a woody headland, most likely in the mid-1200s, presumably to guard Oxwich Bay. Though nothing has survived of its original formation, evidence for the early structure is apparent. Contemporary legal records confirm that this little stretch of paradise on the Gower had been the preserve of the de Penrees family – another of ancient Norman status – since the 1230s. A Swansea-originated charter from 1306 also speaks of 'the ancient knight's fees' at Oxwich, and confirms tenants in situ. An intriguing reference from 1459 speaks of a 'castrum de Oxenwych', which may also confirm the existence of something earlier than the current structure.

The building that welcomes today's visitors is somewhere between late Plantagenet and Tudor. Most aspects, such as the gateway, main hall, dovecote, and large tower at the south-east, were mainly created in the Tudor era at the behest of Sir Rhys Mansel – the same man who owned Old Beaupre. Based on its present condition, the building may have never been intended as more than a fortified manor, which would have reflected the tastes of the time. Nevertheless, when viewing the property, a castle feel pervades. When placed in the context of the references of 1230 and 1459, it seems likely something more defensively sound existed at one time.

Clues among the ruins may also point to at least one of the towers being earlier, albeit subject to change. Above the gateway, the Mansel family coat of arms still occupies pride of place along with those of the Penrices and Scurlages, from which Mansel claimed kin. The Penrices were almost certainly descendants of the de Penrees. Mansel ownership is unlikely to predate the mid-1400s, as the document from 1459 mentioned a Philip Mansel occupying the site. Prior to this, the de la Mere family owned the castle – either successors or an extension of the de Penrees. The Norman church of St Illtyd, located in the nearby woodlands, includes effigies that may be of a knight and lady, both de la Meres, who drowned in Oxwich Bay in the 1300s. Another possibility is they represent Sir John Penrees and Margaret Fleming, who held the manor in the fifteenth century.

On Rhys's death in 1559, his son, Edward, continued the work, notably the extravagant gateway. Including Sir Rhys and Edward's early work, Oxwich's development was regularly ongoing from 1520 to 1580, with Edward overseeing the so-called 'Great House'. Such extravagant works undoubtedly accelerated the estate's fall into bankruptcy. Evidence of Edward's financial problems can be found in the castle's later decline. By 1632 the family was already leasing it out to local farmers.

That the overly ambitious building work was solely responsible for the family's ruin is countered by other factors. Like much of the Welsh coast, Oxwich has a rich history of 'wrecking', which usually involved tricking a ship's crew into running aground. On 27 December 1557, more than a year before Sir Rhys's death, the family plundered a French ship, despite the salvage rights belonging to Sir George Herbert of Swansea – another whose family enjoyed prominent links with many a Welsh castle. In the aftermath, a fierce quarrel broke out. In her attempts to play peacemaker, Sir Rhys's daughter Anne was sadly hit on the head by a rock thrown by Herbert's servant and succumbed to her wounds less than a week later. Sir George was heavily fined yet somehow evaded payment, and the servant was let off. Though the Mansels were prominent salvage wreckers, Herbert's lack of payment proved of enormous consequence.

Due to its isolated location and lack of defensive capability, the castle was unused in the civil war. In the following century, parts of it collapsed due to insufficient care. Over the coming years, the South Range was rebuilt and used as a farmhouse well into the early 1900s. The castle was given to the state around 1950.

As a site synonymous with wrecking, it is perhaps unsurprising that the locality is steeped in legend. Local lore has long connected the church's well with the strange appearance of a ghostly white horse. In Welsh folklore, the creature – known as 'Ceffyl Dwr' in the native tongue – is a mythical water horse. Reputedly, the horse was once seen entering the well and disappearing.

A far greater mystery concerns the castle itself. When work was taking place in 1968, a solid gold brooch was discovered, dating from the first half of the fourteenth century. The find is a rare one and may relate to the area's wrecking past. Another suggestion is that it forms part of Edward II's treasure, which he allegedly hid before he was dethroned in 1327. The brooch now holds pride of place on display at the National Museum in Cardiff.

Oystermouth

Constructed on a hillside overlooking the Mumbles, the ruined walls of Oystermouth Castle are all that remain of one of the finest fortresses on the Gower Peninsula. Home of the Lords of Gower for many centuries, the pattern that set the castle's early history has much in common with its nearby contemporaries. Founded as a motte and bailey early in the twelfth century, the timber walls received an upgrade throughout Henry III's reign.

The man credited with the original work was the Norman warlord William de Londres – the same man in residence at nearby Ogmore. Construction of the primitive structure appears to tally with the Norman occupation of the Gower from 1106 onwards. What significance the castle had in the conflict with the Prince of Deheubarth in the following decade is unclear. The chroniclers recalled that William was forced to flee the mayhem, which saw Gruffudd ap Rhys raze the castle – see also Ogmore Castle. What happened next is difficult to discern. The castle appears to have been rebuilt or restructured when Norman authority was restored a short time later; however, this came to a premature end in 1137 – Gruffudd's final year. That any further rebuilding followed during the see-sawing of fortunes of the prince's sons and successors is unclear. The Londres family died out while John struggled to deal with his rebel barons and the tenacious Llywelyn ap Iorwerth.

By 1220 the early inroads of William Marshal, 2nd Earl of Pembroke – son of Henry III's great regent, William Marshal, 1st Earl of Pembroke – saw the Welsh lose the Gower. For a time, Henry III's government entrusted the barony to John de Braose, Lord of Bramber. At the time, the family had suffered on account of John's infamous grandfather, William, having fled to France to flee King John's wrath. A more welcome outcome for John de Braose was the successful inheritance of his family's lost honours, including the lordship of the Gower, whose influence spread well into the Marcher territories. Intent on rebuilding the family legacy, John concentrated his efforts on Oystermouth and nearby Swansea. An imposing curtain wall was erected around the inner buildings, including a three-storey residential suite and a private chapel. In December 1284, Henry III's son, Edward I, took up lodgings there, at which time the castle was the Braose's primary home.

As the years of carnage came to an end, so too did Oystermouth's importance. The lords of Gower appear to have relocated in the early years of Edward III, after which the castle fell into ruin. Seemingly unused in the civil war, a survey dated 1650 lamented Oystermouth as an 'old decayed castle, no use, but of a very pleasant situation'. As was typical of the 1700s, that pleasant situation didn't go unnoticed by contemporary artists. Nor was its potential for restoration missed by the Swansea antiquarian George Grant Francis in the early Victorian era. After many centuries of neglect by the Somersets – Dukes of Beaufort – the castle entered public ownership in 1927 and is now the responsibility of Swansea Council.

For the modern visitor, the castle's haunting exterior is just the prelude to a fascinating past. In recent years, the remains of pre-Reformation wall paintings have been uncovered in the chapel. In the natural illumination of daylight spilling in through the traceried windows, the body of at least one angel has been discerned. Local tradition tells that the chapel was the work of the castle's final de Braose owner. Not a lord, but a lady.

Discerning Alina de Braose's true history from legend is a frustrating task for any researcher. Daughter of the final de Braose lord of Gower, William, 2nd Baron Braose – himself captured as a child in the Second Barons' War – Alina went to great lengths to create a chapel of rare ostentation. Indeed, few in Britain compare with it. After inheriting the castle, she married John de Mowbray, ultimately leading to the castle's transfer into Mowbray hands.

The marriage, unquestionably, was a forced one. William's heir in the absence of any brothers, the wedding occurred when Alina was just seven years old and John twelve. De Mowbray had previously become William's ward in gratitude for his service to Edward I in Gascony and Flanders. Further complicating the situation was William's declining finances – depleted by his longstanding military campaigns – which forced him to sell the lordship of Gower to the controversial Hugh le Despenser. Worse still, Braose appears to have already promised the lordship to Humphrey VII de Bohun, 4th Earl of Hereford.

It was partly down to Hugh's persuasion of the king to intervene on their behalf that contributed to the Despenser War of 1321-22. In March 1322, John de Mowbray was captured fighting for Thomas, Earl of Lancaster at Boroughbridge and hanged at York. Alina, meanwhile, was relocated to the Tower of London, along with her eldest son John. Four years later, William died. Widowed and fatherless, Alina was forced to wait until Edward III's reign to secure her inheritance. She held the Gower with her second husband, Richard de Peschale until she died in 1331. At this point, her son, John, now 3rd Baron Mowbray, inherited the lordship.

What became of Alina is a mystery. No older than her late thirties on her death, it has long been speculated that she succumbed to an evil end. Local lore has long told that a woman of similar age in a trailing white dress has been seen haunting the castle. Stories describe her as a sombre, weeping lady. On closer inspection, her dress is found to be uncovered at the back and her naked skin is covered in bloodstains.

That Alina de Braose is the entity in question or whether the ghost concerns another wretched soul from the castle's past remains one of the castle's darker mysteries. The story is not without connection to one of Oystermouth's more disturbing features. Amidst the dreariness of the medieval dungeons, a weathered whipping post acts as a stark reminder of the punishment prisoners suffered. It is a sorrowful thought that the lady who worked so hard to develop a chapel with walls illustrating visions of heaven may herself have been the victim of a hellish torment within the castle's darkest pits.

Pennard

The Welsh coastline is famously awash with beautiful beaches. From Carmarthenshire at the nation's most southern point to west along the Gower Peninsula and north out of Pembrokeshire, one is unlikely to run out of places to enjoy a peaceful day enjoying the sights and sounds of the lapping tide.

Of the many, few places rival the beauty of the Three Cliffs Bay. Formed from centuries of coastal erosion, the bay, located close to the village of Pennard on the Gower, is a rare gem easily overlooked. Should one look out across the shore on a calm summer day, as the light begins to fade, it is not difficult to imagine something similar to what Charles Dickens journaled during a stay at Land's End. Though a clear day may offer a sight of the north Devon coast across the Bristol Channel, it is equally easy to feel that one is staring into eternity. And that a trip to the other side could be as easily equated with Avalon as Ilfracombe.

Perhaps to be expected of a coastal fortress, Pennard Castle is highly photogenic. Lying on a golf course's edge in an area where a stiff breeze across dunes can make one's eyes water, the isolated ruins are particularly exposed to the elements. Yet, as is so often true of the castles of Wales, the early allure is far from the whole story. Behind the pleasant veneer, the site is reportedly both haunted and cursed.

The castle's origins lie with Henry de Beaumont, 1st Earl of Warwick. A prominent nobleman who accompanied William the Conqueror on his Midlands campaign of 1068, Warwick established Pennard as one of his demesnes in the early twelfth century. Though little is known of the area's early history, a small settlement developed around the castle. Coupled with the natural protections of the limestone rocks that command the bay, the oval-shaped timber ringwork, ditch, and ramparts provided an effective defence against the warriors of Deheubarth. A long hall was also put up within the walls and a church outside them, around which a local community took shape. A rabbit warren has also been found, which would have been established to stock the locals with meat.

In either the late years of John's reign or early in Henry III's, the king had the original hall upgraded in stone, which served as the focal point of the castle's next phase of evolution. That stage occurred in the thirteenth and fourteenth centuries under the ownership of the de Braose dynasty. In keeping with most castles, other primitive features were replaced with stone. A new double half-circular towered gatehouse was put up at the entrance, from which a portcullis shut off the way to potential intruders. The palisades' removal saw the construction of a curtain wall, while a square tower was also erected on a spur on the west side, complementing a circular one to the north-west.

Despite the impressive progress, the castle ran into problems. An ongoing issue was sand blow. Past historians have speculated that William de Braose's work on Pennard was directly relevant to losing one of the family's earlier deer parks at Penmaen, where a timber castle may have once stood. As time passed, Pennard became untenable and was abandoned in the fifteenth century. A survey from 1650 lamented the site's 'desolate and ruinous' condition. A century later, the south wall was practically beyond salvation. By the turn of the nineteenth century, the damage had been compounded with cracks appearing in the gatehouse's southern tower.

Progressive dilapidation and sand blow would nevertheless whet the imagination of contemporary artists. The golf club attempted repairs; however, extensive costs prohibited a full-scale renovation, and in 1960 the remainder of the wall finally fell. What still stands of the iconic arch and front of the half-towers must count among the most unique of Wales's castle ruins. More survives of the square mural tower to the castle's west and rear, which connects what remains of the curtain wall.

Set in such an enchanting location, its walls depleted by time and the elements, it is no surprise several early fables abound. Among the most intriguing is that the castle was built in the space of a night by a sorcerer to protect himself from the Normans. On the back of a great victory in battle, a powerful chieftain – probably one of the de Braoses – won the hand of the Welsh ruler's daughter in marriage. In one version of the story, the maiden threw herself off Penrice Hill after avenging her lover.

Local lore also tells of strange lights in the valley below interrupting a celebratory feast. On catching up with the source of the lights, the chieftain was shocked to come face to face with a group of fairies – the verry folk. On being threatened by the mortals, the leader of the fairies retorted, 'Stop thy warring ways. Spears or swords cannot harm us. Cursed shall you and your castle be, for spoiling our innocent games'. At this time, the fairies vanished, the sky darkened, and the fortress became a ruin in the wink of an eye. Local legend also tells that the famed old hag of Welsh folklore – Gwrach-y-Rhibyn – curses anyone who dares stay the night within the walls.

St Donat's

Perched on a cliff overlooking the Bristol Channel, splendid St Donat's owes a debt of gratitude to the controversial US newspaper magnate William Randolph Hearst. After more than a century of neglect, Hearst's financial clout resurrected the castle from a dilapidated shell to the unique structure witnessed today.

Since its restoration, many visitors have graced its walls, including John F. Kennedy, Errol Flynn, Sir Winston Churchill, David Lloyd George, Douglas Fairbanks and Charlie Chaplin. Following a visit from the playwright George Bernard Shaw, the author playfully described it as 'what God would have built if he had had the money'. Home to the

United Worlds Colleges since the 1960s, and at times open to the public, the modern-day castle welcomes guests from all over the world to study in its magnificent surroundings and Grade I-listed gardens.

By contrast, St Donat's early history was a far murkier affair. Traditionally, it is placed as the home of the first-century Celtic chieftain Caradog, who spent time at Emperor Claudius's pleasure for resisting the Roman invasion. Archaeological evidence has confirmed that the site has been occupied since the Iron Age. In keeping with Glamorgan's more general history, the Norman encroachment into South Wales in the late eleventh century inspired a motte and bailey formation. A stone successor followed during the late twelfth century and became the residence of the de Hawey family. The keep, inner ward and other parts of the castle were already in place a century later when St Donat's passed to the Stradling family following Sir Peter Stradling's marriage to Joan de Hawey.

Local magistrates, landowners, sheriffs and Members of Parliament, the Stradlings' influence on the area was notable. Family tradition places their origin from the Le Esterlings, who came to England with William the Conqueror, but this was almost certainly a fabrication. Better evidence concerns their early years as Swiss adventurers who arrived in Wales in the late 1200s. Among their number, Sir Edward Stradling – one of nine of that name – fought for Henry V at Agincourt and was rewarded with the hand of Joan – or Jane – Beaufort, a great-granddaughter of Edward III. One of their sons, Henry, was later seized by pirates in the Bristol Channel and only released on receiving a substantial ransom of some 2,000 marks. He later died of a fever in Cyprus on his return from the Holy Land.

The family's dedication to the old faith would continue throughout the Tudor period. Consequently, Sir Thomas Stradling endured time in the Tower of London in 1561 in response to an accusation that he had used the image of a cross in the trunk of an ash tree – whose coming was miraculous – as an illustration of his faith. His son, also Edward, was chiefly responsible for establishing the library at St Donat's, which was considered the jewel in the crown of post-Dissolution intellectual Wales. According to the historian Graham Thomas, the Stradling tradition of educating their sons abroad led to many European works entering the library. It was Edward's writings that created the tale of the Stradling role in the Norman Invasion. His work also gave birth to the legend of the Twelve Knights of Glamorgan.

During the civil war, the stoutly Royalist Stradlings hosted the primate of Ireland, Archbishop James Ussher, when he was required to leave Cardiff. Three family members fought at the Battle of St Fagans in 1648, two of which were driven to exile after Charles I's execution. When the final Stradling heir died childless in 1738, the castle entered a period of decline. Towards the century's end, the great library was sold, and its contents scattered. By the early 1800s, only part of the castle was habitable.

More than fifty years passed before the castle's fortunes slowly began to improve. In 1852 – or 1862 – an alleged Stradling descendant, Dr John Whitlock Nicholl Carne, a magistrate, barrister, and landowner, purchased St Donat's and attempted to revive its fortunes. Better luck occurred on the watch of coal magnate Morgan Stuart Williams before its purchase by Hearst in 1925. Though Hearst's influence was priceless for St Donat's, it was not altogether welcomed, not least due to his acquisition and cannibalisation of parts of Bradenstoke Priory in Wiltshire and St Botolph's Church in Lincolnshire. Ironically, Hearst spent little time at St Donat's and was forced to sell the castle in 1937 on becoming insolvent. Thanks to its purchase by the French philanthropist Antonin Besse and subsequent donation to the Atlantic College, St Donat's future was assured. As such, its record as one of the oldest continuously inhabited castles in Wales remains ongoing.

As expected of the Stradlings' long influence, many of the castle's legends connect with that family. Stories of skirmishes with pirates, battles between the Normans and Welsh princes, victims of betrayal and deceit are merely the tip of the gigantic iceberg of tales that have been passed down. Because the castle fell into disrepair soon after the Stradlings died out, little remains from their time. However, the fortress may still play host to the spirits of at least one of their number.

Possibly the most persistent ghost associated with the castle is that of the final Stradling, Sir Thomas. Heir to the estate and a recent university graduate, Sir Thomas was an extravagant character. A lover of parties, fine wine, and fun, the twenty-eight-year-old chose to embark on a tour of Europe with college friend Sir John Tyrwhitt, whom he had known for many years. Curiously, before the friends departed, they made a pact that the survivor would inherit the other's estates should one of them die.

Barely a month passed before the strange agreement became necessary. After drinking together in Montpellier on 27 September 1738, Sir Thomas was provoked into a duel and killed by a gunshot to the eye.

Shortly after Sir Thomas's gruesome death, the handsome young man's body was brought back to the family home and laid out in the Picture Gallery. Sadly, the tragedy was not over. While his body lay in waiting, the wind blew a candle over, and the room became engulfed in flames. His remains and the family portraits burned to ash.

Although history recalls that Thomas was murdered, the exact circumstances remain unclear. After a lengthy legal battle, Tyrwhitt inherited the castle in 1755, as agreed in the pact. Tyrwhitt claimed that a Frenchman killed him, but other reports suggested Tyrwhitt was personally responsible. Regardless of the exact happenings, sources are consistent that Tyrwhitt successfully conned his friend out of his illustrious estate.

That Thomas died in 1738 has also been called into question. When the young man's body was returned to St Donat's, his nurse noted its unfamiliar appearance. Having acted as guardian for the boy throughout his youth, she knew only too well that Sir Thomas had lost the index finger of his left hand in childhood, but the body that was returned had five fingers on each hand. Is it possible that the body was not Sir Thomas at all? Following the fire, all evidence of the event has been lost. Thomas was reputedly seen on the Continent following the event. An indistinct gravestone with no name is reputed to lie in a graveyard somewhere in France, marked with the ancient family motto 'Without God – without anything'.

The circumstances of Sir Thomas's death may remain unknown, but his time at St Donat's is not forgotten. For many years, his presence reportedly haunted the castle. The family harpsichord was often heard playing even when the lid was closed and the room empty. The bedroom that was once his has hosted countless occupants since. A gigantic ball of light, capable of illuminating the chamber, was reputedly once seen there. Intriguingly, the light was said to resemble an eye. Thomas is not regarded as an evil spirit, but it is curious that something that appears to be an eye should appear in what was once his bedroom considering he was supposedly shot in the eye.

Thomas is not the only Stradling thought to haunt St Donat's. A woman – thought to be Thomas's mother – has also been witnessed at the castle. Mostly seen in the long gallery, her appearance is reputedly a bad omen as she apparently appeared shortly before the outbreak of the Second World War. Respected in life as a grand lady, frequently donning high heels and a long, elegant dress that trailed in her wake, she was supposedly murdered at the castle. As she was the last of the family line after her son's death, she was the only person separating Tyrwhitt from his dubiously gotten gains.

Perhaps unsurprisingly, many of the castle's alleged hauntings are associated with the Stradlings' demise. As recalled in the section on Caerphilly, there is an ancient Glamorgan legend of a hideously ugly, unkempt woman, Gwrach y Rhibyn, who is famed in Welsh folklore as a foreteller of death. Reported sightings of the wraith are frequently near a stream and often accompanied by a phantom hound. When approaching a house, she reputedly knocks on the dying person's window before calling out their name. According to legend, the hag was witnessed at the castle when Thomas died. During an exorcism there during Dr Carne's tenure, she appeared again, the apparent catalyst for a string of paranormal activity.

As recalled in the section on Caerphilly, the exact origins of the hag are unknown. According to a similar yet separate legend, she is not a banshee but the spectre of a once beautiful Norman princess. Recorded in Welsh mythology as Mallt-y-Nos, the hideous crone rides with Arawn, the legendary king of Annwn – the Celtic afterlife, also known as the Otherworld – who hunts for sorrowful souls to take back to his kingdom. A lover of hunting, she reportedly once said, 'If there was no hunting in heaven, then I'd rather not go!'

Supposedly it is not only humans who haunt the Stradlings' former home. A panther reputedly once stalked the halls and bedrooms. Past witnesses reported becoming overcome with great fear on experiencing its bright, mesmerising eyes. The sorrowful apparition of a priest has also been seen walking the corridors. Though his identity remains unclear, the ghost is consistent with the family's adherence to Catholicism.

Plagued by the ghosts of duped former owners, wild animals, and characters from Welsh mythology, it is no surprise that St Donat's has a reputation as one of the most haunted castles in Wales. On the night of the hag's last appearance in the Victorian era, St Donat's was exorcised. Since that time, many of the ghosts are said to be at peace. However, some reports continue centuries after their deaths.

Chapter 7

Monmouthshire

Caldicot

Other than the knowledge that the castle was constructed with a motte and two baileys before being rebuilt in stone in future years, Caldicot's early history remains something of a mystery. The area is mentioned in the *Domesday Book* but without mention of a castle. The structure was put down by the earls of Hereford either late in the eleventh century or early twelfth. The site is close to where Harold Godwinson had earlier established a Saxon burh and was probably chosen for that very reason.

Though William the Conqueror's 'Great Survey' did not mention every castle, it is likely that the area was still to evolve much beyond the sheriff of Gloucestershire's farmland, as was recorded. The sheriff at that time was Durand of Gloucester, whose nephew Walter – son of Durand's older brother Roger – later inherited those lands, in addition to his father's office. In time, Walter's eldest son, Miles de Gloucester, was granted the Earldom of Hereford and made Constable of England – a position Walter may have held. Which of those individuals was behind the castle's initial construction is unclear. Questions also remain over its exact form. Based on others nearby, it was likely timber-based until the Anarchy. Over the following three centuries, gradual enlargement culminated in one of the great castles of Wales.

For this reason alone, Caldicot's journey should be attributed to no one individual. On the deaths of Miles's five sons – seemingly without issue – Caldicot passed to his eldest daughter, Margaret, who married Humphrey II de Bohun. *Ipso facto*, Humphrey also inherited the Earldom of Hereford and the constableship of England. Under Humphrey's son, Humphrey III, Caldicot was upgraded with a stone keep and curtain walls, both of which are c.1170. The castle would remain a de Bohun property for eight generations and more than two centuries.

Replacing the de Bohuns was Thomas of Woodstock: the fifth and youngest surviving son of Edward III, and another to be immortalised by Shakespeare. Thomas gained the dukedom of Gloucester in 1385, nine years after his marriage to Eleanor de Bohun. In 1376, coincidentally the year of the death of his elder brother, Edward, the Black Prince, Caldicot was one of some seventy manors that Thomas inherited on marrying his de Bohun heiress. A year later, on Edward III's death, with the heir to the throne having already predeceased him, Thomas's importance increased dramatically.

Destined not to be the minor brother of a warrior king, Thomas now found himself uncle to a ten-year-old king who possessed little evidence of his father and grandfather's aptitude for warfare. So limited were Richard II's perceived abilities in kingship, and with Lionel of Antwerp also deceased, many responsibilities fell on Thomas. While regency rested primarily with his remaining elder brother, John of Gaunt, Duke of Lancaster, Thomas was granted the usual de Bohun role of Constable of England. As such, stays at Caldicott would be limited. In 1381, when his central estate at Pleshy Castle was partially destroyed in the Peasants' Revolt, he initiated several new buildings, including a gatehouse and drawbridge. A new tower containing private chambers was also named the Woodstock Tower in his honour.

Like many a future Shakespearean tragedy, relations between uncle and king were often far from familial. One of five 'Lords Appellant' who attempted to impeach the five key officials who formed the central pillar of Richard's government, the king deemed his uncle's actions as being in direct conflict with his right of kingship. In 1397 Thomas was kidnapped by Richard's agents and disappears from history. Evidence suggests he was smothered while imprisoned in Calais awaiting trial. Regardless of the exact truth, the coup did little for Richard's popularity. In 1399, Richard was the subject of rebellion by Henry Bolingbroke, the eldest son of the late John of Gaunt, whose inheritance the king had previously deprived. As usual in matters of possible treason, the Crown confiscated Gloucester's property.

Bolingbroke's rebellion successfully ended Richard's reign. As fate decreed, Bolingbroke – now Henry IV – was a widower for his coronation due to the death of his wife, Mary de Bohun, in 1394. Nevertheless, she had lived long enough to give birth to Prince Hal at Monmouth Castle. Twenty years after Mary's death, a division of the de Bohun estates followed the death of Mary's mother, Joan – Mary's sister Eleanor had also passed. Caldicot passed to Henry V and became part of the Duchy of Lancaster. Hal's widow, Catherine of Valois, later held it before it entered the stewardship of the Herbert family and later the Somersets (see also Raglan Castle).

As the castle's importance faltered, neglect inevitably ensued. In 1885 it became the property of J. R. (Joseph Richard) Cobb, whose family continued significant restoration. What was regarded as little more than a farmyard two centuries earlier became a fine Victorian home. As part of the early twentieth-century revamp by Geoffrey Wheatley Cobb, several of Caldicot's rooms were decorated with memorabilia salvaged from Horatio Nelson's first flagship *HMS Foudroyant*, which Cobb himself had previously acquired. The castle remained in the family's hands until Chepstow Rural District Council bought it in 1964. It opened to the public a year later.

Today, the well-restored Victorian home and museum retain much of its medieval charm. The imposing double-fronted gatehouse survives from the days of Thomas of Woodstock. The same is true of some of the towers and the keep. Re-enactments of past events are known to draw the crowds, yet, according to local lore, it is not just actors that bring the past to life. Much ghostly activity has been reported both in and around the walls. The ghosts of monks in brown habits have been spotted, and mysterious chanting has been heard. A wandering beggar boy has been seen throughout the castle; speculation abounds that he is also responsible for previous accounts of poltergeist activity. The hub of that activity appears to be the banqueting hall in the main gatehouse, where moving furniture and mysterious shadows have been noted. Cold spots and bizarre sounds have also been reported.

While no stories exist of Thomas, Duke of Gloucester or any of his male de Bohun predecessors, local lore has long told that his wife returns to her former home. Eleanor's ghost, appearing in a grey dress, has been seen and felt throughout the castle before vanishing without a trace.

Caerleon

It is doubtful that any settlement in Great Britain and Ireland is of greater archaeological importance than Caerleon. The Romans built a legionary fortress – or *castra* – around 75AD, which served as the imperial legion

Legio II Augusta's headquarters until the fourth century. From this the city earned its name: translated from Welsh as 'City of Legions'.

It isn't easy for the modern visitor to imagine Caerleon before the Romans, yet the area was of some importance even before that time. The site had started life as a hillfort in the Iron Age. The name Isca is derived from the nearby River Usk, and though the original fort has long ceased to exist, Roman remains can still be found in the vicinity. The condition of the baths is excellent. Indeed, it is unlikely one will find any better visitor attraction of the type in the UK. Close by, parts of the old barracks are still visible, along with a recently discovered harbour. The Saxon chronicler Gildas – a source for the venerable Bede – noted that the city was the setting of the third-century martyrdom of Julius and Aaron: along with St Alban, the only Christian saints named during the Roman occupation. Based on the evidence discovered, a presence at Caerleon remained in place until the late 300s.

Among the Roman remains at Caerleon, few are more impressive than the amphitheatre. Reminiscent of Rome's famous Coliseum, albeit on a far smaller scale, its condition is excellent and worth the visit to the town alone. There is good evidence that the arena formed a large part of the city's identity and remained of great fascination well into the Norman period. Particularly intriguing are links with King Arthur. The Welsh cleric and historian Geoffrey of Monmouth believed Caerleon was the site of the mythical Camelot. The amphitheatre has also been proposed as the scene of the legendary round table.

In keeping with other Roman settlements in Wales, the colonisers' departure left a vacuum that would not be filled for another six centuries. Between the Romans' going and the coming of the Normans, the only construction of note appears to have been the church of St Cadoc, built on the site of the legionnaires' HQ in the sixth century. Joining the church beyond the eastern corner of the old fort would have been a timber motte and bailey. The *Domesday Book* cites a small colony of eight caracutes of land – a unit of land that eight oxen could plough in a single season – within the lordship of Gwynllwg. Due to its relatively early date, the hypothesis has been put forward that the castle, though Norman in style, was put down by the Welsh lord Caradog ap Gruffydd. If so, his tenure did not last. By the 1086 survey, the lordship was held by Turstin FitzRolf, who some believe the *Bayeux Tapestry* depicts as William the Conqueror's standard-bearer at Hastings.

The exact fate of the castle and town during this period is sadly lost. While one cannot discount the possibility that the area remained a Welsh stronghold, it was almost certainly plagued by violence. Such patterns continued until the reign of Henry II, at which time it became a borough. The castle was presumably in English hands in 1171, when Iorwerth ab Owain and his sons sacked the town and castle. In 1217, William Marshal, 1st Earl of Pembroke, conquered both castle and borough from Morgan ap Hywel, the lord of Gwynllwg, following which the castle was rebuilt in stone. Many of the original Roman buildings were likely stripped of their raw materials and used in the rebuilding.

For the next two centuries, Caerleon appears to have enjoyed a far more peaceful existence. Conquered by the English, it faced no conflict during the wars of Edward I. Those previous campaigns, however, made the town and castle a target of siege during the Welsh revolts of the early 1400s. Rhys Gethin, a general to Owain Glyndŵr, successfully took Caerleon in 1402, along with Newport, Cardiff, Llandaff, Caerphilly, Usk and Abergavenny. Though the castle was returned, it is unclear whether it was restored. Either way, it is unlikely to have been used again. The antiquarian John Leland recorded its standing in 1537, albeit in poor condition. The fact that the Royalists created two forts nearby at Penrhos Farm during the civil war indicates the castle was unfit for purpose. Cromwell also camped at Christchurch Hill on his way to sacking Newport.

A lack of renovation saw the castle's walls finally crumble in 1739, seemingly through exposure to the elements. The one exception is the Round Tower of 1219, which forms part of the Hanbury Arms. The tower's exact purpose is unclear. Most likely, it formed part of the outer bailey. It is a nice epilogue to the castle's story that the Hanbury Arms was a beloved haunt of the Victorian poet laureate Alfred Lord Tennyson. It was there, in 1856, that he enjoyed a drink while working on his acclaimed *Idylls of the King*. And so, a site whose origins may have stemmed from the legendary Arthur has perhaps come full circle with one of Arthurian literature's greatest writers.

Chepstow

Chepstow Castle is a genuinely fine-looking Welsh castle. More beautiful than strong – a trait it shares with Bodiam in Sussex – the castle enjoys the natural defences of being sited on a narrow ridge between a limestone cliff and a wide valley. A view from the opposite bank of the Wye is undoubtedly the best way to enjoy the quadruple bailey layout's immense size. Such has been enjoyed by the English over the centuries.

In keeping with its number of baileys, four key phases define the castle's construction. William the Conqueror's decision to erect the castle on the Welsh side of the old border as early as 1067 confirms the region's importance to England's new king. Sited at a critical crossing of the River Wye, close to Monmouth, Hereford and Gloucester, the new fortress served many important strategic purposes, notably control of the port and the bridge.

Whether the castle was created on the site of something older is now impossible to ascertain. Early construction was the preserve of William's chief supporter, William FitzOsbern, probably late 1067, and appears to have been in stone from the start. The Conqueror's death may predate the Great Tower, which certainly stood in the first decade of his son and successor, William Rufus.

As was standard in Norman military architecture, a large part of the tower's purpose was psychological. Standing on its massive stone plinth, so close to Rhys ap Tewdwr's domain, the tower's height fitted well with the Norman tendency to display outer strength. A band of orange Roman tiles, relocated from Caerwent, circle the outskirts. Further construction of the castle, then known as Striguil – most likely derived from *ystraigyl*, the Welsh for river bend – also set the foundations for the market town and priory to develop alongside it. By the late fourteenth century, the lordship of Striguil had been succeeded by modern Chepstow, which remains today.

Throughout this time, work on the castle continued steadily. A key overseer of construction was the 'greatest knight', William Marshal, 1st Earl of Pembroke, who inherited the lordship of Striguil on marrying Isabel de Clare – Strongbow's daughter, see Pembroke Castle. Throughout Richard the Lionheart's reign, Marshal improved and modernised the castle, building on his experience in France and the crusades.

Key among his additions was the twin-towered gatehouse, quite possibly the earliest in Britain. Also established on his watch were the towers of the middle bailey, and the south-west tower, named in his honour, which included a private chamber. He also upgraded the upper bailey. On William's death in 1219, his sons erected the upper barbican and made improvements to the original Great Tower – notably an additional storey to the gallery with fine windows offering outstanding views of the river. Progress came to a halt when the male line died out in 1245.

The longevity of the female line, however, would be of significant consequence. In 1270 the beneficiary was Roger Bigod, 5th Earl of Norfolk, great-grandson of Marshal through his daughter Maud. During Bigod's time, a series of residential buildings were erected in the lower bailey. Other additions included a castellated wall walk and the widening of the Great Tower's floor. He was also responsible for the town's 'port wall' c.1274-78, which was in place for Edward I's visit in 1284. A short time later, work began on the Marten's Tower, which included apartments for distinguished guests. Further work was also undertaken on the top storey of the Great Tower. Perhaps Bigod's greatest legacy was the sumptuous apartments – La Gloriette – on the cliff edge that allow outstanding views of both castle and the surrounding gorge.

When the wars with Wales came to an end, so too did Chepstow's importance. In 1312 the castle passed to Thomas de Brotherton, Earl of Norfolk, following the impoverished Bigod's death without issue. On Thomas's death, it was inherited by his daughter, Margaret. Though garrisoned for the rebellions of the early 1400s, Owain Glyndŵr's forces avoided the area. In 1468 large swathes of the Norfolk estates were granted to William Herbert, Earl of Pembroke, in exchange for lands in the east of England. Succeeding Pembroke was Sir Charles Somerset, the future Earl of Worcester, who undertook large-scale renovation on acquiring the castle in 1508. In keeping with many castles still in residence, Chepstow's future lay more as a family home than a defensive structure. The Welsh Marches' declining importance, which had begun in 1282, was enforced by a series of laws promulgated by Henry VIII in 1535 and 1542.

Matters changed, however, with the coming of the civil war. Located in Monmouthshire, a home of staunch Royalists, yet on the border of Parliamentarian Gloucestershire, the scene was set for the castle's return to military service. When it was besieged in 1645, the old walls stood firm until the second test in 1648 proved fatal. On 25 May 1648, Roundhead forces took the castle and killed the commander, Sir Nicholas Kemeys. In 1935, a memorial was erected in tribute to his steadfast refusal to surrender.

In keeping with many Parliamentarian-gained castles, Chepstow was Roundhead garrisoned and doubled up as a political prison until the end of the war. Among the prisoners was the famed author and Bishop Jeremy Taylor, and, after the Restoration, regicide Henry Marten, who died at the castle in 1680. Before this, in 1662, the castle's south side was strengthened to withstand cannon fire.

Two years after Marten's death, the castle passed to the Duke of Beaufort, who disbanded the garrison by 1688. Though it avoided the usual slighting, parts of the buildings were dismantled, and others tenanted out or left to rot. Some areas of the land were used for farming or reused as a glass factory. Typical of the time, the ruins became the fascination of many contemporary artists, including Turner. Such was the area's natural beauty, the 'Wye Tour' became a fashionable exercise and a credible alternative to the European tour. As tourism surged, the advent of day trips on steamships from Bristol became all the rage. Not for the first time, the castle's purpose changed again, this time for local fêtes and horticultural shows.

In the twentieth century, Chepstow Castle became the centre of renewed fascination. *Ivanhoe* was filmed there in 1913, and a year later, a successful businessman named William Royse Lysaght acquired the castle from the Beauforts. For four decades, his family engaged in conservation work before handing it to the state. Over the years, more television and filming followed, including an episode of *Dr Who*. It has also been used for large events and even recording part of a heavy metal album.

A castle whose history dates to the early Normans, it is no surprise that Chepstow has its own share of tall tales. One of the most maverick concerns a series of archaeological excavations made around 1910 under Dr Orville Ward Owen's well-publicised leadership. Owen believed that the castle was the hiding place of the lost Shakespeare folios, which he thought had been the work of Sir Francis Bacon.

One of the few surprises is that the castle is host to so few unexplained happenings. A rare exception includes a bizarre story concerning the gift shop. At one time, a grand chess set was kept on display in a glass case. Despite being locked, staff were frequently disturbed to find pieces moved of their own accord. The custodian once placed a hair follicle in the doorway and scattered talcum powder to reveal whatever was responsible. Nothing was disturbed, but the pieces still moved. The process continued until the set was sold. What was behind the strange moves remains a mystery.

The Three Castles of Gwent: Grosmont, Skenfrith and Whitecastle

Overlooking the villages of Grosmont, Skenfrith and Llantilio Crossenny in the Monnow Valley, this enigmatic trio made up a vital medieval lordship.

Like most Marcher castles, Grosmont, Skenfrith and Whitecastle were founded in the immediate years following the Norman Conquest. They were initially primitive earthwork fortifications protected by a timber palisade and ditch and presumably erected to guard the trade route across the border to Hereford. The beneficiary was undoubtedly William FitzOsbern, Earl of Hereford, who put up several motte and baileys following William the Conqueror's subjugation of the south. However, the family connection was cut short due to the rebellion of FitzOsbern's son, Roger de Breteuil, in 1075, which led to the confiscation of the earl's family holdings.

The castles' first date with destiny occurred in 1135 when news of Stephen of Blois's accession saw a revolt break out in the Welsh Marches. Throughout the early twelfth century, Grosmont had been the preserve of the Norman Pain FitzJohn, one of Henry I's so-called 'new men'. After FitzJohn died in 1137, the king amalgamated Grosmont and the neighbouring Skenfrith and Whitecastle to form the lordship of the 'three castles' of Gwent. The move turned out to be one of Stephen's better ones, as this trinity proved of notable importance to Welsh relations. Records from 1183-86 show that Henry II ordered £15 be spent on Grosmont and £128 on Whitecastle. Such transactions, and the work that followed, were carried out by Ralph of Grosmont, a royal official, whose responsibilities extended to nearby Hereford.

Under Ralph's supervision, Skenfrith was largely upgraded in stone on the banks of the Monnow at the cost of just under £44. By 1201 all three were well equipped to withstand attack. That year, King John placed the lordship on the shoulders of a talented clerk named Hubert de Burgh. Hubert had previously served as John's chamberlain while the prince was still Count of Mortain. Hubert's early potential was realised with his appointment as justiciar after events at Runnymede. Following John's death in 1216, Hubert remained at the highest echelons of English government throughout Henry III's minority.

Such was the lack of political stability between 1201 and his death in 1243, Hubert was stripped of the lordship three times. On the first occasion, following his capture in France in 1205, the beneficiary was the powerful William de Braose. Fortunately for Hubert, William's good relations with John lasted less than two years, leading to the castles' return to the Crown. When released from his foreign imprisonment, Hubert worked hard to regain his lost status. John appointed him Seneschal of Poitou before making him justiciar. He finally regained the lordship of Gwent in January 1219 as justiciar to Henry III.

It was at Hubert's behest that the three castles underwent significant rebuilding. After flattening the previous structure at Skenfrith, a new polygonal stonewall with round towers was erected to surround a circular keep. The structure is low lying due to the flattening of the mount. At Grosmont, the stone hall from Hubert's initial tenure was retained and complemented with a curtain wall, a gatehouse, and three mural towers.

All was in place by November 1233 when Henry III, at the head of the royal army, camped at Grosmont. By this time, Hubert had been relieved of his positions, and Henry was seeking to defeat a unique alliance between Llywelyn ap Iorwerth and Richard Marshal, 3rd Earl of Pembroke. On 11 November, Marshal caught Henry's charges off guard and forced them into a hurried escape. When the Marshal War ended the following year, negotiations took place between Hubert and the king under the mediation of the Archbishop of Canterbury, Edmund of Abingdon. Though Hubert never returned to high office, he was once again granted the lordship of Gwent until 1239. For the next fifteen years, care of the castles was the preserve of previous governor Walerund Teutonicus, a German soldier who did himself much credit in the First Barons' War.

It was likely during Walerund's tenure that some of Hubert's work was completed, including an unfinished chamber and a new chapel at Grosmont. At Skenfrith, a chapel and a new roof for the keep were put in. A new hall, buttery and pantry were also established at Whitecastle in 1244. Around this time, Whitecastle was also extensively rebuilt, including new stone curtain walls, four mural towers, a new gatehouse, and the demolition of the original keep. The exact date of the work is unclear and may have followed Hubert and Walerund. Historian Paul Remfry described the result as 'a masterpiece of military engineering'.

Walerund's tenure ended in 1254, most likely the year of his death. On the castles' return to royal ownership, Henry granted the lordship to his eldest son, the future Edward I, as part of a grander plan to keep Llywelyn ap Gruffudd in check. In 1267 the trio passed to the king's second son, Edmund 'Crouchback', Earl of Lancaster, after which it remained part of the Lancaster estate. Grosmont was the likely birthplace of Henry of Grosmont, who Edward III awarded the Dukedom of Lancaster in 1351 as a reward for his exploits in the Hundred Years' War.

It was likely on the duke's watch – if not he, then his father, Henry, Earl of Lancaster – that most of the final additions were made to the castles. The original two-storey rectangular gatehouse at Grosmont was reinforced with a buttressed drawbridge pit. The south-west and west towers were also revamped into multi-storey suites. The north block, from which an octagonal chimney still rises, was erected over the old postern and provided comfortable residence. Today, one can only imagine the sight of the impressive additions set among the beauty of an expansive deer park.

Like many Marcher fortresses, Edward I's conquest of Wales saw a redundancy in the three castles' purpose. This was temporarily reversed in March 1405 when Gruffudd, a son of Owain Glyndŵr, battered the outer walls. The scene had been set the previous year when an English party led by Richard Beauchamp, Earl of Warwick defeated the Welsh close to Grosmont.

Despite a staunch resistance, the castles' lack of purpose saw them fall into ruin by the Tudor era. A survey from 1563 lamented the collapse of Grosmont's bridge and the terrible condition of the interior. In 1613 a further survey described all three as 'ruynous and decayed'. The castles remained in the Duchy of Lancaster's hands until 1825 when they were sold to Henry Somerset, 6th Duke of Beaufort. Three generations later, in 1902, the 9th duke, another Henry, relinquished them to the local historian and soldier Sir Joseph Bradney, whose *A History of Monmouthshire* remains celebrated. In 1922 Grosmont and Whitecastle were taken over by the state, and Skenfrith followed in 1936.

Located in a relatively quiet part of Wales, the three castles of Gwent rarely pay host to the numbers of visitors welcomed by the citadels of Gwynedd. On the other hand, being close to Offa's Dyke, they have found a following among hikers. A well-signposted twenty-mile walk now connects the trio and is a perfect way of seeing them without the hassle of finding a parking space (something this author found tricky in the hilly village of Grosmont).

The challenge, however, was well worth it. In Whitecastle, the treat of a white-walled stone castle surrounded by a compact moat is an idyllic image. At Grosmont, the first sight of the well-preserved walls as one emerges from the path that connects the castle from the narrow high street is almost like something from a fairy tale. Of the three, the riverside fortress of Skenfrith is very visitor friendly. The moat may have been reclaimed by nature, and the walls are subject to occasional flooding, but the reward is also worth the effort.

What is responsible for the alleged hauntings that plague the castles, especially Skenfrith, remains unclear. All this author could find was a vague reputation at the latter. Regardless of the truth behind any local legends, something extraordinary can still be found in the Monnow Valley. For the true castle enthusiast, the lack of tourists only adds to the beauty. On visiting Grosmont, I was privileged to be completely alone. The November weather was typically wet, and under overcast skies the walls seemed to merge with the horizon. I experienced nothing out of the ordinary during my solitude, though that is not to say that the atmosphere didn't prompt occasional anxiety. The piercing wind through unseen holes frequently serves as an awkward backdrop to careful footsteps across puddled floors. Even on a dry day, the crackling of falling masonry or crunching of loose debris beneath heavy hiking boots only adds to the feeling of loneliness as one wanders throughout deserted chambers.

Nevertheless, on this occasion, it was difficult to escape the feeling that I was blessed by an experience particularly rare in the modern day. On taking the one remaining ruined stairway up the south-west tower, the views of the outside world from the walkway between the south-west and west towers were pleasantly unspoiled. Should one be granted the opportunity to visit any of these castles – preferably all three – in a quiet spell, the reward might be more memorable than one could have ever predicted.

The survival of the great castles of Wales is a genuine blessing for many reasons, yet it is also with a tinge of sadness that some have become tainted by modern surroundings. The large car park across Caernarfon Bay may now be as necessary as the modern ticket offices and surveillance equipment; however, in the trinity of Gwent, one can experience something far more rudimentary. The greatest gift a castle can offer us is a window into the way things were. A reminder of our ancestors' past! The spirits who inhabited them may have moved on, but to walk in their unspoilt surroundings is a rare experience. For this author, that marks out Grosmont as a real hidden jewel in Monmouthshire's modest yet fabulous crown. A place where one can share the land as it had been: if only briefly.

Monmouth

Just a few walls remain of the once-mighty Monmouth Castle. Begun as a timber ringwork fortress within three years of the Battle of Hastings, construction was placed on the shoulders of William's chief ally, William FitzOsbern – the same man responsible for nearby Chepstow. Further to standing guard over the Monnow and Wye rivers, the early fortress proved a valuable border castle throughout its first century. Even after FitzOsbern's death, the two castles remained on similar paths. The addition of stonework followed during the Anarchy, with the tower bearing a remarkable resemblance to Chepstow.

In 1233, the fortress witnessed one of the most bizarre nights in any castle's history. Throughout the autumn, parts of England and Wales were embroiled in a strange domestic conflict, dubbed 'The Marshal War'. Richard Marshal, 3rd Earl of Pembroke, the second son of Henry III's great regent, William Marshal, 1st Earl of Pembroke, found himself at the head of a rebellion after a series of disputes with the king's chief advisor, Peter des Roches, Bishop of Winchester. On 25 November, the feast of St Catherine, Marshal attempted to pass the town of Monmouth and its royal fortress with a small band of men at arms. When attacked by the Royalist troops, Marshal somehow defended himself against a dozen men in a scene worthy of his gallant father. Some sources suggest that Richard took possession of Monmouth Castle before razing much of the surrounding area over the following month.

Whatever damage, if any, Marshal brought upon the castle was probably soon repaired. Later that century, the castle was held by Simon de Montfort, 6th Earl of Leicester, before being granted to the king's second son, Edmund 'Crouchback', Earl of Lancaster. Chief among his developments was the main hall, which served as his quarters. Improvements continued under his grandson, Henry of Grosmont, elevated by distant cousin Edward III to 1st Duke of Lancaster. Outside the castle, the town's increase in prominence saw the erection of town walls and a fortified bridge over the Monnow. The bridge exists to this day and is a notable feature of the modern town.

Before Grosmont revamped it, the castle was viewed less fondly by at least one other royal. On being defeated by Roger Mortimer, 1st Earl of March, Edward II was briefly imprisoned at Monmouth before being relocated to Berkeley Castle, where he disappeared from history. A far warmer relationship was enjoyed between the castle and Edward's descendant, Henry IV. In 1386 Henry's wife, Mary de Bohun, gave birth to Henry V within the walls. A statue of King Hal still holds pride of place high on the outer wall of nearby Shire Hall. After avoiding any involvement in the Welsh rebellions of the early 1400s, the castle's defensive capabilities gradually diminished. Reallocation of the outer bailey as a marketplace – now Agincourt Square – saw the site more closely integrated with the town. The Courts of Assize became located in the Great Hall in the Tudor era.

All changed, however, with the arrival of the English Civil War. The castle was initially garrisoned by Royalist troops, then fell and was regained in 1644, only to fall again to the Roundheads in 1645. The following year Cromwell ordered its slighting, and in March 1647, the round tower was obliterated. An usher named More Pye of the local Monmouth School recorded in his diary that the building fell around midday while they were engaged at sermon. In 1673, Henry Somerset, 1st Duke of Beaufort, erected the Great Castle House on the site. This 'house of splendid swagger', in which the Castle and Regimental Museum now exists, was briefly the home of the Assize Court after the castle's slighting before it was relocated to Shire Hall in 1725. While the house thrived, the castle did not.

For the modern-day visitor, the site is disappointingly sparse. Indeed, only one section has survived. Complementary to the museum, the Royal Monmouthshire Royal Engineers Militia have used the site as their HQ since 1875. It is a strange irony that the castle is, officially, one of a rare selection in continuous use. And though the museum and army HQ may be a far cry from the usual Cadw site, Monmouth is a castle whose walls tell a story. During the late 1700s, the English cleric and artist William Gilpin passed the castle by boat as part of his Wye Tour. Among his notes, he lamented the 'ludicrous [...] transmutations of time,' as the site, 'formerly the palace of a king, and birth-place of a mighty prince,' had since been 'converted into a yard for fatting ducks'.

Newport

Local tradition places a motte and bailey *Castell Newyd ar Uysc* – translating as 'the new castle on the Usk' – to around 1075 at Stow Hill, approximately half a mile from the present site. Though a plausible hypothesis, the foundations of any such structure are still to be unearthed. More credible is the work of James Matthew, author of the 1910 publication *Historic Newport,* who noted no mention of the castle before 1126. That this was the year of the castle's construction is unclear.

A garrison is recorded as having been set up by William Fitz Robert, Earl of Gloucester in 1171, the year before it was razed by Iorwerth ab Owain Gwynedd, father of Llywelyn ap Iorwerth. The *Brut chronicle* also states that Henry II visited the castle in 1172, presumably before its destruction. In 1185, four years before the king's death, Henry allocated approximately £6 for repairs, which may suggest that the work was not overly crucial or that the castle was not highly regarded.

Little more is found until 1249, when Henry II's grandson, Henry III, carried out upgrades. During the Second Barons' War, the fortress was defended by Simon de Montfort until Prince Edward – later Edward I – escaped captivity enforced on him since the Royalist defeat at Lewes in May 1264. Thirty years later, Edward ordered repairs be carried out, which may have been ongoing when his son, Edward II, granted the castle to his favourite, Hugh le Despenser, 1st Earl of Winchester. Two years later, in 1322, Roger Mortimer razed it as a personal attack on the 'pharisee' Despenser, but not before relieving him of its furnishings. Some 300 trees were used in the rebuild between 1326 and 1386, at the behest of either Despenser's successor, Hugh de Audley, 1st Earl of Gloucester, or his son-in-law, Ralph, Earl of Stafford. By that time, the town had become the centre of the lordship of Wentlooge.

The new castle first appeared in 1405 in the aftermath of its sacking in 1402 by Owain Glyndŵr. Thirty years on, the lord of Newport, Humphrey Stafford, later 1st Duke of Buckingham, oversaw a second rebuild. Much of that work was completed in 1460 when Sir Owen Tudor – second husband of Henry V's widow, Catherine of Valois, and founder of the Tudor dynasty – spent time incarcerated within the walls. Owen's second son, Jasper Tudor, Duke of Bedford, briefly followed in his father's footsteps, albeit more voluntarily.

While one must give Humphrey Stafford credit for much of the castle's developments, the opposite is true of the 3rd duke for its decline. Son of Henry Stafford, the 2nd duke, and great-grandson of the industrious 1st duke, Edward Stafford lost favour with Henry VIII and was beheaded for treason in May 1521. As was usual in such matters, his property was requisitioned by an act of attainder. Due to the lack of upkeep, Edward VI decided to part with the castle and granted the lease to William Herbert in 1548. A century later, his descendant, Colonel Henry Herbert, established a small garrison of fifty troops there. Despite surviving until 1648, Cromwell's Roundheads eventually cracked the walls.

Whether any detailed restoration occurred in the aftermath is unclear. In 1743 the castle was recorded as being a ruin. Under the Morgan family, the inner site found a new purpose in the Victorian era as a tannery and, later, a brewery. In 1883, when the inner ward remained the preserve of the brewery, a fire destroyed much of the interior. Among the losses were the traceried windows, which were most likely of Tudor origin.

Before the century was over, the castle changed hands again. At some point before 1950, the then-owner, Lord Tredegar, entrusted it to the Office of Works. Sadly, a combination of a nearby ring road from the 1970s, the closure of a public footpath and the permanent fencing rendered the castle off-limits for a decade. Due to recent developments, the romanticised views that inspired Turner in 1796 are unlikely to be repeated.

Closed, fenced off and isolated, Newport is just the type of structure one might expect to be haunted. Local lore has long connected the castle with the spirit of its Fitzhamon founder. Reputedly a giant of a man, Robert Fitzhamon's ghost has reportedly been seen wandering the ruins. While some may argue that a ghostly giant's roaming could be deemed a safety concern, the more significant threat undoubtedly comes from health and safety laws. Until such aspects are addressed, one could easily argue that a poem penned in 1911 by W.H. Davies sums up the castle's time: 'Days that have been'.

Raglan

Nestled among the Monmouthshire hills, magnificent Raglan remains a genuine jewel in Wales's crown.

Many questions remain unanswered regarding the castle's beginnings. On conquering the locality in the late eleventh century, the area surrounding the modern village became the preserve of the earl of Hereford, William FitzOsbern. It has long been speculated that William put down a motte and bailey on the present site. Despite some archaeological evidence, nothing definitive has been found about what existed or when and how it was built. Records from the next century prove that the Bloet family held the manor until the reign of Richard II. Though it is unlikely that the manor or early motte and bailey was anything out of the ordinary, its situation, set in the heart of the parkland in which herds of deer grazed, was undoubtedly stunning.

On firmer ground are documented recordings of the modern castle. Begun in 1432 under Sir William ap Thomas, the fortress was constructed in stone from the start. Records confirm that William had previously been a tenant before parting with 1,000 marks to purchase it outright. How Sir William afforded the enterprise is itself a subject of some intrigue. The lesser son of a minor lord, William profited greatly from holding local offices. Good fortune followed with two marriages to wealthy heiresses. The second of whom, Gwladus ferch Dafydd Gam, enjoyed much local influence as the daughter of the prominent Welsh warrior Dafydd Gam.

Such tales of rags to riches compare favourably with many English and Welsh active in the Hundred Years' War. Similarly, the early story of Raglan has more than a passing comparison with Bodiam and Herstmonceux: a castle built for splendour as much as defence. Raglan's story is ironic for many reasons. Though by no means the largest in Wales, it was the largest built by a man of Welsh birth. The design was unusual, not least as the keep was located outside the main walls. The great tower, which still dominates much of the site, remains a contemporary illustration of William's wealth and power. The same is true of the south gate, which once had a moat and drawbridge before a double portcullis and three imposing double doors. An array of gun loops in the walls complemented the projecting arches or machicolations, from which large rocks or burning objects would be dropped. The grand stairway –

restored in 2011 – leading up to apartments set around the Fountain Court was Herbert's work.

Raglan's rise continued under Sir William's son, another William. Unlike his father, the younger man went by the English surname Herbert instead of the usual Welsh ap and the father's name. A fighter in the Hundred Years' War and a supporter of the Yorkists in the Rose Wars, he profited greatly from his enemies' spoils and the wine trade with Gascony (until 1450, Gascony was still an English domain). On being made Earl of Pembroke – ironically, he was the first of Welsh birth to be awarded an earldom – he was regarded, in certain circles, as a chosen one or 'national deliverer': the man capable of completing the efforts of the Princes of Gwynedd and bringing in a new age of Welsh independence.

Unrequited though William's ambitions were on the matter of Welsh independence, his status skyrocketed. The family's rise is no better illustrated than by the wedding of his son and namesake, the second earl, to Mary Wydville, sister of Elizabeth Wydville – queen to Edward IV. It was also the first earl who, on seizing Pembroke Castle in 1461, discovered the four-year-old Henry Tudor inside. On being made Herbert's ward, Tudor spent the next few years at Raglan as somewhere between a distinguished guest and prisoner. Had Herbert got his way, Tudor may have married his daughter Maude.

Despite the marriage setback, throughout the 1460s, he used his wealth to expand and furnish Raglan on an otherwise unparalleled scale. The polygonal towers – which many have speculated were inspired by Caernarfon's – date from his tenure. Complementary to the development of the deer parks, the grounds were rich with orchards, rabbit warrens and fishponds. The bard Dafydd Llwyd remarked later that century of the castle's 'hundred rooms filled with festive fare, its hundred towers, parlours and doors, its hundred heaped-up fires of long dried fuel, its hundred chimneys for men of high degree.' While some past historians have rightly remarked that the castle has more in common with an Oxbridge college than a Norman citadel, coupled with the late date, one could easily make the case Raglan was the last proper castle to be built in England or Wales.

Herbert's lot, alas, ended in disgrace. Earlier denounced by Clarence and Warwick the Kingmaker as an 'evil advisor', the committed Yorkist was executed in 1469 following the Warwick-led Lancastrians' victory at Edgecote Moor. No sooner was Herbert dead did Henry Tudor leave

Raglan for exile in France. It has been speculated that work on the castle ceased before beginning again under the third William, 2nd Earl of Pembroke, throughout the next decade. In 1491 the second earl's death without a male heir saw the castle pass to his daughter, Elizabeth, wife of Sir Charles Somerset: the later legitimised bastard of Henry Beaufort, 3rd Duke of Somerset. Henry Tudor, now Henry VII, arranged the marriage in gratitude for his earlier treatment at Raglan. Sir Charles enjoyed great success under the first two Tudor kings, culminating in him being granted the earldom of Worcester. Throughout that time, work on Raglan proceeded. Following Charles's death, his son, Henry, oversaw the relocation of the lead from Tintern Abbey during the Dissolution of the Monasteries.

Throughout the Tudor era, improvements and expansion of the castle continued. Most of this came under Henry's son and grandson: William and Edward Somerset, respectively, who also owned Chepstow. Described by one John Kenyon as 'wealthy, brilliant and cultured men,' chief among William's achievements was the long gallery that overlooked an artificial lake, extensive gardens, and expansion of the Pitched Stone Court. After Edward took control in 1589, the changes were more external. Complementary to a moat walk that circled the great tower, work on the greens around 1606 received national acclaim. While both were made a Knight of the Garter, Edward's achievements included being appointed to the Council of Wales and Master of the Horse under Elizabeth I. He later organised James I's coronation before serving as Lord Privy Seal in the 1620s.

Such things were in place when Edward's son, Henry, the fifth earl of Worcester, took the reins in 1628. Henry enjoyed a particularly resplendent lifestyle at Raglan, albeit 'sober and respectful'. The red gate was his work. Under his scientifically minded son, Edward, work on the gardens included a 'water commanding machine' located within the great tower. The unusual mechanism appears to have created a fountain effect by spurting moat water into the air, a little like modern-day Versailles. The steam pump may have been the first of practical use ever recorded.

Sadly for Raglan, the castle's rise came to a halt when the English Civil War reached the former Marcher lands. In 1642, Raglan remained the property of the fifth earl, Henry, now in his sixties. As expected of Catholic nobles, the family were committed Royalists. When Charles

I sent his son and heir – the future Charles II – on a tour of his supporters to raise funds for the war effort, Henry responded in October 1642 by donating approximately £1m in modern money to the Royalist cause. In gratitude, Charles upgraded him from earl to marquess.

For both king and castle, such promotions merely papered over emerging cracks. As the local religious tension rose, the Catholic marquess became a target of local apathy. Amusingly, it was fear of Edward's ingenious steam engine that scared off a motley crew of local protestants. To combat the rising threat, Henry invested around £40,000 in modern bastions around the castle and a powder mill. A garrison of 300 was also stationed within the walls and equipped with the latest cannons. In Edward's absence, the king visited Henry twice in the hope of securing extra funds and enjoyed a game of bowls on the green. As the war continued to turn Parliament's way post-Naseby, Henry planned for many of his valuables, including paintings and oak panelling, to be transferred to his brother at Troy House, also in Monmouthshire.

The decision proved wise. When Edward was captured in Ireland, a garrison of 800 troops encountered a Roundhead siege in early June. Also present were distant family and several retreated Royalist leaders. In preparation for the attack, the long avenue of trees was chopped down, and many local buildings were razed to increase visibility and deprive the enemy of provisions. After initially putting up a formidable defence against Colonel Morgan and Sir Trevor Williams, General Fairfax's arrival and the Roaring Meg proved a bridge too far. The garrison held out for three brave months before Somerset surrendered on 19 August 1646.

Though Henry accepted good terms for the garrison, he was sent to Windsor. His beloved castle was subsequently stripped of all valuables and left to the elements. For Edward, the son of one of the wealthiest magnates in England, he inherited debts but no land. After escaping to France in 1648, he returned four years later and was imprisoned. An income of £24,000 per year in his prime dropped to a measly £3 per week and he died penniless. His many inventions, including the steam pump, recorded in his work, *A Century of Inventions*, remain unfound.

Whether on Parliament's demand or Fairfax alone, orders were issued for the castle's destruction. The man charged with the task was Henry Herbert, ironically a descendant of the original William ap Thomas. The process was scandalous. In what was described as a 'carnival atmosphere', locals stripped the raw materials and dredged the moat. Arguably Fairfax's most unforgivable crime was burning the library located between the old gatehouse and state apartments. The windows were deliberately tall to allow light to enter. As it transpired, Henry would never live to deal with the fallout. He was granted permission to be interred in the vault at Windsor, inspiring him to quip, 'Why then I shall have a better castle when I am dead, than they took from me when alive.'

Depleted, demeaned, and deprived for the duration of the Protectorate, Raglan was left to rot. The one saving grace was that the strong walls proved impossible to destroy. When Charles II succeeded Richard Cromwell at the end of the Interregnum, the Somersets regained the castle and their other properties, albeit with no commitment by Charles to repay the family's earlier offerings to fund the war effort. Due to the high restoration costs, Henry Somerset, 3rd Marquess, concentrated instead on nearby Troy House and Badminton House in Gloucestershire. Consequently, the castle suffered throughout the next century, and the stone was often reused elsewhere. Noted among the most remarkable criminals was one Hopkins, dubbed in certain quarters as the 'Grand Dilapidator' due to his removal of chimneys, stairways, and windows.

In 1756 Raglan's fortunes improved during the ownership of another Henry Somerset, 5th Duke of Beaufort. Due to its immense size, the ruins became an integral stop on the Wye Tour. In addition to the erection of benches and other viewing platforms, the Great Hall was reroofed in the 1820s and became a site of 'Grand Entertainment'. A decade later, the grand staircase was also reinserted. In 1881 the Prince of Wales, later Edward VII, and his wife, Alexandra, visited the ruins. In 1938 it was taken into state ownership and is now the property of Cadw.

It is an exceptional castle indeed that rivals the majesty of Raglan. On a warm summer's day, a lovely atmosphere pervades, despite the eeriness of repugnant gargoyles. Complementing the sightless glares, heraldic coats of arms worthy of Hampton Court or Windsor still hang from many of the walls. While other signs survive of its early splendour, sadly, just a quick perusal of the contemporary accounts confirms what has been lost. Before the civil war, reports spoke of the walls being hung with vibrant tapestries from Arras in France's Pas-de-Calais region. An inventory from 1639 also describes the plethora of silver and gilt plate stored in the Great Tower.

A far greater tragedy concerns the loss of the library. Whether the contents were destroyed in the razing or stolen remains unclear. The enormity cannot be understated. Such was the treasure trove of unique Welsh manuscripts, in literary terms, only the Dissolution of the Monasteries and the fire at Alexandria can compare. A few are believed to now reside at Hereford Cathedral; however, most are lost.

Intriguingly, sightings of a 'bardic' figure have been witnessed, generally from the vicinity of the former library. Some have suggested that he was the librarian who hid many books in a secret tunnel beneath the castle. No records survive of the man's identity and fate. For the modern tourist, the fake books on the winding staircase are an amusing gimmick that fails to highlight the importance of what once filled the chamber above.

A depleted shell may now be all that survives of what was once arguably the most glorious of all Welsh castles, yet there is little doubt that in Raglan, Monmouthshire retains a genuine jewel in the nation's crown. As the historian Anthony Emery rightly pointed out, Raglan served as one of the 'last formidable displays of medieval defensive architecture'. One can only hope that the books were saved and will one day be found.

Chapter 8

The Welsh Marches: Gloucestershire, Herefordshire and Shropshire

Clun

Before the Norman conquest, Clun was a small Saxon village formed around a parish church. The lands previously possessed by Eadric the Wild were taken by the early-Norman baron Robert de Say, who erected a substantial motte with two baileys.

Located on a bend of the River Clun and overlooking the modern town, the castle was blessed with many natural defences. In response to the recurring skirmishes in the Marcher region, notably those by Gruffudd ap Cynan, Henry I established a castle-guard system to protect Clun consisting of several fiefs located along the old Roman road. Later that century, the Lords of Clun laid out plans for a new town close to Clun Castle. The area surrounding the castle was also declared a Marcher Barony, which led to the 'Honour of Clun'.

The early lords were the FitzAlans, among whose number William spent fifteen years in exile for supporting Matilda. He returned on the accession of Henry II and regained his castle. On his wife's death, it passed to their son, also William, whose outstanding contribution was the magnificent four-storey great tower to the north of the motte. William had been present with Richard I at the building of Château Gaillard in Normandy, whose surrounding circular towers almost certainly inspired him at Clun. When William died in 1210, King John's demand of a fee of 10,000 marks prohibited the next William from his rightful inheritance. After William died in 1215, his brother John, an ally of Llywelyn ap Iorwerth, seized Clun and nearby Oswestry. Though the king recovered the castle, payment of the 10,000 to Henry III saw the FitzAlans regain the property.

Suspicions of John's loyalty would again be raised during the Marshal War. The castle was Royalist-garrisoned in 1233 and resisted the attack that destroyed the town. In 1244, John's son and namesake inherited the castle. The death of his father's cousin without issue also made him *de jure* Earl of Arundel. A marriage between another John and Isabella, a daughter of the Mortimers of Wigmore, strengthened the family further. At this time, the castle was described as 'small but strongly built' but needed repair.

When such repairs occurred is unclear. A combination of the lack of purpose following Edward I's conquest and the FitzAlans' acquisition of Arundel Castle in England contributed to Clun's loss of prestige. Over the coming century, it was transformed into a hunting lodge with pleasure gardens and a horse stud. On Richard FitzAlan's execution in 1397, Richard II deprived the family of the property; however, Henry IV restored it. Thomas FitzAlan successfully oversaw the castle's defences during Owain Glyndŵr's rebellion, after which its purpose further dwindled. A century later, John Leland recorded the castle's ongoing fall from grace. It was unused in the civil war and slighted by Parliament in 1646. Future owners included Clive of India. A final claim to fame is its inspiration for Sir Walter Scott's Guard Doleureuse in his 1825 novel *The Betrothed.*

Croft

Standing among 1,500 acres of gorgeous woodland, parkland and farmland, elegant Croft Castle is a nature lovers' dream. Six miles north-west of the market town of Leominster, the estate is one of the least spoilt in England.

True to the standard of many National Trust properties, significant emphasis is placed on the gardens. A long avenue of Spanish chestnut trees complements a lovely array of beech and oak trees that line the main drive and appear timeless in the evening light. Within the grounds, a stunning three-acre walled garden includes a vineyard, orchard, and glasshouse from the turn of the previous century, all of which add to the feel of ongoing habitation. The thirteenth-century chapel of St Michael gives off the aura of many a parish church and contains the tombs of past residents. Perhaps the most famous is the impressive joint tomb of Sir Richard and Eleanor Croft. Eleanor was previously the wife of Sir Hugh Mortimer, who met his fate at the Battle of Wakefield in December 1460.

Some form of structure is believed to have existed on the site since the eleventh century. A Norman clan of some status, the original Crofts are believed to have arrived in England during St Edward the Confessor's reign. The estate is recorded in the *Domesday Book* as founded by a Norman knight, Bernard de Croft, whose family were closely linked with their neighbours, the Mortimers of Wigmore and Ludlow (see Wigmore Castle and Ludlow Castle). A nearby Croft-owned field staged the Battle of Mortimer's Cross on 2 February 1461. The conflict was one of the most significant of the Wars of the Roses as the House of York's armies, led by Edward, Earl of March – the future Edward IV – comprehensively defeated Henry VI and Jasper Tudor. The well-loved recreational walk, The Mortimer Trail that meanders from Shropshire to Herefordshire, passes through the estate and is named in their honour.

The present castle was begun in the fourteenth century and has been much altered since, including a rebuild in the 1660s. Among its owners was one Sir John Croft, who married Janet, a daughter of the famed Welsh hero Owain Glyndŵr. It was most likely from their connection with Owain the Crofts adopted the famous Welsh dragon – the Wyvern – as their new crest. On Henry VII's accession, Sir Richard Croft was appointed treasurer to the king's household and later steward to Prince Arthur. Prior to this, he fought alongside the future Edward IV at Mortimer's Cross, while his wife, Eleanor – Hugh's widow – served as governess to the future 'Princes in the Tower'. As previously recalled, their tombs can be found at the local church.

Royalists to the core, the owners proudly accepted their castle being dismantled instead of falling into Roundhead hands after being captured in the civil war. Under Herbert Croft, Bishop of Hereford, the slighted fortress rose like a phoenix from the ashes, and the country house-style property that exists now has been excellently preserved. Despite bad debts on the back of the South Sea Bubble forcing a sale in 1746 to the Knight family, the Crofts rebought the castle in 1923. During the Knights' tenure, the powerful ironworks magnates remodelled the castle in Rococo-Gothic in the 1760s. In 1799, it was acquired by Somerset Davies, a Ludlow MP, whose descendants sold the property to Lady Katherine Croft. The modern castle, though open to the public, still serves as the family residence.

A family home for almost a thousand years, the castle is reputedly haunted by the ghost of Owain Glyndŵr. Exactly what became of

Owain – officially the last native Welshman to hold the title Prince of Wales – remains one of history's great mysteries. Ousted from Harlech Castle, his chief remaining stronghold, in 1409 after rebelling against Henry IV in September 1400, he reportedly avoided capture and was last seen in 1412. Despite offers from Henry V to come to terms, he never surrendered and does not appear to have been betrayed. According to one of his followers, he died in 1415 of unknown causes. Since that time, the much-revered leader has acquired something of mythical status in Wales. He is often reported in various parts, leather-clad and donning his armour. Many questions remain unanswered about his precise connections with the castle, notably in its present state. A bishop staying there in the early twentieth century remains the most prominent eyewitness of his haunting.

Joining Glyndŵr, the wailing of a ghostly baby, along with a figure wearing a grey doublet, have also been seen. More prominent still is a lady donning a close-fitting cap, who is believed to have been a Croft. Often seen staring out of a window, she reputedly requested financial aid from an Irish relative, most likely in the 1740s, and remains in constant watch for its arrival. One can only hope it might calm her spirit to know that the modern castle is in safe hands and beloved by both descendants and visitors worldwide.

Goodrich

Few castles in medieval England played a more critical role in guarding the Welsh border than the mighty Goodrich.

Evidence suggests that the Anglo-Saxon thane and landowner Godric of Mappestone put down a motte and bailey shortly after the Norman Conquest. Godric appears in the *Domesday Book* as a tenant of Howle Hill in the same county. The name Goodrich originates from Godric. Theories have been put forward that part of the site dates to King Canute, but this is unproven.

Following Godric's creation of a timber and earthworks fortification, the imposing three-storey stone keep was added in the mid-twelfth century. The views from the summit are still among the most expansive in the area, which was particularly important for a Marcher castle. Earlier in the twelfth century William Fitz Baderon, most likely Godric's son-in-law, had succeeded Godric. In the 1120s, William's castle passed to his son, Baderon of Monmouth, who held it during the Anarchy. Recorded as Lord of Monmouth from 1125 till his death in 1176, Baderon's marriage to Rohese de Clare, whose family tended to support King Stephen, brought problems as the area in general backed Matilda. Stories from the time indicate that Baderon was forced to storm his castle to recover it from Matilda supporters. Stephen later granted the fortress to Gilbert de Clare, Earl of Pembroke, Rohese's brother. Gilbert was succeeded by his son Richard, aka 'Strongbow', who was later stripped of it by Henry II in 1154. Who built the keep is now a mystery. The theory that Baderon did so to withstand Matilda's supporters is plausible but by no means definitive.

Strongbow's loss was initially the Crown's gain. In 1203 John granted the castle and manor to William Marshal, 1st Earl of Pembroke. Marshal's castle was the subject of a Welsh attack in late October 1216 when the nine-year-old Henry III was crowned at nearby Gloucester. Fortunately for the royal camp, the attack was soon thwarted. The castle's expansion was most likely undertaken during William's time, most notably a curtain wall that circled the keep. On Marshal's death, the castle passed through his adult sons. During the Marshal War of 1233-34, Richard Marshal, 3rd Earl of Pembroke, fortified the castle but failed to withstand a Royalist siege. In the 1240s, by which time both Richard and his younger brother, Gilbert, were dead, the king granted the castle to Walter, now 5th earl. Remarkably all of William Marshal's adult sons died childless by 1245.

Later that century, the castle was expanded into the present concentric design, which included luxurious living quarters and the somewhat ominously coloured red sandstone walls we see today. Most of this occurred under the Marshals' successor as Earl of Pembroke, the powerful magnate Willian de Valence, a half-brother of Henry III from his mother's marriage to Hugh de Lusignan after King John's death. Valence had also taken the 'greatest knight's' granddaughter, Joan, as his wife. Over the next decade, the rise of Llywelyn ap Gruffudd presented many challenges to the Marcher areas. From 1280 Valence spent vast sums on revamping the castle. It may well have been under his violent tenure that a small dungeon, narrow and windowless, was created below the keep.

Succeeding Valence was his son, Aymer, who added a further line of defences. On his death in 1324, the castle passed to his niece on his mother's side, Elizabeth de Comyn. No sooner had she inherited the property than she was kidnapped. The culprits were none other than the king's royal favourites and advisors, the Despensers, who forced her to sign over the castle in April 1325. Fortunately for Elizabeth, the Despensers' luck did not last. Both father and son – Hugh the Elder and Hugh the Younger – were executed within a month of one another in October and November 1326. That year, Elizabeth married Richard Talbot, 2nd Baron Talbot, who regained the castle by force. From 1326 the Talbots held Goodrich as their most favoured home and were successful in withstanding the forces of Owain Glyndŵr in 1404-05. The Talbots were made Earls of Shrewsbury in 1442, after which they remained firm supporters of the House of Lancaster.

By the time the family fell out with the Tudors, Goodrich was no longer the fashionable place it had once been. The Wars of the Roses had significantly interrupted the family's prolonged stays there. After John Talbot died at the Battle of Northampton in 1460, the Yorkist William Herbert became the beneficiary before Talbot's son (also John) won back control. According to the acclaimed antiquarian John Leland, by 1540, some of the castle was used to hold local prisoners and confiscated livestock. In 1616 the final Talbot, Gilbert, died without an heir, and the castle passed to Henry Grey, Earl of Kent.

Like many a great castle, Goodrich's date with destiny came during the civil war. Concerted attempts by Richard Tyler, the constable in the 1630s, ensured the walls were in a fit state. By December 1643, Henry Grey, 1st Earl of Stamford established a garrison with Tyler's support. Unlike at most castles, Goodrich's soldiers were on Cromwell's side until nearby Royalist pressure inspired their retreat to Gloucester, and Sir Henry Lingen installed his own forces. Over the next year or so, Royalist raids of local Parliament-supporting homesteads became commonplace. Siege in June 1646 saw the castle ruined beyond repair.

In the eighteenth century, this once mighty guardian of the English border had become a picturesque ruin. In 1740 the property passed from the Grey family to Admiral Thomas Griffin, who attempted restoration. The famed local clergyman William Gilpin wrote lovingly of the castle in his *Observations on the River Wye* of 1782. It also held appeal among many watercolour artists, while the famed writer William Wordsworth cited it as the 'noblest ruin in Herefordshire'. It would prove the inspiration for Wordsworth's *We Are Seven*. Less pleased was the famed poet when Sir Samuel Rush Meyrick built Goodrich Court next door. In 1920 it was taken over by the state and is now in the care of English Heritage. Goodrich Court was largely demolished in 1949.

Established as an imposing defensive fortress on the border with Wales, it is hardly surprising that Goodrich's history has given rise to legends and alleged hauntings. In 1646, the Royalist garrison suffered a violent siege from the Parliamentarian commander Colonel John Birch. The Roundhead arsenal included the 'Roaring Meg', made especially for the occasion. Incidentally, in recent times the castle has become reacquainted with Roaring Meg. After being seated outside a local museum for a time, it now rests within the castle's courtyard.

It was mainly this state-of-the-art weapon's mortar lobbing capabilities that ultimately culminated in Goodrich's slighting. Local legend tells that one Alice Birch, the colonel's niece, took refuge there with her Royalist lover, Charles Clifford. As the Parliamentarians raised the siege, the illicit couple left the castle at nightfall on horseback only to find that heavy rains had muddied the banks and swelled the river, causing them to be swept away by the current. Their ghosts have been seen, usually gazing despondently down from the ruined ramparts. Alice is also believed to be the lady in white who has been seen on horseback.

The keep has also been described as possessed of a dark atmosphere. Edward III later gave his blessing for local prisoners to be kept in Valence's dungeon. To this day, a hole in the stonework close to the old doorframe confirms where the iron bar opened and closed. Curiously, the building was once dubbed the 'Macbeth Tower' in honour of a former Irish chieftain who was held there. The keep is also reputedly haunted by the man in question who died trying to escape.

Beloved by the military historian, artist, writer, and folklorist alike, there is no doubt that in Goodrich Castle the county of Herefordshire has something genuinely exceptional. The views of the Wye Valley remain as expansive as ever. Impressive as Colonel Birch may have been as a soldier, his claim to Parliament of Goodrich, 'I humbly conceive it is useless', was as arrogant as it was wrong. Perhaps allowance can be made that the castle had caused him many problems. Fortunately, his advice was roundly ignored. As the historian Adrian Pettifer rightly pointed out, not only is it the finest in the county but 'one of the best examples of English military architecture' in existence.

Hopton

Little now remains of Hopton Castle in Shropshire. Initially constructed as a motte and bailey in the twelfth century in the village of the same name, the castle was reconstructed in stone by Walter de Hopton, most likely around the Second Barons' War of 1263-67. Walter's descendants maintained it until the direct line died out during the Wars of the Roses when the castle passed in marriage to the Corbet family of Moreton Corbet Castle. In the 1600s, the final female heir, Elizabeth Corbet, married Sir Henry Wallop, who modernised the interior and strengthened the defences for the Roundhead cause. Hopton and nearby Brampton Bryan were two of the few Parliamentarian castles in the Marcher region and thus avoided being slighted. By 1700 the property remained inhabited; however, a lack of appropriate financing saw it become outdated and fall into disrepair. Since 2006, the Hopton Castle preservation trust has looked after the ruins.

For the modern visitor, there is much to love about Hopton Castle. Erected as a tower house, most likely on the site of the original keep, the castle is ironically more in keeping with those of the Scottish Marches than the Welsh. Unlike many of the region, the design was intended to be one of status and used as a hunting lodge. Set among the gorgeous surroundings of the Shropshire Hills AONB, a visit is worth making for the views alone.

Despite the glorious countryside, the area also hides a darker side. Successful in avoiding a long siege by the Parliamentarians, the castle was, ironically, the victim of a Royalist attack. In 1644 – at which point the direction of the war was still unclear – Sir Michael Woodhouse and 500 Royalist troops laid siege to the walls and set fire to the surrounding buildings. Defended by a mere thirty-one Parliamentarians, the garrison, under the command of Samuel More, faced a mammoth task.

Precisely what happened next has drifted into the realms of legend. After setting fire to a house on the northern perimeter, apparently the lodgings of one Richard Steward, the Royalists failed to entice More into surrendering. A week later, the Cavaliers returned in greater numbers. On initially breaking in through the chimney in Richard Steward's house – according to some reports, already a wreck by now – the intruders became trapped and were killed. The discovery of a small hole inside the garderobe is believed to denote the point of entry.

After another week of cooling off, the Royalists returned with heavy artillery. At this point, More was warned that no mercy would be granted should surrender not be swift. Again refusing, hand to hand fighting allegedly saw the loss of some 150 Royalists compared to just one Roundhead. The next night, the Royalists set fire to a brick tower among the outer defences. On fleeing, More's men apparently set fire to Gregory's house on taking refuge in the central tower. All the while, the Royalists mined beneath the tower's south side. Trapped, More surrendered on the belief his men would be taken to Shrewsbury.

According to More himself, the Royalists failed to honour their word, and the remaining 28 members of the garrison were butchered. Another version states that More's refusal to surrender until the three-week siege culminated in the bailey's fall and fire to the keep cost his men. Woodhouse opted not to grant the Roundheads mercy and put them to the sword. Tradition holds that the garrison's ghosts have been seen in the cold waters of the moat, where their bodies were unceremoniously tossed. Joining them are the spirits of four Royalists and Elizabeth Mayrick, a Royalist widow. Legend claims that she has been seen aimlessly wandering the tower house, lamenting her husband.

The victims of cruelty or a delayed surrender, the understaffed garrison succumbed to inevitable defeat. An intriguing epilogue to the story is the coining of the phrase Hopton Quarter: a byword for treacherous treatment by an enemy. The Cavaliers' decision not to refortify the castle would later come back to haunt them.

Ludlow

Magnificent Ludlow is one of Britain's most recognisable castles. Constructed on a headland overlooking the River Teme, the castle was among the first erected in stone from the offset.

The man responsible was one Walter de Lacy, a Norman nobleman of ancient ancestry. As the second-in-command to William FitzOsbern, Earl of Hereford, Walter was a man of some prominence in his own right. He began his castle within the manor of Stanton Lacy around 1075; today, one can find a small village of that name close to the modern town. The fortress was initially called Dinham Castle before being renamed: Ludlow. Walter took a keen interest in the castle's rise. As the decade progressed, the manor became the fulcrum of his estates.

On Walter's death in 1085 – ironically after falling off some scaffolding while inspecting building work at St Guthlac's Priory, Hereford – his estates passed to his son Roger. Although early work around the inner bailey was finished by 1115, including four towers and a gatehouse, Roger's participation in the rebellion against William Rufus in 1088 and conspiracy of 1095 saw him deprived of the castle in favour of his brother, Hugh. When Hugh died without issue in 1115, Henry I gave it to Hugh's niece, Sybil, who married Pain FitzJohn, one of Henry I's 'new men'. When Pain died in 1137, Ludlow became a hostage to the Nineteen-Year-Winter's seesawing of fortunes. In 1139 Stephen took the castle after several failed attempts and successfully rescued Prince Henry of Scotland.

For the remainder of the century, the castle tooed and froed between the de Lacys and their rivals. During this time, the family established the rectangular outer bailey and great tower. Henry II temporarily confiscated Ludlow during Hugh de Lacy's absence in the 1172 invasion of Ireland, most likely to ensure his loyalty. Hugh's heir, Walter, was similarly deprived on the back of Prince John's rebellion of 1194. Within a year of travelling to Ireland in 1201, he was again denied his recovered properties; again, most likely a gambit on John's part to ensure he did not change sides. Refusal to pay a fine inspired John to pass the property to William de Braose – Walter's father-in-law – but this was reversed following William's own dispute with John. As Walter again fell out with John, prompting him to join William in Ireland, Ludlow was confiscated until 1215. By this time, the innermost bailey appears to have been finished.

Following John's death, life at Ludlow resumed some normality. Henry III and Llywelyn ap Iorwerth met there for peace talks in 1223; however, this failed to end three years of recurring conflict in the Welsh Marches. Concerns over Walter's activities in Ireland also saw Ludlow again requisitioned for two years. Though Walter performed well for Henry, an inability to repay his debts forced him to pawn the castle to the Crown in 1238 before regaining it before his death in 1241.

As Walter had no living male heir, Henry III granted Ludlow to Walter's granddaughter Maud, who he married to his favourite, Peter de Geneva. After Peter's death, Maud married Geoffrey de Geneville, a friend of the future Edward I. This close relationship inspired Simon de Montfort, 6th Earl of Leicester, to seize Ludlow in 1264 following the Battle of Lewes. Geneville soon recaptured it, and it was there in 1265 that a liberated Edward met up with the Royalist camp. Around this time, Geoffrey rebuilt the inner bailey, which dates with the construction of the town walls.

These improvements would cement Ludlow's importance throughout the next century. The marriage of Geoffrey's eldest granddaughter, Joan, to Roger Mortimer, later 1st Earl of March, in 1301 was of particular consequence. Over the next twenty years, further additions included the Great Chamber block and a chapel dedicated to St Peter in the outer bailey. Mortimer is likely to have entertained the teenage Edward III there in 1329 following Edward II's dethronement and probable death.

Despite Mortimer's downfall and execution in 1330, Joan retained the castle. Inherited by various descendants, Richard II took advantage of the fourth earl's youth – another Roger – and placed the castle in the control of a committee of nobles. On his dethronement, Ludlow was in the wardship of Henry IV, albeit officially still Mortimer property. A force led by Edmund Mortimer engaged with Owain Glyndŵr's at the Battle of Bryn Glas in June 1402, in which Edmund was captured. The king refused to pay the ransom, which led to Edmund marrying Owain's daughter, Catrin. Except for Richard II's brief deprivations and Henry IV's wardship, Mortimer's descendants held the castle until 1425, when Edmund died childless. He was replaced in 1432 by Edmund's nephew, Richard, 3rd Duke of York.

For the next twenty-eight years, the castle served as the duke's home. Improvements followed, including the rebuilding of part of the Great Tower. A largely straightforward victory for the Lancastrians in the 1459 Battle of Ludford Bridge, just outside the town, saw Henry VI make John Talbot, Earl of Shrewsbury lord, and place Edmund de la Mare as constable. York died at Wakefield the following year; however, the castle passed to the Crown on Edward IV's accession and became one of Edward's favourites. In 1473, his eldest sons – the Princes in the Tower – were sent there.

Unlike many Marcher castles, Ludlow had many good years ahead of it. Due to its prominent location and newfound royal status, it was chosen as the seat of the Council in the Marches of Wales, making it the *de facto* capital of Wales. Following that, Henry VII sent his eldest son and heir, Prince Arthur, to Ludlow to perform his duties as Regent of Wales. It was here in 1502 the prince took his new bride, Catherine of Aragon, and established an alternate court. Had Arthur lived longer, his younger brother, Henry, would have been in line to be Archbishop of Canterbury. As fate had it, the man who married six times would still become head of the Church in England. Between 1525 and 1528, the castle was regularly the residence of Princess Mary, later Mary I. Under Elizabeth I, it was the home of the antiquarian Sir Henry Sidney, also the council's president.

Throughout this period, Ludlow was extensively developed. So much so that it was selected to host many cultural events, including John Milton's debut of *Comus*. Such times came to a premature end in 1641 when an Act of Parliament stripped the council of its powers. Just five years later, the castle suffered a more physical body blow. Despite boasting impressive defences under Sir Michael Woodhouse, the Roundhead army under Sir William Brereton and Colonel John Birch forced a surrender on 26 May 1646. Though its contents were sold off, Cromwell kept a garrison at the castle throughout the Interregnum. Following the Restoration, Charles II had it repaired, yet in 1689 the abolition of the recently reinstated Council of the Marches saw the castle enter a period of neglect. In 1772 the Earl of Powis, Henry Herbert, leased it from the Crown, after which it was continued by his son, George. In 1811 it was sold to George's brother-in-law, Edward Clive, who built a mansion overlooking the outer bailey. His descendants now operate the castle as one of the finest tourist attractions in the region.

Inhabited for nearly a thousand years, an important fortress in a critical location, it is hardly surprising that Ludlow has acquired many legends. Among the most prominent is Lady Marion de la Bruere, whose ghost haunts the Pendover (or Pendovin) Tower. In the 1160s, the castle was under the control of the prominent Marcher lord Josse de Dinant, who struggled to hold Ludlow against the rampaging Welsh and the noble pair Hugh de Mortimer and Walter de Lacy. Josse captured Mortimer and extracted a ransom after holding him in the tower that still bears his name. In 1166, a pitched battle before the walls injured Dinant. Things might have been worse had it not been for his young protégé, Fulk de Metz, who ensured de Lacy's capture, as well as two of his knights. Thanks to Marion's collaboration, the trio escaped using a rope of knotted linen. The reason for her agreeing to aid them? She had fallen in love with the imprisoned Arnold de Lys.

A short time later, when Josse was away, Marion invited Arnold to Ludlow, unaware that the lustful knight secretly conspired with de Lacy to storm the castle. As Arnold climbed the rope and embraced Marion, de Lacy and several of his men followed him, slew the watchmen and opened the gates. Marion realised her foolishness and reached for Arnold's sword and killed him before plunging to her death in the valley below.

Hearing of the news, Josse was furious. His best efforts to regain the castle failed, thanks primarily to de Lacy's decision to join the Welsh. Josse was locked up, and a furious Henry II demanded de Lacy ensure his release and end his agreement with the Welsh. Though the former was quickly established, the departure of the Welsh took four years of bribery.

Since that time, the distraught Marion's ghost has been reported many times, destined to replay the horrific circumstances of her suicide. Many have also claimed to hear a terrible piercing scream, followed by silence. Joining her in her haunting is believed to be a ghostly soldier whose audible breathing has been heard. Both are reputed to haunt the Pendover Tower, which is also known as the hanging tower.

Moreton Corbet

Barren, desolate, exposed to the elements, the decrepit walls and empty windows of Moreton Corbet are a sad reminder of a castle that time forgot. Intended as a luxury Tudor residence, this dilapidated mess that stands tall over the local Shropshire landscape was another roundly depleted by the artillery of the Roundhead army. Whether the revamped mansion was ever completed or fully restored is unclear. According to local lore, the construction of the castle was hindered by a vicious curse.

The castle was planned as the home of the English landowner and MP Robert Corbet on the site once occupied by two Anglo-Saxon thegns. They likely built some form of fortified structure here; however, the castle's early records are murky. In the thirteenth century, an English family, the Torets, took over the manor, which probably included a castle. In 1216, William Marshal, 1st Earl of Pembroke, and later regent of England under Henry III, conquered the property, then owned by Bartholomew Toret and named Moreton Toret. The site was renamed when the fortress was inherited by his son-in-law, Richard de Corbet. Somewhat alluringly, the family coat of arms is a Corbeau or raven, which may well be the origin of the family name.

For the next 350 years, the property remained in the same family's hands, during which the structure's evolution was ongoing. Robert's father, Sir Andrew, oversaw many changes to the perimeter wall and gatehouse, much of which has survived. Construction of the new castle began around 1579 when Robert returned with grand plans inspired by a trip to Italy. Building work was delayed by Corbet's untimely death from the plague in 1583, after which his brothers, Richard and Vincent, took over the project.

As progress continued, things took on a bitter twist. Bizarrely, the cause was not related to money, materials, or war, but the dire circumstances inflicted on the religious minorities following James I's accession as King of England. James's hardline policy caused massive unrest among the puritan community.

One of those affected was a local named Paul Homeyard, a friend of Vincent yet a staunch critic of the king. Sadly, Vincent's generosity in offering Homeyard sanctuary placed him on a collision course with the authorities. When the puritan's religious ideals became ever more fanatical and vociferous, an uneasy Vincent forced Homeyard to flee to the surrounding countryside.

As the puritan adapted to life as a hermit in local caves, life for the Corbet family returned to normal. Work on the castle progressed, and after many years of hard work, it was all set to become the family home. Unfortunately for Vincent, a combination of his initial kindness and subsequent insecurity placed him on Homeyard's revenge list. One fateful day, the puritan fugitive returned to the developing castle and placed the following curse on the family:

> Woe unto thee, hard hearted man, the lord has hardened thy heart as he hardened the heart of the Pharaoh, to thine own destruction.
>
> Rejoice not in thy riches, not in monuments of thy pride, for neither thou, nor thy children, nor thy children's children shall inhabit these halls.
>
> They shall be given up to desolation; snakes, vipers and unclean beasts shall make it their refuge, and thy home shall be full of doleful creatures.

As fate transpired, the Corbets were plagued by countless delays. From its appearance alone, one could easily argue that the skeletal ruins bare all the hallmarks of a property plagued by a supernatural curse. In the civil war years, the castle was besieged and damaged at least once. So limited were the defences, a Parliamentary unit of just ten soldiers were needed to take it. Although partially repaired, the buildings fell into complete disuse in the eighteenth century.

Although Robert Corbet's dream home was probably never completed, the remains are a depressing sight. When the moon rises over the horizon, the skeletal outline of the unfinished mansion appears particularly ominous. Paul Homeyard may have long departed the empty halls, yet local legend has long told that his ghost continues to reside there. Strange noises are said to emanate from the cellar, in which an oppressive atmosphere has often been reported. Of the puritan's reason for haunting the castle, one can only imagine. Whether seeking refuge at the site where he was briefly welcomed or forever cursed to wander the empty walls, there is no doubt Moreton Corbet is destined to remain a sad reminder of what might have been. The nearby church houses the family tombs.

St Briavels

Overlooking the River Wye in the heart of the Gloucestershire countryside, the beautifully located St Briavels is the archetypal site of many uses. A busy administrative centre for the Forest of Dean, the castle was also a favoured royal hunting lodge, weapons' factory, and legal venue.

Though the local village appears to be pre-Norman, early work on the castle occurred between 1075 and 1129. William the Conqueror had previously granted control of the village to the ever-busy William FitzOsbern; however, in 1075, four years after the earl's death, William's son, Roger de Breteuil, was stripped of it as punishment for his role in the 'Revolt of the Earls'. The castle was created soon after under a royal mandate, while the royal bailiffs took the village.

Under Walter de Gloucester and later his son, Miles, the castle became the administrative centre for the Royal Forest of Dean. Though its purpose appears to have been more legal than defensive, Miles took sole possession of St Briavels on the death of Pain FitzJohn early in the

Anarchy and set about improving it. In 1160, then back in royal control, Henry II upgraded the defences in stone.

It was at that time the castle began to develop as a hunting lodge and forestry office. Locally made iron goods were often stored there before being shipped in large quantities. Richard the Lionheart is recorded as having taken some 50,000 St Briavels-made horseshoes to the Holy Land. In later years, his brother enjoyed many hunting trips in the forest and often stayed there. In 1207 he also entertained the native lord Gruffyd ap Cadwallon within the walls.

On the back of such visits, John invested almost £300 on a stone wall, tower, gateway and several buildings within the bailey, including a lodge. A timber chapel followed in 1236-37, by which time the castle was a place of incarceration for those who had fallen foul of forest law and fine court. The surrounding ditch most likely preceded the arrival of a Royalist garrison during the Marshal War of 1233-34. Edward I later added a gatehouse and a further wall while the timber chapel was made permanent.

Throughout the thirteenth and fourteenth centuries, the castle earned a reputation for the creation of crossbow bolts. A forge within the bailey dates to around 1228, and during the Hundred Years' War was producing more than 1000 quarrels a day. Iron was also used in the formation of local siege engines. The castle remained in royal favour under Edward II, who often visited. Fresh renovation, however, became unstable when Edward ousted the castellan, Roger d'Amory, in favour of Hugh le Despenser the Younger, a move that persuaded d'Amory to take up arms. As the Despensers' influence increased, the threat of violence rose with it. One of the most unfortunate victims was the deputy constable, Robert Sapy, who was brutally attacked on his way to London. After being relieved of his possessions, his arms and legs were broken, and his eyes torn out. A short time later, Queen Isabella took control of the castle before it reverted to the Crown on the accession of her son, Edward III.

For the next two centuries, ownership remained at the mercy of the changing fortunes of English governance. Property for a time of Thomas, Duke of Gloucester – youngest son of Edward III and an uncle of Richard II – it passed to Thomas le Despenser by a grant for life in 1397. Two years later, following Henry IV's usurpation, it passed to John of Lancaster, Duke of Bedford. Changes of ownership among various royal favourites included Warwick the Kingmaker, whose widow, Anne, took possession on his death.

The lack of stability, alas, would take a steady toll on St Briavels. When the civil war broke out, it was the property of Philip Herbert, 4th Earl of Pembroke. Though a good friend of the king, Herbert sided with the Roundheads, thus sparing the castle siege. At the restoration, Charles II granted it to the Royalist Edward Somerset, 2nd Marquess of Worcester. Throughout the next century, the castle's fortunes continued to ebb and flow. Much of the inner bailey was removed in the 1700s, while 1777 saw the collapse of the keep. Also lost was the 'forester's horn' chimney, a famous local relic.

In the absence of a permanent resident, the castle was transformed into a court and debtors' prison, where conditions became the stuff of notoriety, as documented by the early prison reformer John Howard in 1775. A series of riots in the 1780s and again in 1831 led by the notorious local rebel Warren James, and a damning Parliamentary investigation into its inhumane conditions, led to its closure. Following the Parliamentary report, the commissioners' conclusion lamented the terrible conditions: not least that there was 'no water within for the prisoners' liberty, and they are obliged to get some person to fetch it.' The prison finally relocated in 1842 and the castle remained uninhabitable until around 1906. After extensive renovations, the castle reopened in 1948 as a youth hostel, and the drained moat turned into a garden in 1961.

Though much of the castle's history went unrecorded, this welcoming location has retained much of its atmosphere. So much so, it is reputedly one of the most haunted castles in England.

Much of the activity is believed to occur in 'King John's bedroom', which also served as a courtroom. A large stone in the fireplace is well worn, apparently from repeated strikes against it for every criminal sentenced to death. The prison room is renowned for its strange atmosphere, a feeling intensified by the graffiti scrawled on the walls. One fascinating example by Robin Belcher reads, 'The Day will come that thou shalt answer for it for thou hast sworn against me, 1671.'

That Belcher's ghost haunts the castle is a matter for conjecture. Nevertheless, local tales tell of many former inhabitants who still make their presence known. A knight in armour reportedly appears on moonlit nights. Darkened figures also stalk the chaplain's room. A similar spirit has been spotted in the 'hanging' room, while the feeling of being strangled has been reported inside the constable's room. Among the most haunted parts of the castle are the state apartments, which are reputedly the domain of a young girl in a white dress. Other unexplained phenomena range from flashes of light, strange sounds and smells. The worst seem to centre around a small oubliette or 'little place of forgetting'. Such locations were usually reserved for the most dangerous prisoners, whose cries for mercy mainly went unheard.

Of all the stories associated with this modern retreat, among the most disturbing are the ethereal sounds of a crying child throughout the solar room. During renovations, the corpse of a baby wrapped in linen reportedly fell from the ceiling. Exactly how the poor child came to be there is a mystery. Sadly, it seems almost inevitable from the location that the child's death was not peaceful.

Stokesay

Stokesay Castle is rightly regarded among the finest fortified manor houses in England. Built during the 1280s and 90s by the leading wool merchant Laurence de Ludlow, the present structure stands on the original de Lacy castle site. The *Domesday Book* records Roger de Lacy holding 'stoches' of the king: stoches being an Anglo-Saxon word for cattle farm. In the early 1100s, the area was managed on the de Lacys' behalf by the de Say family, from whom Stokesay was born.

Throughout the de Lacy years, tenants seem to have been common. A marriage between a de Lacy granddaughter, Margery, and Sir John de Verdun of Alton Castle had included the deeds to Stokesay. To raise funds for his crusade in September 1270, de Verdun rented out the property for three years to one Philip de Whichecote. In 1281, seven years after de Verdun's death, Laurence de Ludlow bought Whichecote's tenancy for around £266. Thanks to his success in the wool trade, Laurence was well on his way to making a fortune.

Work on Ludlow's masterpiece began around 1285 and took at least five years. In 1291 he received the king's permission to crenellate and built the southern tower. Sadly, Laurence drowned off the south coast in November 1294, presumably after a trip to the Continent. Since that time, Stokesay has remained mostly in its original state and incorporates parts of the original de Lacy castle. After being retained by Ludlow's descendants through his son, William, until the sixteenth century, the tower passed into the Vernon family through marriage. Come the civil war, the fortress was owned by the staunch Royalist William Craven, 1st Earl of Craven, who held the castle until 1645 when a short Parliamentarian siege ensured the garrison's surrender.

Fortunately for the castle and its future owners, the slighting only resulted in minor damage. Owned subsequently by the Baldwyn family, who rented parts out for agricultural purposes, it gradually fell into disrepair before it was saved by the Craven Estate, descendants of William Craven. The castle underwent significant restoration between 1830 and 1850 and again after the Craven Estate was sold to new owners. The repair was undertaken with great care and a commitment to retain its original form – a rarity for the time. The declining fortunes of the modern descendants saw the castle gifted to English Heritage in 1986.

A site famed for its impressive condition and authenticity, Stokesay Castle's story is more social history than military. Before de Ludlow's ownership, local legend tells that two brothers – both giants – lived above the site: one on View Edge, the other Norton Camp. Like most giants, the family had enormous wealth stored in a ginormous treasure chest kept at the castle. When in need of funds, the lazy giants, who possessed only one key, would toss it between each other. One day, one of the brother's fell short with their throw, causing the key to become lost in the moat. Supposedly the chest remains hidden in the castle, and the brothers' ghosts still wander the land mourning their lost wealth. The tale also states that any searcher will encounter the giants' pet raven if they get close to finding the treasure.

Perhaps unsurprisingly, the treasure has never been found. Most likely, it originated from de Ludlow's success as a wool merchant.

Whittington

Few fortresses are richer in mystery and romance than fairy-tale Whittington Castle. Located close to the Roman city of *Viroconium Cornoviorum* – modern-day Wroxeter – on the English side of Offa's Dyke in northern Shropshire, the castle was initially a motte and bailey fortified for the Norman knight Sir William Peverel, a Matilda supporter, around 1138.

The original castle may have been built on a Norman manor house, though evidence has yet to be found. Prior to the Roman invasion, an Iron

Age fort had already been erected at nearby Old Oswestry, which formed a nearby lordship. In 1149, Madog ap Maredudd annexed both as part of the Kingdom of Powys, which lasted till 1165, five years after Madog's death. On reclaiming the area, Henry II entrusted the castle to Roger de Powys with financial backing to carry out repairs. Complicating the matter, Fulk FitzWarin (often dubbed Fulk III) also possessed a claim to the castle. There is a beautiful legend that early in the castle's history, Sir William Peverel held a grand tournament to find a suitor for his daughter, Mellet, as he prepared to grant her the castle. The winner was Warin de Metz of Lorraine, henceforth founder of the FitzWarins.

According to the famous ancestral romance, *Fouke le Fitz Waryn*, Fulk and Prince John became childhood friends at Henry II's court. This changed one fateful day when a petulant John lost his temper on losing to Fulk at chess. In later years, the outlawed Fulk rebelled against his former friend and sought to recover his familial right to Whittington Castle, which John had given to a Welsh claimant. Fulk was eventually pardoned, and his claim was recognised in 1204.

Located at the heart of the Marcher lands, it is unsurprising that Whittington's involvement with the Welsh was far from over. Destroyed by Llywelyn ap Iorwerth in 1223, the castle was returned to the English as part of a peace treaty made between the Prince of Gwynedd and Henry III, after which Henry had the castle rebuilt in stone. Though the garrison surrendered to the Welsh in 1267 and was not recovered until 1276, it officially remained in FitzWarin hands. After Llywelyn ap Gruffudd died in 1282, Whittington enjoyed a relatively peaceful existence under the FitzWarins until Fulk XI died in 1420. The one exception was in 1404 when Owain Glyndŵr laid waste to the surrounding lordship. He failed, however, to capture the castle.

When the FitzWarin line died out, the castle passed to Fulk XI's sister, Elizabeth, who married Richard Hankeford. In 1422 William FitzWarin – an alleged relative and claimant – scaled the walls, but his success was short-lived. The castle later passed by marriage into the Bourchier family until John Bourchier, 2nd Earl of Bath, swapped the castle and title with Henry VIII for some confiscated monastic lands closer to the family home in Devon. It is doubtful that the fortress has been inhabited since.

Recorded as being in some decay at the time of the trade, Whittington passed through various owners. By the 1630s, the gatehouse was leased out, and the tenant granted permission to take freestone from the castle. In 1643 it was taken by the Roundheads, yet there is no evidence that it was directly involved in the conflict.

Even without the burden of war or slighting, the castle's condition continued to worsen. In 1760 one of the towers collapsed into the moat. Other parts were quarried, notably for laying local roads. In 1808 William Lloyd attempted to revive its fortunes by restoring the gatehouse. As recently as the 1990s, it was still being let out as a farmhouse. Finally, in 2002, it became the property of the Whittington Castle Preservation Trust, whose excellent work has sparked a revival in its fortunes.

Though the stonework is much depleted, the castle is full of legends and hauntings. To this day, the arms of the FitzWarins continues to hang over the gateway. According to local legend, the coat of arms is not the only reminder of former times. A hooded figure has reputedly been spotted in the grounds. The same is true of a blacksmith wearing a battered apron.

Among the most bizarre of Whittington's tales is that of a cursed chest. Local lore states that considerable misfortune awaits the castle's heir if one should open it. The chest, believed to be a casket from the Elizabethan period, was removed from the castle in recent years. It is unclear whether this is related to the curse or simply for its safekeeping. Intriguingly, it is also alleged that someone tossed the key into the moat to avoid the temptation. The curse's origin is unknown, though another story tells that two children died on opening it. It is reputedly their ghosts that have been seen peering out through a window. This may well be the same room that certain staff members have been reluctant to enter.

Undoubtedly the most alluring of Whittington's legends concerns King Arthur and the Knights of the Holy Grail. According to local legend, the grail was kept in the castle chapel during the thirteenth century, becoming the possession of Fulk FitzWarin, who was the great-grandson of Payne Peverel, one of the original guardians. Furthermore, Arthurian lore speaks of the white castle in the white town. Whittington derives from 'white town', so the castle was indeed located in the white town. More compelling still, its proximity to *Viroconium*, a candidate some have conjectured for a historical Camelot, potentially merits a connection with Arthurian Britain.

Perhaps most intriguing was the discovery of the so-called 'Marian Chalice' in a nearby cave. The origin of this strange, tiny article is unknown. Tests in recent years have concluded it to be an ointment jar, with persuasive evidence that it consists of the type of material used in the Holy Land in the first century AD. Though it is improbable that it was used to drink wine at the last supper, the 'Marian Chalice' is, nevertheless, a rare trinket. Some claim it was once used by Mary Magdalene to store ointments or perfume and brought to England as part of the fabled voyage with Joseph of Arimathea. Proof, alas, remains elusive.

Wigmore

A seat of aristocratic power in its prime, little now remains of Wigmore Castle. Located a steep one-mile walk from the Herefordshire village of the same name, it was built between 1067 and 1071 under the watchful eye of the powerful Norman, William FitzOsbern, 1st Earl of Hereford. Despite putting significant effort into its construction, William the Conqueror stripped FitzOsbern's son, Roger de Breteuil, of the castle for participating in the unsuccessful 'Revolt of the Earls' in 1075.

At Roger's expense, the castle served as the home of the influential Mortimer family, who expanded it and upgraded it in stone. Sited on a narrow ridge, its natural defences were among the most impressive in the region. It remained in the family's possession despite being besieged by Henry II in the summer of 1155 due to Hugh de Mortimer's refusal to return nearby Bridgnorth Castle to the Crown. The inner gatehouse and D-shaped east tower are the main survivors from the Mortimer era.

In time, Hugh's descendants would endure similarly fraught relations with the monarchs. Most prominent among their number was that 'greatest traitor' Roger Mortimer, 1st Earl of March, who suffered time in the Tower and execution at Tyburn following his rebellion against Edward II and later role in Edward's usurpation. In 1329 Roger held a tournament near Wigmore with the young Edward III in attendance.

When Edward III confiscated the family estates, Wigmore was one of many properties taken by the Crown. The king enjoyed several weeks there in the summer of 1332. Ten years later, he returned the fortress to the Mortimers. Roger's grandson and namesake, Roger, 2nd Earl of March, was a founder member of the Knights of the Garter. His grandson, Roger 4th Earl, was briefly Richard II's chosen heir. When the male Mortimer line ended in 1424, it was granted to Richard, 3rd Duke of York, whose son, later Edward IV, pitched battle nearby at Mortimer's Cross in 1461. It seems likely that Edward was stationed at Wigmore. Though at least one document describes the castle as derelict at that time, archaeological evidence suggests building work followed.

What occurred at Wigmore in the years that followed is something of an enigma. In the centuries since, the castle found use as a prison. The Elizabethan scientist and alleged alchemist and conjurer, Dr John Dee, apparently viewed Wigmore Abbey's records in a chapel in the inner bailey in 1574. In 1601 the owner, Sir Gelli Meyrick, was executed for his role in the Essex rebellion, and Elizabeth I sold the castle to Sir Thomas Harley. After it avoided use in the civil war, during which the lady of the castle had its defences dismantled to prevent Royalist occupation, its decline continued.

Now overgrown, the castle is a tranquil ruin over which an air of mystery hangs. It is to English Heritage's great credit they have maintained the wildness, not least as many rare flowers and bats have thrived. The climb from the local town is among the steepest one will encounter, albeit worth the likely solitude and expansive views.

Though free of hauntings, there is a strange story that one of the Mortimers was appointed co-guardian of the orphaned sons of one of the lords of Dinâs Bran. Intent on keeping the young boys' inheritance, soldiers serving him and the earl of Warenne threw the innocent lads into the River Dee, supposedly at the bridge at Holt, near Wrexham, where the meagre remains of Holt Castle can still be found. The story is courtesy of the Georgian author Thomas Pennant, who cites a manuscript described by the Reverend Price, who was then keeper of the Bodleian Library. Local lore also claims that one can still hear the boys' desperate screams amidst the sound of the cascading water. Sadly, it is unclear which characters were involved.

Chapter 9

The Best of the Rest

Further to the castles already mentioned, the following section is my best attempt at including some of Wales's other wonderful fortresses. Some of these are now particularly sparse or so far off the beaten track they are tough to find. Others are privately owned and not open to the public. Nevertheless, in my opinion, they are worthy of inclusion.

No castle in Wales 'has been oftner stain'd with the infamy of treachery'. So wrote the acclaimed antiquarian William Camden of **Abergavenny Castle**. Located in the lovely market town of the same name in the shadow of the black mountains, the castle was established around 1087 by Hamelin de Balun to guard the Usk valley.

The reasons for Camden's gloomy commentary undoubtedly concern one particularly nasty moment in the castle's early history. In the 1160s, Miles de Gloucester's son, Henry Fitzmiles, Lord of Abergavenny, was murdered. The prime suspect was Seisyll ap Dyfnwal of Castell Arnallt. On Henry's death, the castle passed to his daughter Bertha, and her husband, William de Braose, who rebuilt parts of it. At Christmas 1175, de Braose requested Seisyll's company, along with his son, Geoffrey, and many leaders of Gwent. Then, in a scene worthy of *Game of Thrones*, William had his visitors slaughtered in the great hall. The genocide and subsequent land grab led to William's forced retirement, after which the family name remained tainted. In 1182, Hywel ap Iorwerth, Lord of Caerleon, ordered the castle's razing in revenge. Though William was absent, most of his men were captured.

In 1190, the castle was rebuilt in red sandstone and was visited by King John in 1215. The Hastings family expanded it in the following centuries, after which Owain Glyndŵr sacked the town. No resident lord occupied the castle after that time. As the Roundheads neared, Charles I ordered its slighting to prevent occupation. At its prime, a curtain wall and ditch surrounded a stone keep, chapel and towers. A hunting lodge was built atop the motte in the nineteenth century, by which time it was renowned among walkers for lovely views. A public garden followed, and it is now home to a museum.

Sometimes known as Queen's Hope, **Caergwrle Castle's** timeline is quite possibly the shortest of any Welsh castle. The castle's story began with the breakdown of relations between Llywelyn ap Gruffudd and his brothers. After their father, Gruffudd – the son of Llywelyn ap Iorwerth – died in 1244, Llywelyn ap Gruffudd defied the Welsh law of 'equal shares' and claimed Gwynedd for himself, to his brothers' expense. Dafydd, the third brother, took his grievances to Edward I, who took Dafydd into his service and granted him funds to start the castle at Caergwrle. The castle was erected at Dafydd's behest in 1277, a short distance to the south of Flint and Ewloe.

Things changed, however, when Dafydd rebelled against Edward, prompting the king to send Reginald de Grey, 1st Baron Grey de Wilton to claim the castle in June 1282. On Grey's arrival, Dafydd had already retreated and compromised the structure. Edward granted the castle to his queen, Eleanor, and a town was planned. This was shelved when a fire broke out in the royals' presence in September 1283. Dafydd was executed on 3 October 1283 and was the last independent ruler of Wales.

Despite surviving only six years, its contributions to Edward's conquest remain noteworthy. In the sixteenth century, a millstone quarry opened beneath the cliffs and caused at least one of the walls to collapse. In 1823, a Bronze Age bowl was discovered at the castle, dubbed 'the Caergwrle Bowl'. The ghost of an elderly woman in Victorian garb has reportedly been seen near the castle. The same is true of a ghostly black Labrador. Nearby, the historic Packhorse Bridge also has a reputation for being haunted.

Located in the heart of Glamorgan, the Cadw-owned ruins of **Coity Castle** began life as a simple timber ringwork – most likely on the remains of something preexisting. Among the usual stone upgrades were a rectangular keep and a strong curtain wall, which were added by the de Turberville family in the 1100s. Over the next two centuries, the Gamage family's further work included stone vaults, an octagonal pier, domestic quarters, and a chapel.

Consistent with many castles of that age, inheritance favoured the male heir, and property often left the family through marriage. When Thomas de la Bere – a minor – died in October 1414, the castle became the property of Sarah de Turberville, the younger sister of the previous owner, Richard Turberville. At least two years earlier, Sarah had married Sir William Gamage of Roggiett, at which time Thomas de la Bere was still alive. In 1412, William embarked on a month-long siege to rid the castle of the Verneys, who had attempted to claim the castle. Lady Joan, the wife of Sir Richard Verney, was of Turberville stock as the daughter of Lady Margaret. Due to her status as a childless widow, her claim was granted little respect by the authorities of the day. Despite their later success in obtaining ownership, Gamage and his associate, Sir Gilbert Denys, were sent to the Tower of London as punishment for the unlawful siege. They were finally released on the death of Henry IV.

For more than a century and a half, the Gamages added to the castle before leaving it in 1584. Whether the fortress ever had another owner is unclear. Abandoned no later than the reign of Charles I, Coity was sold in the 1700s to the Edwins of Llanharry and later the earls of Dunraven before entering public ownership.

Close to the small town of Dolgellau exists a rare example of a twelfth-century native Welsh castle. Though what now exists of **Cymer Castle** is little more than a tree-covered pile, the structure is rare for being stone-built of native pedigree. The motte appears to have been in existence by 1116, courtesy of the Welsh prince, Uchdryd ab Edwin of Tegeingl. It can still be found near Cymer Abbey, which was an important site throughout the medieval period.

Two imposing mounts and a series of ditches are the highlights of what once made up **Deganwy Castle**. Tradition places Deganwy as the chief fortress of Maelgwn Gwynedd, who ruled Gwynedd during the sixth century. A nearby hill, Bryn Maelgwyn, was named in the prince's honour. Roman occupation before that is also likely. Excavations in the past century have unearthed early medieval pottery, while a chance discovery in July 1979 revealed a hoard of 204 silver Cnut (Canute) pennies.

Even as a timber structure, the castle proved an effective defence against Irish raiders. Though the primitive fortress was struck by lightning around 812 and abandoned, Henry III chose to rebuild the castle at the cost of £2,200 to strengthen his control over Gwynedd. Unfortunately for the king, work came undone early in the Second Barons' War when Llywelyn ap Gruffudd razed it. Edward I erected a new, more impressive fortress at Conwy. Long-standing tradition claims that the first stone of Conwy came from Deganwy.

Dolforwyn Castle is a special one in Welsh history. Native as opposed to Norman, the castle has little in common with most in this book. On invading the area in 1257, Llywelyn ap Gruffudd constructed the castle between 1273 and 1277 to affirm his hold on his newly conquered lands. Rectangular in design and primitive compared to the mighty Norman citadels, the castle was hewn from the rock and consisted of a rectangular keep and circular tower. Later additions included the construction of ramparts.

Having failed to obtain Edward I's permission for the new build, tensions grew. No sooner had the castle been created, Roger Mortimer, 1st Baron Wigmore and Henry de Lacy, Earl of Lincoln launched an attack. It fell on 8 April 1277 due to a combination of its limited design and lack of water supply. Custody was granted initially to Gruffydd ap Gwenwynwyn and later Roger Mortimer, who upgraded its defences. It remained in the family's hands until Mortimer's famous descendant and namesake, Roger Mortimer, 1st Earl of March, revolted against Edward II. It appears to have been occupied until the reign of Richard II, by which time it was in poor condition. Ownership later passed to the earls of Powis and eventually Cadw.

Local legend tells that a maiden named Sabrina drowned nearby and became the Goddess of the Severn: Dolforwyn literally translates as 'maiden's meadow'. Sabrina is mentioned in John's Milton's masque *Comus*. The castle also features in the work of Bernard Cornwell. Ironically, excavations have included part of a leather book cover, a small die, a silver coin, and catapult balls.

Close to the village of the same name in Conwy County Borough, the rectangular-towered **Dolwyddelan Castle** is another underappreciated gem. Famed for its stunning views, the fortress was another of native origin that served the princes of Gwynedd. Though no written accounts exist of its construction, it is believed to have been the birthplace of

Llywelyn ap Iorwerth. Another possibility is that Llywelyn was born within the nearby tower of Tomen Castell and personally oversaw Dolwyddelan's construction.

Edward I's conquest of the castle in 1283 proved a critical step in the war with Wales, not least as it deprived the Welsh of a key lookout point. During its capture, Edward took an inspired decision to issue troops with white uniforms to camouflage them in the winter landscape. After taking the castle on 18 January, he ordered the addition of the second tower. Repairs and other additions followed over the next three years, including a curtain wall to link the pair. Edward is also recorded as having kept a permanent garrison there until 1290.

After playing no role in any of the later wars, the castle's purpose dwindled. Following Owain Glyndŵr's rebellion of the early 1400s, further improvements were made by the local lord, Maredudd ab Ieuan ap Robert, on being granted the lease in 1488. Restoration during the middle of the nineteenth century by Lord Willoughby de Eresby, following damage to one of the towers, saw the addition of the battlements. It entered public hands in 1930.

Close to Dinefwr Castle, **Dryslwyn Castle** also enjoys a position of prominence over the Towy Valley. Though a prehistoric origin cannot be ruled out, its story is also intrinsically connected with the Princes of Deheubarth. On Lord Rhys's death in 1197, his sons engaged in a bitter dispute concerning their inheritance.

Exactly which prince built Dryslwyn is unknown. Evidence suggests construction mainly occurred in the 1220s, which may connect it to Rhys Gryg. The castle has similarities with nearby Dinefwr, notably the round keep, which is also visible from a distance. The *Annales Cambrie* recall that a siege by the Seneschal of Carmarthen was laid in 1246 in support of the 'rightful owner' – whoever that was.

The castle was expanded around Edward's conquest and remained in Welsh hands after Dafydd's death in 1283. Rhys ap Maredudd held the castle until his revolt in 1287 culminated in Edward laying a bloody three-week siege that required 11,000 men and at least one trebuchet. Owain Glyndŵr seized the fortress in the summer of 1403. On its recapture, the English removed much of the stonework and blocked off the gatehouse. A fire also gutted some of the interior timber buildings.

Only earthworks remain of the castle at **Ewyas Harold**. Its early construction was probably of Saxon origin, which survived until 1052. William FitzOsbern rebuilt the castle before the *Domesday Book*'s compiling, after which a priory was established in the bailey. The castle gradually decayed after involvement in many border skirmishes, including the Marshal War of 1233-34. Refortification occurred under William Beauchamp, Lord Abergavenny, to withstand Owain Glyndŵr, who appears to have concentrated on other areas.

On the outskirts of the village of the same name in the Vale of Glamorgan, **Fonmon Castle** has little in common with its Norman ancestry. It is unusual for being one of the few revamped in the nineteenth century, yet not of neo-Gothic architecture.

Though minimal records exist of its formation, the castle was clearly of Norman origin. Its evolution likely followed the pattern of an eleventh-century motte and bailey, upgraded in stone no later than the early 1200s. A now-debunked local legend long told that the castle was created at the behest of Oliver St John of Fonmon, one of the legendary Twelve Knights of Glamorgan who proved so instrumental in the Norman Conquest. Sadly, the story was fabricated by the influential Stradling family (see St Donat's Castle).

While a small rectangular stone keep was added no later than the early 1200s, around the same time as the original curtain wall, its significant developments occurred later that century, notably an L-shaped structure that included a tower at the south-east corner. Bizarrely, the broadest of the defensive walls is the one that overlooks the ravine, which would typically have been the weakest side as it was already impenetrable. The owners at that time were the St John family, predecessors of the Viscounts Bolingbroke. Despite avoiding conflict in the civil war, they were unable to foot the bill for its upkeep and sold the castle to Colonel Philip Jones, who created the east range and a further wing on the north side.

Further developments, including mock battlements, took place in the mid-1700s under the colonel's great-great-grandson, Robert Jones III. After a period of decline, improvements were made in the second half of the nineteenth century before Fonmon entered the Boothby baronetcy through marriage. Though little remains of the early castle, it is unique in being home to a dinosaur park, medieval village, and the setting of various environmental initiatives.

Only one round tower survives of **Hawarden Castle**. Another of possible Iron Age pedigree, the medieval fortress rose as a Norman motte and bailey, which lasted until the thirteenth century. Re-erected in stone, Hawarden was besieged by Dafydd ap Gruffudd in Easter 1282, thus reigniting hostilities with Edward. The *Lanercost Chronicle* was especially scathing of Dafydd's actions occurring on Palm Sunday.

Twelve years later, Madog ap Llywelyn took the castle, after which things remained quiet until the civil war. The remains were slighted on Cromwell's orders and now form part of the New Hawarden Castle estate, which occasionally welcomes visitors.

Few castles are richer in history than **Llawhaden.** Owned by the Bishopric of the Diocese of St David since around 1115, the site's history reaches back to the Bronze Age. Local excavations have revealed the vicinity to possess the most significant number of defended sites in West Wales, most of which were established in the Iron Age. Sections of a Roman road have also been uncovered nearby. Saint Aidan is believed to have founded a *clas* at the site, which preceded the stone church.

Often known as one of the 'seven Bishop Houses', Llawhaden Castle's time may have begun as a timber fortress atop something prehistoric like nearby ones. The early castle, most likely built by Bishop Bernard in the reign of Henry I, was razed by the Welsh in 1193, after which the Bishop of St David's, most likely Peter de Leia, rebuilt it as a *caput* of his barony. While only the moat and earthbank survive from Bernard's castle, the stone ruins mostly date to Bishop Adam de Houghton 1362-89, whose additions included the Great Hall and iconic gatehouse.

The local village, which included a hospice for paupers and pilgrims, suffered during the Dissolution and for a time fell into decline. Similar was true of the castle, both a bishop's house and a Marcher lordship. Shortly before the Dissolution, Bishop William Barlow sold the lead from the roof for his daughter's dowry, after which the building never recovered. Renovation work began in 1930 under the Commission of Works. Today, the ruins are well looked after by Cadw and offer stunning views of the wider countryside.

Located on a bend of the River Teifi, in the market town of **Newcastle Emlyn** in Carmarthenshire, the ruins of the thirteenth-century castle are both rugged and picturesque.

The *Brut y Tywysogion* (the Brut Chronicle) recorded that Llywelyn ap Iorwerth took a local castle in 1215, which may have been Newcastle Emlyn, if not something more primitive. Most of the ruins post-date Llywelyn, albeit marginally. Local tradition holds that Maredudd ap Rhys built the castle around 1240, which would be a rarity in Welsh history, as the area was traditionally Norman ruled. Maredudd was himself of esteemed stock as the grandson of Rhys ap Gruffudd, Prince of Deheubarth.

In 1287 Maredudd's son, Rhys ap Maredudd, was actively in rebellion against Edward I and fled to Newcastle Emlyn after being besieged at Dryslwyn Castle (another stone native Welsh castle on a hilltop close to Carmarthen). When an English force that included forty – then later sixty – oxen dragged the siege engine from Dryslwyn Castle to Newcastle Emlyn via Cardigan, the garrison held firm before being forced to surrender.

When Edward completed his conquest, for a time, Newcastle Emlyn was at peace. In 1343 the castle became one of twenty-six to be held by Edward, the Black Prince when installed as Prince of Wales. For nineteen years, it enjoyed stability under Edward's castellan, Richard de la Bere. When Owain Glyndŵr's forces laid siege in 1403, the castle briefly fell before being repaired later that century.

With close attention, one can discern clues as to its appearance at that time. Due to the river's natural bends, access was only possible from the west. The triangular inner ward, which included a great hall, kitchen, and chapel, was protected by a curtain wall and a twin-towered gatehouse. The towers were rectangular on the inside and semi-octagonal on the outside, which accounts for the bizarre shape. An external stairway to the first floor allowed access to the curtain wall. During the early Tudor era, Sir Rhys ap Thomas installed glass windows.

By the early 1600s, a survey concluded the castle was in good condition, which inspired King Charles to set up a garrison there. The castle was besieged around 1645 and conquered at least once. Though the exact circumstances are either lost or unrecorded, a record from early the following century states Newcastle Emlyn was 'dismantled in the late Civill warres and plundered and ever since neglected'. Little survives besides the outer defences.

Overlooking the town of Bridgend in Glamorgan, **Newcastle** was one of three Norman castles constructed at the western limit of early Norman occupancy: the others being Coity and Ogmore.

Though details of its early years are somewhat vague, a timber ringwork fortress appears to have been put down early in Henry I's reign. The legendary William de Londres – one of the Twelve Knights of Glamorgan – allegedly built the castle to help augment Norman rule over east Wales. At the time, the area was the preserve of the Norman Robert Fitzhamon, to whom de Londres was devoted.

Towards the end of Henry II's reign, the castle was upgraded by either William Fitz Robert, 2nd Earl of Gloucester, or the king himself when the Crown absorbed the lordship on the earl's death in 1183. Chief among the works was the thickening of the outer wall to combat the uprising of Morgan ap Caradog, the lord of Afan. After the castle was granted to John, at that time styled count of Mortain, he gifted it to Morgan on his father's death. In 1208 it passed to Morgan's son, Lleison, and then to John's divorced first wife, Isabella, Countess of Gloucester, on Lleison's death in 1214. After Isabella's death in October 1217, the castle changed hands at least twice, culminating in its passing to the de Turberville clan of Coity Castle.

Records of the castle's later history are frustratingly scant. As the de Turbervilles preferred Coity, Newcastle later passed to the Berkerolles and Gamages, who left it largely untouched. While most of the stonework dates from the late twelfth century, the three-storey south tower was revamped with fine windows and fireplaces in the Tudor era. By the end of the century, the castle was seemingly abandoned. Like the Gamages' other castles, it was sold in 1718 to Samuel Edwin of Llanmihangel Place and later the earls of Dunraven.

Wales also has two Newports. While the one in Monmouthshire has been mentioned, the less spectacular Pembrokeshire namesake was built on land the Normans seized from Rhys ap Tewdwr. A later Norman Marcher lord William Fitz Martin founded **Newport** in 1197 on abandoning his base at nearby Nevern. In 1215 and 1257, Llywelyn ap Iorwerth and Llywelyn ap Gruffudd, respectively, conquered the Royalist garrisons. In both cases, the Fitz Martins later reclaimed it.

None of the original castle has survived – a fact mainly attributable to Owain Glyndŵr. After a time in the Crown's custody after the owner James Tuchet, Lord Audley was executed for treason against Henry VII in 1497, Newport was returned to his son, John Audley. Audley sold the castle in 1539, by which time the Marcher lordships had been abolished.

In 1859 a more modern property was built on the site of the gatehouse. The present building is a privately owned hotchpotch of additions that post-date Llywelyn ap Gruffudd's attack and isn't open to the public.

Old Beaupre's appearance is similarly mixed. That a proper castle ever existed on the site is unclear. Based on the available evidence, the L-shaped building's development continued from the original construction in the early fourteenth century until the 1700s.

During the Tudor period, the house underwent significant remodelling under Vice-Admiral Sir Rhys Mansel, then William Basset, whose family owned the castle for much of its history. William's work was continued by his son, Richard, by which time the gatehouse and triple storeyed Renaissance porch were all completed. Work in the Tudor era may have seen the demise of an earlier castle in favour of the farmhouse-style building that exists now.

Due to its lack of defences, Old Beaupre was never garrisoned and experienced no Roundhead siege. Such developments, however, did not prevent the family from falling on hard times. Around the turn of the eighteenth century, the castle passed to the Jones family, who took up residence in the smaller adjacent building, dubbed New Beaupre. When the Joneses sold in 1709, it was barely habitable. Today, only the south-eastern block remains a residence.

Over the years, this amalgamation of old and more recent has led to some interesting ghost stories. Like many others in South Wales, Old Beaupre is allegedly haunted by the banshee-like Gwrach y Rhibyn. Local legend tells that she would rise out of the nearby river at twilight, her arms flapping, bat-like. Reports also tell of workers seeing her wailing and sobbing among the ruins. Though New Beaupre is a private residence, the castle is Cadw-owned and welcomes visitors.

Open to visitors in 1978-2002 before being purchased by a private owner, **Penhow Castle** is also the setting of some strange ghost stories. Built by Sir Roger de St Maur, a Norman who served the Lord of Striguil (Chepstow), the castle was inhabited no later than 1129.

It was from the St Maur line that the infamous Seymours descended. Indeed, Penhow is their first documented home. Much of the modern castle dates from the reign of Henry VII, thus preceding Queen Jane, the third wife of Henry VIII. The Seymours later vacated the property for

Hatch Beauchamp in Somerset and Wulfhall in Wiltshire, at which time Penhow was sold to the Lewis family of St Pierre. Around 1674, they converted the castle into something more contemporary. Their claims to fame included Thomas Lewis as high sheriff, who was also married to the daughter of the Lord Mayor of London, Sir Richard Levett.

Described by some as the 'oldest continuously inhabited castle in Wales', the attractive castellated manor house has many alleged apparitions. A young girl dressed in a blue-grey apron haunts the castle's great hall. Intriguingly, the top bedroom also experienced misfortune involving a young girl. Next door to the fortress stands the church of St John the Baptist. Buried in the churchyard is the nine-year-old Anne Keene, who is believed to have been the girl in question.

One evening, a dinner party was interrupted by the music of a 'ghostly string quartet'. A bearded man of around forty has been seen in the Banqueting Hall, the site of another alleged tragedy. Another male, allegedly a Seymour, has been seen in the courtyard. A female spirit has been seen on the staircase, where the sounds of mysterious footsteps have also been heard. Orbs, strange lights, and cold spots have also been reported in various parts. The castle's proximity to the thirteenth-century church and a historic coaching inn are further reminders of the area's past.

Just the mount survives of the castle at **Radnor**. Found close to the Norman church, the original motte and bailey – recorded in the native tongue as *Trefaesyfed* – was most likely erected at the behest of William FitzOsbern, Earl of Hereford, within five years of the Norman Conquest.

Around the time the *Domesday Book* was compiled, the castle was granted to Philip de Braose, 2nd Lord of Bramber, an early magnate of the imperious de Braose clan. It remained in safe hands until the Welsh took it following the Battle of Dingestow. In 1188 Rhys ap Gruffudd, Prince of Deheubarth, and his son-in-law Einion o'r Porth hosted Baldwin, Archbishop of Canterbury, and Gerald of Wales there as they sought pledges for the Third Crusade. While Einion was the victim of fratricide three years later, in 1195, William de Braose's wife, Maud, played an integral part in retaking the castle. On hearing of the coup, Rhys laid siege to it and subsequently defeated Roger Mortimer in the Battle of Radnor.

At the turn of the next century, by which time Rhys was dead, William de Braose retook Radnor. Around 1208 fortunes changed when John carried out his infamous vendetta against William, culminating in his exile in France and the death of his wife and child at Corfe Castle. In August 1216, while John sought the Pope's assistance in annulling the charter signed at Runnymede, he had the castle burned to restrict the family's activities after Giles de Braose, Bishop of Hereford claimed it. After Giles's death in 1215, the castle became Crown property.

In 1231, as Henry III struggled to halt Llywelyn ap Iorwerth's advances, the castle was again razed. Two years later, as Llywelyn allied himself with the rebel baron, Richard Marshal, 3rd Earl of Pembroke, Richard's brother-in-law, Richard, Earl of Cornwall – younger brother of Henry III – had the castle 'illegally' rebuilt. When the Marshal War was over, the fortress became the property of the Mortimers. When the king engaged in hostilities with Simon de Montfort, 6th Earl of Leicester, Radnor was again destroyed: this time, permanently.

So scant are sources for **Rhayader Castle**, it is no longer discernible whether records concern the motte and bailey in the town or a mound across the river. At least one of the two was likely erected by Rhys ap Gruffudd, c. 1177. At the time, Rhys had recently conquered Buellt; however, five years later, the warring pair made peace, and Rhys returned Buellt to William. Rhys rebuilt the castle in 1194 after Maelgwn ap Cadwallon destroyed it six years earlier.

After Rhys's death in 1197, the castle was caught up in an inheritance war between two of his children and again destroyed. Roger Mortimer – a forebear of the 'greatest traitor' – began a third castle in the early 1200s; however, work was halted when it was captured. Llywelyn ap Iorwerth destroyed the castle for the final time in 1231.

Though the castle no longer stands, a bizarre story is associated. At some point in the twelfth century, a knight held captive was granted a 'magic bell' and told it could break down his cell walls. On testing it, the walls remained solid, and his wardens laughed their heads off. A short time later, lightning struck the castle, reputedly destroying all but the wall on which the bell hung. The nearby hotel is reputedly the subject of paranormal happenings.

Even less now exists of the castle in the Marcher village of **St Clears**. The formation of the nearby Cluniac priory no later than the early reign of Henry I probably indicates that the castle was erected around that time. The 30-ft-high motte is still identifiable from its shape; earthworks and a few traces of former stone walls also offer evidence of the past establishment. Following the castle's formation, a Marcher borough grew around it.

The castle is recorded as having been conquered up to three times by the Welsh. A reference to Rhys ap Gruffudd's taking of 'Ystrad Cyngen' in 1153 almost certainly concerns St Clears. Gerald of Wales also mentions it as the residence of twelve archers who murdered a young Welshman 'devoutly hastening to meet the archbishop': most likely to offer his services as a crusader. As penance, the guilty dozen took up the cross.

In 1189 Rhys took the castle a second time and granted it to his son, Hywel Sais. In 1195, William de Braose recovered it for King John before Llywelyn ap Iorwerth conquered it in 1215. When hostilities ended, the castle was granted to William Marshal, 2nd Earl of Pembroke – son of Henry III's great regent – and presumably strengthened. In its heyday, the stone surroundings initially proved effective in withstanding Owain Glyndŵr before the garrison surrendered in 1405. The castle was situated between the rivers Tâf and Cynin and possessed an impressive support network. A local quay on the Tâf was reputedly capable of accommodating ships of 500 tons.

The ruined riverside castle in the centre of **Swansea** was once among the great fortresses of the Gower. On being granted the lordship in 1106, Henry de Beaumont, 1st Earl of Warwick established a timber motte and bailey, which was completed by 1116. At approximately 170ft in diameter, the motte was one of the largest in Wales until urban sprawl claimed it in the early 1900s.

A far more sophisticated castle awaited Rhys ap Gruffudd in 1192. While the original had failed to see out 1116, a ten-week siege that brought the garrison to the brink of starvation could not defeat them. Better luck awaited Llywelyn ap Iorwerth in 1217; however, the castle was restored to Henry III three years later. It is likely that work began on the new castle almost immediately and continued until the Statute of Rhuddlan in 1284. Mention of the 'New Castle' was first recorded in the thirteenth century.

Throughout the 1300s, the castle was the property of the de Mowbray family, among whose number, John de Mowbray, was Lord of the Gower from 1331 until his death in October 1361. Over the following three centuries, the owners' regular absence saw the castle fall into decay. By the late 1600s, the tower had become a bottle factory, and a town hall was erected within the walls. The great hall was being used as a workhouse and later a drill room within fifty years, while the town hall was replaced with a post office.

Work on redirecting the river, and the motte's dismantling, followed in the next two centuries, the latter being replaced with a newspaper office. Among those in the employ of the *South Wales Daily Post* was a certain Dylan Thomas. The office was removed in 1976, and the castle opened to the public.

Visually, few towns in Wales compare with stunning **Tenby**. Its beautifully coloured buildings, quaint harbour and sandy beaches have long been the delight of holidaymakers. The town walls have also been well preserved. Their presence offers another bizarre irony. The walls of this most English Pembrokeshire town were erected to keep the Welsh out and still form a significant part of its identity.

Central to the town's development was its castle. The fortress was constructed on a nearby headland following the Norman domination of the early 1100s. A stone tower formed the heart of the structure, around which strong curtain walls, littered with a series of smaller towers, attempted to ensure the town's security. While the walls proved no match for Rhys ap Gruffudd or his brother Maredudd, the English garrison put up a better defence in 1187. A successful sacking of the town by Llywelyn ap Gruffudd in 1260 failed to take the castle.

Following Edward I's subjugation of 1277-83, Tenby was incorporated into the Marcher Lordship of Pembroke, the earl of which was William de Valence. The half-brother of Henry III and husband to William Marshal's granddaughter, Joan, William oversaw the construction of the town walls. Other defensive features followed under Edward III, including a barbican.

In 1457, by which time the earldom had lapsed, Henry VI granted the castle and lordship to Jasper Tudor. Jasper revamped the castle and town, the cost of which impoverished the local merchants. Further additions were made in preparation for post-1588 Spanish armadas. Typically of many defensive fortresses, the civil war was a watershed in Tenby's history. A ten-week Roundhead siege against the refortified castle in 1648 ultimately ended in surrender when the garrison ran low on provisions.

The most important of Jasper's additions was a parapet walk, which forms part of the legendary ghost walk route. The town's wealth of stories of witches, fairies and other strange happenings is especially popular with tourists. Though little of the medieval castle has survived, a path from the picturesque harbour up to castle hill allows a tour of the main gateway and tower. Another walk also offers a complete circuit of the old curtain walls. The museum and art gallery now stands on the site of the great hall.

Another castle that was once the preserve of the Marshals is beautiful **Usk**. Now under private ownership but open to visitors, the earliest records date from 1138 and refer to its being captured by the Welsh. The castle was clearly already in existence by that time, which probably points to its creation no later than the town's establishment about twenty years earlier. Such dates would also tie in with nearby Monmouth and Abergavenny. Far older evidence also confirms a Roman settlement there that predates Caerleon.

The exact circumstances of its construction notwithstanding, the castle's first century was consistent with the ebb and flow of the wider area. After being returned to the English, the Welsh retook it in 1174, despite earlier attempts by the Marcher lord Richard de Clare to strengthen it. The English recaptured it in 1184.

Better efforts followed courtesy of William Marshal, 1st Earl of Pembroke, notably a masonry wall with round towers. In the late summer of 1233, Henry III laid siege to the castle, which was then the property of Richard Marshal, 3rd Earl of Pembroke. Despite the chroniclers speaking of a general weariness among the Royalist troops, Marshal agreed to a fifteen-day surrender, thus allowing Henry to correct 'whatever needed to be correct in the kingdom, with the counsel of the bishops'.

Though Marshal perished the following year, duped by his Irish enemies in league with Henry's chief counsellor, Peter des Roches, Bishop of Winchester, Usk survived unscathed. In 1314 the castle's owner, Gilbert de Clare, 7th Earl of Hertford, was killed at Bannockburn. The fortress also served as the birthplace of the famous chronicler Adam of Usk in 1352.

Usk's next date with destiny corresponded with Owain Glyndŵr's rebellion. In 1402 Owain's forces sacked the town, leading to a significant battle at nearby Pwll Melyn, a quarter-mile walk from the castle. Despite Owain's impressive efforts, calm was brought by the prominent Welsh warrior Dafydd ap Llewelyn ap Hywel, better known as Dafydd Gam. Usk subsequently became the property of the Duchy of Lancaster, whose line occupied the throne of England. After that, the castle suffered a period of neglect. A lack of action in the civil war saw only partial slighting. Since late in the reign of Charles II, the castle gatehouse has been reused as a residence.

Standing high above the Loughor Estuary on the Gower Peninsula, fourteenth-century **Weobley** is another whose designation as a castle is open to debate. The property is another of connection with the de la Beres. A deed from 1318 signed by Adam de la Bere confirms the building's status and association with the original de Braose stewards.

Whether a motte and bailey or something older still preceded the now-ruined stonework is unclear. Far clearer is the origin of the surviving walls, which spanned the reign of Edward II. The death of John de la Bere in 1403 most likely coincides with Owain Glyndŵr's rebellion. Fortunately, the castle remained standing, and the century ended with it under the control of Sir Rhys ap Thomas. When his grandson, Rhys ap Gruffydd, was condemned to death for treason in 1531, Weobley became the property of the Crown. A series of owners and tenants followed until it was presented to the state in 1911.

A final Welsh castle worthy of inclusion is **Wiston**. Erected by the mysterious Flemish settler Wizo (see also Piston Castle), Wiston's destiny began with Henry I's decision to grant land to the Flemish around 1108 after terrible floods in the Low Countries. In later years, the castle veered between royal and native ownership before ultimately returning to English control.

The first prominent example of this came in 1147. Despite Hywel ab Owain's success, the endeavours of Wizo's son, Walter, ensured the castle was reclaimed. In 1193 another Hywel, this time Sais, son of Rhys ap Gruffudd, took it as part of an attempt to reconsolidate Deheubarth. During the siege, Walter's brother, Philip, was taken captive. Two years later, they recovered the castle. Llywelyn ap Iorwerth's sacking in 1220 came within a year of the death of the great William Marshal. Eventually, William's son, heir and namesake, the second earl of Pembroke, oversaw the castle's return. Erection of the newer stone buildings at the expense of the wooden ones duly followed.

Despite William's early progress, work came to a halt shortly after. Whether Llywelyn's continued rampaging of the marches or the deaths of William Marshal, 2nd Earl of Pembroke and his younger siblings without issue by 1245 was the more significant factor is subject to debate. Though records confirm it became the property of one Sir John Wogan under Edward I, his favouring of neighbouring Piston saw the property become abandoned. The Royalists' use of it as a minor outpost in 1643 proved a one-off footnote, and no record of a skirmish exists. When Major-General Rowland Laugharne marched his Roundheads on the area, the only action of note occurred at nearby Colby Moor.

Despite being abandoned for many years, Wiston is noteworthy for remaining a stone motte and bailey. The site, set atop a steep set of steps opposite the local church, is a genuine jewel in the Welsh crown. A reminder that castles come in all shapes and sizes and that sometimes the most basic are also the most special.

On the English side of the border, there are also further castles of interest. The manor house at **Acton Burnell** was built by Robert Burnell, Bishop of Bath and Wells in 1284. The bishop was a close advisor of Edward I, and the manor was close to Watling Street. A combination of both factors saw Burnell granted permission to crenellate that year.

Following Burnell's death in 1292, the estate passed through his descendants and then the Lovels of Titchmarsh through marriage. Henry VII confiscated the land after the Battle of Stoke Field in 1487 and granted it to the Howards, Dukes of Norfolk. The property was largely demolished by the civil war and never sieged.

Ironically, the property's outstanding claim to fame occurred in 1283. It was here, most likely in the barn, Edward held a Parliament. The occasion was notable for being the first that included the House of Commons. The Statute of Acton Burnell is also noteworthy for giving protection to creditors. The ghost of a young girl in white lace has reportedly been seen wandering the ruins. Another has been seen in the nearby hall.

In its prime, **Brampton Bryan Castle** guarded a vital route from Ludlow to Knighton along the Teme Valley: one of the main ways in and out of mid-Wales.

Little is known of the early structure. Recorded as a demesne in the *Domesday Book*, the first reference to the sandstone and ashlar fortress was in 1295 as a 'tower with curtilage'. The owner Bryan de Brampton had died the previous year, after which his son-in-law Robert Harley inherited the castle. In the civil war, a garrison of 100 under the command of Lady Brilliana Harley miraculously withstood 700 Royalists.

Though the castle was ruined and Brilliana succumbed to illness later that year, Brampton Bryan Hall was erected among the ruins. Remarkably the estate has remained under Harley ownership for seven centuries. Local legend tells that the Devil in possession of Cromwell's soul returns to the park every 3 September. In more recent times, it has been used for filming, including *Howard's End.*

The first motte and bailey at **Clifford Castle** was established in 1070 by William FitzOsbern, 1st Earl of Hereford on a cliff overlooking a ford on the Wye. Its location on the flood plain offered an extra form of defence with the occasional creation of a shallow lake. After FitzOsbern succumbed to his wounds in Flanders, his son, Roger de Breteuil, forfeited Clifford and his other lands for engaging in the 'Revolt of the Earls' in 1075. The castle was granted to Ralph Tosny, who rebuilt it in stone with the Crown's permission. The marriage of Ralph's daughter, Margaret, to Walter Fitz Richard saw Walter adopt the name Walter de Clifford no later than 1162. His daughter, Rosamund, was the same 'Fair Rosamund' who allegedly became Henry II's mistress.

Walter's grandson of the same name was at the helm in September 1233 when Henry III laid siege to the castle due to Walter's alliance with Richard Marshal, 3rd Earl of Pembroke. Only a few days followed before Walter and Henry came to peace. Sadly, Walter dishonestly led his troops against Llywelyn ap Iorwerth, his father-in-law, who had only engaged against Henry on Walter's behalf. About twenty years later, Walter's hot-headedness saw another rebellion. Among his vulgar traits, he forced a royal messenger to eat a royal writ – wax seal and all. Consequently, Henry III stripped him of Marcher lord privileges.

A lack of a male heir saw Walter's daughter, Matilda, inherit the castle in the 1260s. John Giffard conquered it during the Second Barons' War and kidnapped and raped Matilda. In keeping with the abhorrent laws of the time, rape was followed by marriage. On Giffard's death in 1299, the castle passed to the Mortimers of Wigmore and diminished in value. It was garrisoned against Owain Glyndŵr but never repaired. Excavations between 1925 and 1953 revealed the foundations of several buildings, including twin towers, animal remains, pottery, iron, arrowheads, and a Roman brooch. William FitzOsbern's great motte now occupies the heart of the remains.

The red sandstone ruins of the castle of **Ruyton-XI-Towns** stand in the village churchyard. The Welsh destroyed the original castle in 1202 and again by the forces of Owain Glyndŵr after being rebuilt in the early fourteenth century. The village is small and atmospheric, comprised of the amalgamation of 11 hamlets.

The castle ruins have something of a dreamy quality and are an interesting visit. Local lore states that the ruins are plagued by a strange mist in the dead of night that rises from the valley below, only to reveal a headless horseman.

The final castle worthy of inclusion is **Amroth Castle**. Though little, if anything, remains of the fifteenth-century residence on which the eighteenth-century castellated mansion now stands, it was at this caravan park I first became acquainted with the castles of Wales. Thank you for the memories, Amroth!

Postscript

Writing this book has been an enormous pleasure – not least as it gave me the perfect opportunity to revisit old ground. Equally rewarding was the chance to study different eras of history and visit some truly fascinating locations for the first time. As I recounted in the introduction, attempts at gaining a deeper understanding of Britain's history very much forms the heart of my personal story. One that remains ongoing!

As is true of all my books, many people were of great help to me throughout the journey, not least the fabulous staff at the castles in question. As usual, a great many obstacles needed overcoming. My greatest regret – as I'm sure all readers will be able to sympathise with – is that much of the writing took place in lockdown. Few things whet a history lover's appetite like exploring castles, so it was indescribably frustrating that I began this book when the castles were closed. The more I thought about this, the more I found a bizarre irony. For much of 2020-21, the people of Britain – and the wider world – have been forced to stay at home. Similarly, during the Middle Ages, the castle's primary focus was to keep the outside world at bay.

In many ways, we, too, have been forced to adopt something of a siege mentality throughout the pandemic. For this reason alone, I will find it particularly interesting to return to this in future years to see how life has changed when Covid-19 fades into normality. This will be especially fascinating for subsequent editions. Will recent times change our visiting patterns, or will most things soon go back to how they were? From a research perspective, such things are already making me look at history differently. Throughout the medieval period, the average citizen was perpetually on guard against possible threats. Not only were they frequently worried about their livelihoods and personal liberties, even prepared to go to war over them, but they also spent much of their lives trying to stave off a deadly plague. It has often been said that history repeats. Never have I understood this more clearly. As they say, the more things change, the more they stay the same.

Despite the challenges of writing during lockdown, I must also admit to being incredibly lucky. In the case of this book, I was not forced to rely on my experiences of this last year alone. As I have mentioned many times already, my love of castles has been lifelong. This is particularly true concerning the castles of Wales. I am, therefore, most grateful that both of my recent castle books have been possible to write.

I would love to say that this book is in some way fully comprehensive on Wales's castles, but that would be a simplification. As far as I'm aware, no practical guide containing anything like a complete list has ever been published. A few very reasonable efforts have been made, especially online, yet none would claim to be finished. Frankly, I doubt such a database is possible. An estimated 600 historical castle sites have been identified in Wales. Most of these have little or nothing remaining. In some instances, any surviving earthworks are either minor or hidden beneath dense greenery. I say this not to deprive them of their significance – quite the contrary. Several of the type have been included in this book. I chose them because their story is worthy of telling. While I have tried, where possible, to focus on castles that can be visited – at least under normal circumstances – it is not the historian's job to discriminate or to fall into the trap of judging books by covers. The story of what is now a barren hill may be every bit as important as a mighty citadel. At times like this, it is essential to remember that any history writer's first job is to judge their chosen subject by the standards of its time rather than our own. Never, under any circumstances, should history become tainted by the complications of the present.

Fortunately for the castle lover, no better country exists than Wales for its natural tendency to honour its past and keep it alive. Neither is there a country that takes the preservation of its historical sites more seriously. From the fortresses of the princes of Gwynedd to Edward I's Iron Ring, Wales is the proud home to no fewer than 200 visitable castles. Of these, ten were added from scratch by Edward I. Many more, of course, were of Norman pedigree. While the former are undoubtedly among the most famous, not to mention the most visited, practically every region of Wales is stocked with its share of sights capable of thrilling locals and tourists.

As we have learned, English subjugation was just one reason for a castle to be established. Further to the ongoing wars, a key reason for the large number is geography. There is no doubt that Wales's natural scenery lent itself to the castle. A land of rivers, coasts, valleys and mountains, the possibilities were endless. Natural water supplies were also far more common than many of Wales's European counterparts, thanks to the rain. Being a hillier land than England, it is also no surprise that they were built on sites that previously served as hill forts. No matter what part of Wales a native or Norman warlord ventured into, there would rarely have been any shortage of higher ground to establish a fortress.

Wales's pre-Norman history should not be overlooked in this regard. Throughout the period 950-1063, many key events were imperative to creating early fortresses. No fewer than thirty-five Welsh rulers died during that period, and consequently, the land grabs saw Wales divided into smaller kingdoms. On the one hand, such circumstances allowed Gruffudd ap Llywelyn to emerge as universal ruler; on the other, it also led to his death and the early Norman inroads.

Throughout the period 1066-1410, the kingdoms of Gwynedd and Deheubarth were nearly always the origin of Welsh resurgence. During that time, almost every Plantagenet king of England had a native antagonist. While in some cases, the relations between the Welsh princes and the English Crown were tolerable, if not cordial, at other times, violence flared. During the long reigns of Henry II and Rhys ap Gruffudd, both were true. In their differing ways, both men were masters of diplomacy, yet, when relations were at their worst, things got very nasty. No better example of this concerns Henry's blinding of Rhys's son, Maredudd, after taking him hostage. In some instances, we are also left dealing with questions of what if? How different history could have been had Henry's employment of Irish mercenaries to raid Gwynedd proved more effective! How different things could have been had armies been better prepared or marching in good weather!

On Henry II's death, Lord Rhys's already imperfect relationship with the Crown broke down. As the following years demonstrated, all the usual requirements that are traditionally indispensable in keeping the peace were tested. In addition to Richard the Lionheart's absence on crusade, peace between the two nations was never more difficult than when the royal households were divided. Like Edward III in the build-up to the Wars of the Roses, Rhys had too many children. Unlike England's 'perfect king', Rhys's additional problem was that they were out of wedlock. Consequently, trouble in Deheubarth and Gwynedd inevitably followed. How significant this would be for the castle.

In the reigns of John and Henry III, Welsh nationalism reached something of a zenith – again, in Gwynedd especially. When Wales needed a hero, up stepped Llywelyn ap Iorwerth: 'The Great', as his English epithet concedes. Llywelyn was no ordinary warrior. Even as a young man, the tenacious grandson of Owain Gwynedd had demonstrated the full-blooded confidence needed to eject his uncles, Rhodri and Dafydd, from their lands. By 1197, still not yet twenty-five years old, he was close to achieving complete control of Gwynedd. It was he who, in 1201, oversaw the nation's first formal treaty with an English king. It is equally significant that John offered him his daughter in marriage. Joan may have been illegitimate, but the dynastic benefits were clear, especially as John had still to father a legitimate child. It also speaks volumes of John's respect for Llywelyn that the prince joined him on his march on Scotland in 1209.

Throughout that first decade of the thirteenth century, Llywelyn's march to greatness continued. By 1208 he controlled Powys, and had it not been for his relationship with William de Braose, consolidation of his lands would have been assured. True, John's invasion of 1211 forced a pitiful surrender, but his failure to consolidate early progress allowed Llywelyn to reclaim what he had lost. While John's position in Europe became increasingly precarious, Llywelyn's stock was rising. In 1216, history was also made at Aberdyfi when the once warring Welsh princes agreed to support Llywelyn. The contrast between Wales and England at that time could not have been starker. As John's subjects sought to consolidate the terms sealed at Runnymede, Llywelyn's were ready to unite under one banner.

For the young Henry III, the havoc Llywelyn wreaked on the Marcher lands and those of William Marshal, 1st Earl of Pembroke, were just two of several unwanted distractions. When young Henry's government, led by Marshal himself, finally saw off the dauphin of France – later Louis VIII – peace with Wales was highly sought. Though Llywelyn was initially reluctant, the Treaty of Worcester in March 1218 brought a temporary halt to hostilities. Confirmation of Llywelyn as Prince of Wales in Henry's eyes by 1220, and those of the other Welsh princes by 1226, failed to bring permanent peace. Until the Pact of Middle in 1234, trouble in the Marches remained a regular thorn in the king's side.

Throughout that time, the importance of the castle cannot be overstated. The rise of Hubert de Burgh, Henry's justiciar, had posed Llywelyn an extra threat, yet one he proved capable of withstanding. Similar was true of Marshal's heir and successor, William Marshal the Younger, 2nd Earl of Pembroke. When the strange circumstances of the Marshal War put Henry on a collision course with William's second son, Richard, Llywelyn found an unlikely ally. Following Richard's death and the Archbishop of Canterbury's brokering of peace in 1234, Llywelyn came out on top. No further violence would occur between the king and Welsh prince in Llywelyn's lifetime.

For Wales, Llywelyn's death would prove a significant turning point. An emblematic figure around which Welsh independence had long rested, his achievements did not survive him for long. While his grandson, Llywelyn ap Gruffudd, was of a similar mould, he faced an altogether different foe in Longshanks. As the castles on both sides of the border met busy times in the service of English Marcher and Welsh lord, war between England and Wales came to an overdue, if not anticlimactic, conclusion on Llywelyn's death in 1282. With this, another bizarre irony presents itself. The creation of the castles and town walls for which Wales is now famous was the ultimate symbol of native oppression.

As was so often the case at the end of a war, the victor's marks of conquest proved more psychologically intimidating than practical. True enough, the Iron Ring served an essential purpose, not least in thwarting Madog ap Llywelyn, but it was their power as a deterrent to further uprising that justified the high cost. As feats of engineering, they stand alone as the champions of Wales, if not Europe. Architecturally, they remain unique chapters in the story of the castle's evolution, especially concerning Middle Eastern and Savoyard influences. For more than a century, they ruled a kingdom at peace. Only one person dared attempt to topple them.

Alongside the two Llywelyns, Owain Glyndŵr is often revered as something of a medieval superman figure. According to J.E. Lloyd's biography of 1931, he was 'the father of Welsh nationalism'. Indeed, in many a patriot's eyes, Owain may even surpass Llywelyn ap Iorwerth as the national hero. How much of his life is firmly grounded in history or has become lost in legend is impossible to discern. There seems little doubt that he was as aware as any of the prophecies of Geoffrey of Monmouth and certain other bards. His actions, especially early in the revolt, also suggest that he leaned on these. Even now, it is unclear what became of him. Did he perish during the conflict with Henry IV? Perhaps struck down by a blade or illness? Or did he survive for a time? Among the most outlandish theories is that he became the chaplain on his daughter's estate.

Regardless of what became of him – and from where he came – Owain's raising of the rebel flag brought an end to a century of Welsh obedience to the Plantagenets. Though the reasons for his uprising are challenging to report concisely, none of royal birth captured the spirit and zeitgeist of the Welsh better in the Plantagenet era. As for the castles of Wales, never since Edward's subjugation had they been so important. Owain stands alone as the only man of the medieval era to consistently conquer some of Edward's fortresses: a sign, perhaps, that royal authority could be toppled. Whether this says more about the lack of maintenance and capabilities of individual garrisons or Owain himself is subject to debate.

The chroniclers paint a startling picture of him. A fierce warrior with a knack for warcraft, he was a rare breed of medieval leader. Indeed, he is one of the few whose achievements rival Longshanks, Wallace, and Bruce. That he was always honourable in battle is subject to criticism – his refusal to grant the women of Carreg Cennen safe passage during the castle's siege stands as a clear example of this. On the other hand, he was a man of his time and in the business of leading a war. The revolt's longevity indicates he had a rare ability to survive and instil loyalty in his followers. As was true of Edward, control of the Iron Ring was integral to his success. When Owain lost Harlech in 1409, the rebel flag quickly fell with it. While the Tower of London awaited his nearest and dearest, he disappeared into obscurity. Like King Arthur and his knights, there is a certain nostalgia attached to him. Even today, many hold out hope that a future prince will one day return to aid Wales in her hour of need. A far sadder reality is that his rebellion set back the Welsh cause by 150 years.

For many a Welsh castle, Owain's rebellion would be a swansong. Due to their geography, many played no role in the English Civil War. For those that did, it rarely ended well. While some enjoyed something of a cultural renaissance in later years, just like their English counterparts, most were not so lucky. Or perhaps they were the most fortunate of all. While the grand country houses command respect and adoration out of reach to the typical home, for the purists, there is nothing quite like a ruin. The inhabitants have long since moved out, yet their soul remains intact. Along with the rugged remains of the abbeys and priories – and in certain rare cases those of the pre-Norman eras – nothing offers a more tangible connection to those who came before us.

If I have taken one unexpected thing from writing this book, it is a genuine pride that our ancestors have not been forgotten. Nor are they likely to be so anytime soon. Like all Brits, the Welsh are rightly proud of their history and go to great pains to preserve and celebrate it. In common with the Scots, Irish, and parts of England that claim a Celtic heritage, such distinct levels of identity are incredibly special. While the trend towards globalisation has many benefits, in this author's opinion, it is equally right that one's national identity is guarded. If an individual should be celebrated for their uniqueness and have their past respected, surely the same must be true of a nation. After all, is a nation's history nothing more than the collective heartbeat of all who came before us – good and bad? It is in them we find wisdom; in some cases, solace and understanding. It is also through them we learn valuable lessons. The castles of Wales are not only Wales's past but humanity's past. For this reason alone, the 'Land of Castles' is incredibly precious. As UNESCO quite rightly pointed out, the castles of Wales are among the most important ever built and include some of the 'finest examples of late thirteenth- and early fourteenth-century military architecture in Europe'.

Appendix A

Edward I's Ring of Iron

Flint Castle (1277)
Hawarden Castle (1277)
Rhuddlan Castle (1277)
Builth Castle (1277)
Aberystwyth Castle (1277)
Denbigh Castle and town walls (1283)
Caernarfon Castle and town walls (1283)
Conwy Castle and town walls (1283)
Harlech Castle (1283)
Beaumaris Castle (1295)

Appendix B

Further Castles in Wales or the Welsh Marches

Barry Castle – most of the gatehouse remains.
Bryn Bras Castle – a country house converted into apartments.
Candleston Castle – a fourteenth-century fortified manor house.
Crickhowell Castle – some tower ruins remain.
Dyserth Castle – scant ruins.
Holt Castle – scant ruins.
Llandovery Castle – some ruins.
Longtown Castle – a ruined stone motte and bailey.
Morlais Castle – scant ruins.
Neath Castle – some ruins.
Pembridge Castle – reconstructed and now under private ownership.
Penrhyn Castle – reconstructed since the 1780s.
Penrice Castle – scant ruins in the grounds of a neo-classical mansion.
Richard's Castle – some earthworks remain.
Shrewsbury Castle – now a museum.
St Fagans Castle – now a museum.

Bibliography

AA, *Exploring Britain's Castles*, Basingstoke: AA Publishing, 2011

Treasures of Britain and Treasures of Ireland, London: Drive Publications Ltd, 1968

Abrahams, Paul and Marc Alexander, *In Search of Britain's Haunted Castles*, Stroud: The History Press, 2011

Alexander, Marc, *Phantom Britain*, London: Muller, 1975

Ashbridge, Thomas, *The Greatest Knight – The Remarkable Life of William Marshal, The Power Behind Five English Thrones*

Ashe, Geoffrey, *Mythology of the British Isles*, York: Methuen Publishing, 1990

Baker, Mark, *Myths and Legends of the Gwrych Castle Estate*, 2014

Bartlett, Robert, *England Under the Angevin Kings 1075–1225,* Oxford: Oxford University Press, 2000

Bartlett, Robert, *The Making of Europe: Conquest, Colonization and Cultural Change, 950–1350,* Harmondsworth: Allen Lane, 1993

Barlow, Frank, *William Rufus*, New Haven and London: Yale University Press, 2000

Borman, Tracy, *Henry VIII and the Men who Made Him: The Secret History Behind the Tudor Throne*, London: Hodder & Stoughton, 2018

Borman, Tracy, *Thomas Cromwell: The Untold Story of Henry VIII's Most Faithful Servant*, London: Hodder & Stoughton, 2014

Bradbury, Jim, *Stephen and Matilda: The Civil War of 1139-53*, Stroud, Gloucestershire: The History Press, 2005

Brown, R. Allen, *English Castles*, London: B.T. Batsford, 1976

Bumpus, T. Francis, *The Cathedrals of England and Wales*, T. Wener Laurie, 1921

Camm, Bede, *Forgotten Shrines: An Account of some old Catholic Halls and Families in England and of Relics and Memorials of the English Martyrs*, London: MacDonald & Evans, 1910

Carpenter, D. A., *Henry III*, New Haven: Yale University Press, 2020

Carpenter, D. A, *The Minority of Henry III*, Berkeley and Los Angeles: University of California Press, 1990

Carpenter, D. A, *The Struggle for Mastery – Britain 1066-1284*, Oxford: Oxford University Press, 2003

Cathcart, King, D. J., *Castellarium Anglicanum – an index and Bibliography of the Castles in England, wales and the Islands: Vols 1-2*, London & New York: Kraus International Publications, 1983

Chandler, David, *Sedgemoor 1685: From Monmouth's Invasion to the Bloody Assizes (Spellmount Classics)*, Staplehurst: Spellmount, 1999

Church, S.D. (ed.) *King John: New Interpretations,* Woodbridge: Boyd & Brewer, 1999

Clancy, Michael, *England and its Rulers,* Oxford: Oxford University Press, 1998

Cogswell, Thomas, *James I (Penguin Monarchs): The Phoenix King*, London: Phoenix, 2017

Crouch, David, *William Marshal: Knighthood, War and Chivalry, 1147-1219*, London: Routledge, 2016

Curran, Bob, *Lost Lands, Forgotten Realms – Sunken Continents, Vanished Cities, and the Kingdoms that History Misplaced*, Franklin Lakes, New Jersey: New Page Books, 2007

Danziger, Danny, Gillingham, John, *1215: The Year of Magna Carta*, London: Hodder and Stoughton, 2004

Davies, John, Jenkins, Nigel, Baines, Menna, Lynch, Peredur I., *The Welsh Academy Encyclopaedia of Wales*, Cardiff: University of Wales Press, 2008

Davies, Michael, *The Last King of Wales: Gruffudd ap Llywelyn, c. 1013-63*, Stroud: The History Press, 2012

Davies R. R., *Owain Glyn Dŵr*, Y Lolfa, 2011

Davis, John Paul, *A Hidden History of the Tower of London*, Barnsley: Pen & Sword History, 2020

Davis, John Paul, *King John, Henry III and England's Lost Civil War*, Barnsley: Pen & Sword History, 2021

Davis, John Paul, *Pity for the Guy: A Biography of Guy Fawkes*, London and Chicago: Peter Owen Publishers, 2010

Davis, John Paul, *Robin Hood: The Unknown Templar,* Peter Owen, 2009

Davis, John Paul, *The Gothic King: A Biography of Henry III*, London and Chicago: Peter Owen Publishers, 2013

Denholm-Young, N., *Richard of Cornwall*, Oxford: Basil Blackwell, 1947

Dougherty, Martin J., *Celts – The History and Legacy of One of the Oldest Cultures in Europe*, London: Amber Publishing, 2016

Dunne, John J., *Folklore, Myths and Legends of Britain*, London: Readers Digest Association Ltd, 1977

Edwards, John, *Mary I: England's Catholic Queen (The English Monarchs Series)*, New Haven and London: Yale University Press, 2011

Fanthorpe, Patricia, *The World's Most Mysterious Castles*, Toronto: The Dundurn Group, 2005

Foss, Arthur, *Country House Treasures*, London: Book Club Associates, 1980

Fraser, Antonia, *Cromwell, Our Chief Of Men*, London: Phoenix, 2002

Fraser, Antonia, *King Charles II*, London: Phoenix, 2002

Fraser, Antonia, *The Six Wives of Henry VIII*, London: Phoenix, 2002

Fry, Plantagenet Somerset, *Castles: England, Scotland, Wales, Ireland – The definitive guide to the most impressive buildings and intriguing sites*, Newton Abbot: David & Charles, 2001

Gascoigne, Christina, and Gascoigne, Bamber, *Castles of Britain*, Book Club Associates, 1976

Giles, J.A., *The Life and Times of Alfred the Great,* London: George Bell, 1848

Giles, J.A, *Roger of Wendover's Flowers of History, Comprising the History of England from the Descent of the Saxons to AD 1235,* Vols 1–2, London: Henry. G. Bohn, 1849

Giles, J.A *Matthew Paris's English History from the Year 1235 to 1273,* Vols 1–3, London: Henry. G. Bohn, 1852-4

Gillingham, John, *Richard I (The English Monarchs Series)*, New Haven and London: Yale University Press, 1999

Gillingham, John, *The Wars of the Roses: Peace & Conflict in 15th Century England*, London: Phoenix, 2001

Gower, Jon, *The Story of Wales*, BBC Digital, 2012

Hallam, Dr Elizabeth (General Editor), *Chronicles of the Age of Chivalry: The Plantagenet dynasty from 1216 to 1377: Henry III and the Three Edwards, the Era of the Black Prince and the Black Death*, London: Salamander Books Ltd., 2002

Hallam, Dr Elizabeth (General Editor), *The Plantagenet Chronicles: Medieval Europe's Most Tempestuous Family, Henry II and his Wife, Eleanor of Aquitaine, Richard the Lionheart, and his Brother King*

John, Seen Through the Eyes of their Contemporaries, London: Salamander Books Ltd., 2002

Hamilton, Dave, *Wild Ruins – The explorer's guide to Britain's lost castles, follies, relics and remains*, Bath: Wild Things Publishing, 2015

Harwood, Brian, *Fixer and Fighter – The Life of Hubert de Burgh, Earl of Kent, 1170–1243*

Hennings, Margaret, *England Under Henry III*, New York: Longmans, Green, 1924

Hicks, Michael, *Richard III*, Stroud: Tempus, 2003

Higham, Robert and Philip Barker, *Timber Castles*, Exeter: University of Exeter Press, 2004

Holt, J.C., *Magna Carta*, Cambridge: Cambridge University Press, 1965

Holt, J.C., *The Northerners: A Study in the Reign of King John*, Oxford: Oxford University Press, 1961

Horspool, David, *The English Rebel: One Thousand Years of Trouble-making from the Normans to the Nineties*, London: Viking, 2009

Hume, David, *History of England from the Invasion of Julius Caesar to the Abdication of James the Second,* Vol. III, Boston, MA: Phillips, Sampson & Co, 1858

Hunt, Tristram, *The English Civil War At First Hand*, London: Phoenix, 2003

Hunt, William, *The English Church in the Middle Ages*, Longmans, Green & Co, 1888

Hunt, William, *Eleanor of Castile, Queen of Edward I: A Short Biography,* Oxford: Oxford University Press, 1900

Hunt, William, *King Henry I of England: A Short Biography*, Oxford: Oxford University Press, 1900

Hunt, William, *King Henry III of England: A Short Biography*, Oxford: Oxford University Press, 1900

Hunt, William, *King John of England: A Short Biography*, Oxford: Oxford University Press, 1900

Hutchinson, Robert, *House of Treason: The Rise and Fall of a Tudor Dynasty*, London: Phoenix, 2009

Jenkins, Simon, *A Short History of England*, London: Profile Books, 2012

Jenkins, Simon, *Churches, Houses, Castles*, London: Penguin Books, 2008

Johnson, Matthew, *Behind the Castle Gate: From Medieval to Renaissance*, London: Routledge, 2002

Johnson, Paul, *The National Trust Book of British Castles*, London: Book Club Associates, 1978

Jones, Craig Owen, *Compact History of Welsh Heroes: The Revolt of Madog ap Llywelyn*, Llygad Gwalch Cyf, 2008

Jones, Dan, *Magna Carta: The Making and Legacy of the Great Charter*, London: Head of Zeus Ltd., 2014

Jones, Dan, *Summer of Blood: The Peasants' Revolt of 1381*, London: HarperCollins Publishers, 2010

Jones, Dan, *The Hollow Crown – The Wars of the Roses and the Rise of the Tudors*, London: Faber & Faber, 2015

Jones, Dan, *The Plantagenets: The Kings Who Made England*, London: HarperCollins Publishers, 2012

Jones, Richard, *Haunted Castles of Britain and Ireland*, London: New Holland, 2003

Jones, Richard, *Myths and Legends of Britain and Ireland*, London: New Holland, 2006

Keen, Maurice (ed.), *Medieval Warfare: A History,* Oxford: Oxford University Press, 1999

Lander, J. R., *The Wars of the Roses*, Stroud, Gloucestershire: Sutton, 2000

Kinross, John, *Discovering Castles in England and Wales*, Princes Risborough: Shire Publications Ltd, 1995

Knight, Stephen, and Ohlgren, Thomas, *Robin Hood and Other Outlaw Tales*, Kalamazoo, MI: Medieval Institute Publications, 1997

Leland, John, Smith, Lucy Toulmin, *The Itinerary in Wales of John Leland in or about the years 1536-1539. Extracted from his Mss. Arranged and Edited,* Leopold Classic Library

Luard, Henry Richards, *Annales Monastici, Vols I-V*, Longmans, Green, Reader & Dyer, 1866-73

McLynn, Frank, *Lionheart & Lackland, King Richard, King John and the Wars of Conquest*, London: Vintage Books, 2007

Marsden, Sir Simon, *Phantoms of the Isles – Further tales from The Haunted Realm*, London: Guild Publishing, 1990

Marsden, Sir Simon, *The Haunted Realm – Ghosts, Witches and Other Strange Tales*, Exeter: Webb and Bower, 1986

Messer, Danna R., *Joan, Lady of Wales – Power and Politics of King John's Daughter*, Barnsley: Pen & Sword, 2020

Mason, Emma, *William II: Rufus, the Red King*, Stroud, Gloucestershire: Tempus, 2005

Mason, John, *Haunted Heritage*, London: Collins and Brown, 1999
Maunt, K. L., *The Welsh Kings: Warriors, Warlords and Princes*, Stroud: The History Press, 2006
Maurer, Helen E., *Margaret of Anjou: Queenship and Power in Late Medieval England*, London: Boydell Press, 2005
Miller, John, *James II (The English Monarchs Series)*, New Haven and London: Yale University Press, 2000
Morris, Jan, *A Writer's House in Wales*, Washington D.C.: The National Geographic Society, 2002
Morris, Marc, *A Great and Terrible King: Edward I and the Forging of Britain*, London: Windmill Books, 2009
Morris, Marc, *Castle: A History of the Buildings that Shaped Medieval Britain*, London: Windmill Books, 2012
Morris, Marc, *King John: Treachery, Tyranny and the Road to Magna Carta*, London: Windmill Books, 2016
Morris, Marc, *Kings and Castles*, London: Endeavour Press, 2018
Morris, Marc, *The Norman Conquest*, London: Windmill Books, 2013
Mortimer, Ian, *The Fears of Henry IV: The Life of England's Self-Made King*, London: Vintage, 2008
Mortimer, Ian, *The Greatest Traitor: The Life of Sir Roger Mortimer*, London: Vintage, 2010
Mortimer, Ian, *The Perfect King: The Life of Edward III, Father of the English Nation*, London: Vintage Books, 2008
Mortimer, Ian, *The Time Traveller's Guide to Medieval England*, Vintage, 2009
Mortimer, Richard, *Angevin England 1154–1258,* Oxford: Blackwell, 1994
Nicolle, David, *Medieval Siege Weapons: Western Europe AD 585–1385*, Oxford: Osprey Publishing, 2002
Norgate, Kate, *The Minority of Henry III*
Ohlgren, Thomas (1998), *Medieval Outlaws*, Stroud: Sutton Publishing
Pearse, B., *Ghost Hunters Casebook: The Investigations of Andrew Green*, Stroud: The History Press, 2007
Penn, Thomas, *Winter King: The Dawn of Tudor England*, London: Penguin Books, 2012
Pettifer, Adam, *English Castles: A Guide by Counties,* Woodbridge: Boydell Press, 1995

Phillips, Alan, *Castles of Wales*, Stroud: Amberley, 2014
Pitkin Guides, *Castles of Wales and the Welsh Marches*, London: Pitkin Publishing, 2001
Plowden, Alison, *Lady Jane Grey: Nine Days Queen (Classic Histories Series)*, Stroud: The History Press, 2016
Pollard, A. J., *The Wars of the Roses (British History in Perspective)*, Basingstoke: Palgrave MacMillan, 2013
Powicke, Maurice, *King Henry III and the Lord Edward*, Vols 1–2, Oxford: Clarendon Press, 1947
Powicke, Maurice, *The Oxford History of England: The Thirteenth Century 1216–1377*, Oxford: Clarendon Press, 1962
Prestwich, Michael, *Edward I (Yale English Monarchs)*, New Haven and London: Yale University Press, 1997
Prestwich, Michael, Britnell, Richard, and Frame, Robin, *Thirteenth Century England X*, Woodbridge: Boydell Press, 2005
Purkiss, Diane, *The English Civil War: A People's History*, London: Harper Perennial, 2007
Readers Digest, *The Most Amazing Places of Folklore & Legend in Britain*, London: Vivat Direct Ltd, 2011
Reese, Peter, *The Life of General George Monck: For King and Cromwell*, Barnsley: Pen & Sword Military, 2008
Rex, Peter, *1066: A New History of the Norman Conquest*, Stroud: Amberley Publishing, 2011
Ross, Charles, *Edward IV (The English Monarchs Series)*, New Haven and London: Yale University Press, 1997
Saul, Nigel, *Richard II (The English Monarchs Series)*, New Haven and London: Yale University Press, 1999
Seward, Desmond, *A Brief History of the Wars of the Roses*, London: Robinson, 2007
Seward, Desmond, *The Last White Rose: The Secret Wars of the Tudors*, London: Constable, 2010
Seward, Desmond, *Richard III – England's Black Legend*, London: Thistle Publishing, 2013
Shirley, Walter Waddington, *Royal and Other Historical Letters Illustrative of the Reign of Henry III,* Vols 1–2, Longmans, Green, Reader and Dyer, 1862–6
Skidmore, Chris, *Bosworth: The Birth of the Tudors*, London: Weidenfeld & Nicolson, 2013

Skidmore, Chris, *Edward VI: The Lost King of England*, London: Phoenix, 2008
Smith, J. Beverley, Llywelyn ap Gruffudd: Princes of Wales, Cardiff: University of Wales Press, 1998
Somerset, Anne, *Elizabeth I (Women in History)*, London: Phoenix, 1997
Somerset, Anne, *Unnatural Murder: Poison at the Court of James I*, London: Phoenix, 1998
Spencer, Dan, *The Castle in the Wars of the Roses*, Barnsley: Pen&Sword Military, 2020
Spencer, Dan, *The Castle at War in Medieval England and Wales*, Stroud: Amberley, 2018
Spencer, Charles, *Killers of the King: The Men Who Dared to Execute Charles I*, London: Bloomsbury, 2014
Stephens, Meic, *The Oxford Companion to the Literature of Wales*, Oxford: Oxford University Press, 1986
Stubbs, William, *Select Charters and Other Illustrations of English Constitutional History*, Oxford: Clarendon Press, 1870
Swanton, Michael (ed.), *The Anglo-Saxon Chronicles*, London: Dent, 1996
Thompson, M. W., *The Decline of the Castle*, Cambridge: Cambridge University Press, 1987
Thompson, M. W., *The Rise of the Castle*, Cambridge: Cambridge University, 1991
Tout, Thomas Frederick, *The History of England: From the Accession of Henry III to the Death of Edward III (1216–1377)*, London: Longmans, Green & Co., 1906
Trevelyan, Raleigh, *Sir Walter Raleigh*, London: Allen Lane, 2002
Turvey, Roger K., *The Welsh Princes, 1063-1283*, London: Routledge, 2002
Underwood, Peter, *A Gazetteer of British, Scottish and Irish Ghosts – Two Volumes*, New York: Bell, 1985
Vincent, Nicholas, *A Brief History of Britain 1066–1485 – The Birth of a Nation*, London: Constable and Robinson, 2011
Vincent, Nicholas, *Peter des Roches – an alien in English Politics*, 1205–1238
Warner, Kathryn, *Blood Roses: The Houses of Lancaster and York before the Wars of the Roses*, Stroud: The History Press, 2018

Warner, Philip, *Sieges of the Middle Ages*, Barnsley: Pen&Sword Military, 2004

Warren, W. L., *King John*, London and New Haven: Yale University Press, 1997

Weir, Alison, *Henry VIII: King and Court*, London: Pimlico, 2002

Weir, Alison, *Lancaster and York: The Wars of the Roses*, London: Vintage, 2009

Weir, Alison, *The Princes in the Tower*, London: Pimlico, 1992

Westwood, Jennifer, *Albion, A Guide to Legendary Britain*, London: Book Club Associates, 1986

Wolffe, Bertram, *Henry VI (The English Monarchs Series)*, New Haven and London: Yale University Press, 2001

Further to the above, the many guidebooks of the castles in this book were very useful study aids.

Websites

http://www.gatehouse-gazetteer.info/home.html
http://www.castlefacts.info
http://www.castlestudiesgroup.org.uk/
http://www.castlestudiestrust.org
http://www.castlewales.com/home.html
http://www.ecastles.co.uk
http://www.castlesfortsbattles.co.uk
https://www.english-heritage.org.uk
https://www.nationaltrust.org.uk
https://cadw.gov.wales
https://rcahmw.gov.uk
https://coflein.gov.uk/en/
https://councilforbritisharchaeologywales.wordpress.com

Index